Russian Transformations

The transition of Russia to a 'developed market economy' has been slower, more contradictory and less predictable than expected. This book examines contemporary Russian socio-economic development in several of its regions and sectors, and explores the degree to which Russian experiences can be incorporated into current social science theories. The regions examined include Moscow, Novosibirsk, Tatarstan and Bashkortostan. The book draws on a range of theories and methodologies. In particular, it questions how far the concept of 'globalization' is applicable to the situation in Russia.

Leo McCann is Lecturer in Human Resource Management at Cardiff Business School. Having completed his Ph.D. on postsocialist development in Tatarstan, Russia, at the University of Kent, he has gone on to examine the transformation of employment relations in other societies, including the United Kingdom, United States and Japan.

BASEES/RoutledgeCurzon Series on Russian and East European Studies

Series editor: Richard Sakwa

Department of Politics and International Relations, University of Kent

This series is published on behalf of BASEES (the British Association for Slavonic and East European Studies). The series comprises original, high-quality, research-level work by both new and established scholars on all aspects of Russian, Soviet, post-Soviet and East European Studies in humanities and social science subjects.

1 **Ukraine's Foreign and Security Policy, 1991–2000**
Roman Wolczuk

2 **Political Parties in the Russian Regions**
Derek S. Hutcheson

3 **Local Communities and Post-Communist Transformation**
Edited by Simon Smith

4 **Repression and Resistance in Communist Europe**
J.C. Sharman

5 **Political Elites and the New Russia**
Anton Steen

6 **Dostoevsky and the Idea of Russianness**
Sarah Hudspith

7 **Performing Russia**
Folk revival and Russian identity
Laura J. Olson

8 **Russian Transformations**
Edited by Leo McCann

Russian Transformations

Challenging the global narrative

Edited by
Leo McCann

Routledge
Taylor & Francis Group
LONDON AND NEW YORK

First published 2005 by Routledge

Published 2022 by Routledge
2 Park Square, Milton Park, Abingdon, Oxon OX14 4RN
605 Third Avenue, New York, NY 10017

Routledge is an imprint of the Taylor & Francis Group, an informa business

Typeset in Times by
Taylor & Francis Books

Publisher's Note

The publisher has gone to great lengths to ensure the quality of this reprint but points out that some imperfections in the original copies may be apparent.

British Library Cataloguing in Publication Data
A catalogue record for this book is available from the British Library

Library of Congress Cataloging in Publication Data
A catalog record for this book has been requested

ISBN 978-0-415-32371-0 (hbk)
ISBN 978-0-415-65414-2 (pbk)

Contents

Illustrations

Figure

Tables

Acknowledgements

It was a great pleasure to put this volume together, and I have a number of people to thank. All of them were instrumental in making the book happen. First of all I would like to express my gratitude to the ten other authors. Many of them had to work to very tight deadlines, and all of them had to cope with the increasing intensification of the academic labour process! Of course, without the help and support of Peter Sowden, my editor at RoutledgeCurzon, the book would never have materialized. Thanks must also go to the anonymous reviewer for comments and suggestions and to Sarah Moore for her work on the manuscript. Finally, I would like to thank my partner Kate for all the happiness and companionship she has provided.

Leo McCann
Cardiff, August 2003

Contributors

Ella Akerman is currently a Ph.D. candidate at the School of Mediterranean Studies, King's College London, having formerly been a Research Associate at the Scottish Centre for International Security, University of Aberdeen. Her area of expertise includes Central Asian and Middle Eastern politics, as well as Russian foreign and security politics. Her articles have been published in *The Review of International Affairs*, *The Journal for Conflict, Security and Development*, *Security Dialogue* and *The Central Asian Survey*. She graduated from the University of Sorbonne in History (MA) and from the University of Aberdeen in Commercial Law (LLM).

Pınar Bedirhanoğlu is Assistant Professor in the Department of International Relations at the Middle East Technical University in Ankara, Turkey. She received her Ph.D. in International Relations from the University of Sussex in 2002. Besides the topics of capitalist transformation process in Russia and the critique of the 'transition' discourse, her research interests include global political economy, neoliberalism, the state and the neo-Gramscian school in international relations.

Sarah Busse Spencer received her Ph.D. in Sociology from the University of Chicago. Her research examines the effect of post-Soviet social relations on the development of capitalism in Russia.

Leontina Hormel is a Ph.D. candidate in the Department of Sociology at the University of Oregon. Her dissertation examines gendered forms of informal labour market participation in Ukraine. She is currently researching the trend of eastward labour migration from a medium-sized, central Ukrainian city and the influences of gender and skill dynamics on this group of labourers.

Leo McCann is Lecturer in Human Resource Management at Cardiff Business School. Having completed his Ph.D. on postsocialist development in Tatarstan at the School of Social Policy, Sociology and Social Research at the University of Kent, he has gone on to examine the transformation of employment relations in other societies, including the United Kingdom, Japan and the United States. He is currently working on a book on Tatarstan with RoutledgeCurzon.

Anastasia Nesvetailova is Lecturer in Political Economy in the Geography Department of the University of Liverpool. After studying for her MA at the University of Manchester's Department of Government, she completed her Ph.D. on 'The political economy of international crises' at the University of Wales, Aberystwyth. Her research interests include the political economy of financial capitalism, contemporary economic transformations and the evolution of capitalist relations in Eastern Europe and the CIS.

Richard Sakwa is Professor of Russian and European Politics and Head of the Department of Politics and International Relations at the University of Kent. He is the author of 12 books on Russia and the Soviet Union. His most recent work includes the third edition of *Russian Politics and Society* (Routledge 2002), *Putin and Russian Politics* (Routledge 2003), *Postcommunism* (Open University Press 1999) and *The Rise and Fall of the Soviet Union* (Routledge 1999).

Yakov Schukin is a doctoral candidate in Sociology at the University of Minnesota. His interests include globalization and class formation in post-Soviet Russia. His work on globalization, Russian political landscape and educational reform appeared in the Russian journal *Private Stock* (*Neprikosnovennyi Zapas*).

Gregory Schwartz is Lecturer in Human Resource Management at Cardiff Business School. His most recent articles, dealing with employment decision-making, wages and management restructuring in Russian industrial enterprises, have appeared in *Europe-Asia Studies* and *Work, Employment and Society*.

Olga Shevchenko is Assistant Professor of Sociology at Williams College, Massachusetts. She is currently working on a book manuscript dedicated to the public rhetoric of the late 1990s in Russia, and to the transformations that occur in this context to the everyday notions of autonomy, competence and trust among contemporary urban Russians. Her recent articles include 'Between the holes: emerging identities and hybrid patterns of consumption in post-socialist Russia' in *Europe-Asia Studies*, and '"In case of fire emergency": consumption, security, and the meaning of durables in a transforming society' in *Journal of Consumer Culture*.

Caleb Southworth is Assistant Professor of Sociology at the University of Oregon. He has two survey projects on labour markets in the field, one in central Ukraine and the other in the Russian Republic of Bashkortostan. He is currently working on a book on paternalism in Russian factories during the 1990s.

1 Introduction to *Russian Transformations*

Leo McCann[1]

The new, postcommunist, Russia is now well over a decade old. Yet its 'transition' to a 'developed market economy' has been slower, more contradictory, and less predictable than nearly all observers back in 1992 might have guessed. This volume examines theories and evidence regarding contemporary Russian socio-economic development, and explores different ways in which the Russian experiences can be incorporated into broader social science theories.

During this period of transition a major social science concept has also developed. 'Globalization' emerged as one of the key themes of Western social science, and its growth, at least initially, went hand in hand with the development of theory and research in postcommunism. The end of the Soviet Union was a major element of the early work of global theory (Fukuyama 1993). There followed an explosion in academic publishing on the issue of globalization and globality (Busch 2000: 23). By 2004 the globalization publishing craze appears to have calmed down somewhat.

Perhaps oddly, however, the development of postcommunist Russia is very rarely mentioned in the mainstream globalization literature. Whereas the collapse of the Soviet system is often seen as a major result of globalization, or one of the main markers of its starting point, globalization writers have little to say about Russia's progress since the collapse. Instead, its progress is covered widely in neoliberal 'transition' theories, which essentially make up the East European 'wing' of the globalization literature. Analyses of Russian transformations have been largely limited to the neoliberal economic definitions of transition. This book embeds the experiences of Russia into the globalization literature, but at the same time challenges the neoliberal approach to globalization. It attempts to offer alternative views built from a range of theoretical and empirical approaches.

At present there are, generally speaking, three broad approaches to understanding globalization. The development of these approaches follows a fairly simple dialectical process of thesis-antithesis-synthesis. First, there is the radical thesis, or 'hyperglobalist' view (to use the terminology of Giddens (2000: 7–10) and Held *et al.* (1999: 10)). This is also known as the 'first wave literature' (Hay and Marsh 2000: 4). This view posits a new global age that has fundamentally transformed the nature of all societies.

Second, there is the counterargument to this view, known as the sceptical position (Giddens 2000: 7–10; Held *et al.* 1999: 10), or the 'second wave literature' (Hay and Marsh 2000: 4–5). Analysts of this school do not buy the argument that a new global age has been ushered in. They tend to claim that, given a longer historical view, the period 1990–2000 is simply one phase of expansive capitalism, and there have been other phases in the past with greater levels of world interaction.

Third, something of a synthesis of these two positions has been formed since the mid- to late 1990s, known as the 'transformationalist' position (Held *et al.* 1999: 10), or the 'third wave literature' (Hay and Marsh 2000: 7–14). This view tends to be accompanied by a broader discussion of what globalization (if anything) *actually is*. In particular, more attention has been paid to the role of individual agency as opposed to sweeping structural transitions. Unfortunately, such an open and diverse approach, (in keeping with the traditions of postmodernism which, arguably, have inspired the development of the third wave global literature) tends to render impossible the job of creating broader theories of action and structure.

This book tends to view Russia's changes in a similar approach to Hay and Marsh's 'third wave literature' or Held *et al.*'s 'transformationalist' view of globalization. There have been significant changes in some parts of the country, little change in others, and unexpected, lesser-known forms of change in still others. We particularly want to shed light on that final area – the parts of the country that bear little resemblance to the usual litany of globalization's supposed benign or pernicious effects. Instead, these features are fairly unique to Russia and the former Soviet Union but are nevertheless related to the confusing, contradictory and creative forces associated with so-called 'global change'. Capitalism is capable of transforming itself and recreating itself in myriad ways, and human beings are equally capable of all kinds of ingenious and original responses to such change.[2]

The transition paradigm, located mostly in the 'first wave' literature, remains the dominant position amongst policymakers and the media in explaining postsocialist development. It tends to assume a goal-based analysis of systemic transformation. The progress of Russia (and all other former socialist societies) is calculated according to its proximity to specific performance targets (EBRD 2002). Typically, Russia is seen by Western governments as having made good progress in liberalizing prices, controlling inflation, and opening its economy to foreign investors, but has made patchy and unsustained efforts towards reforming its industrial firms and management structures, and its legal sphere (which remains unclear, poorly enforced and open to abuse). The fiscal regime, and land and property laws are inadequately developed and occasionally contradictory. Concerns are also raised regarding recent developments in the state control of media. Year on year the EBRD Transition Report reads like the words of a frustrated schoolteacher: Russia is a gifted but difficult pupil, and must try harder. It would appear to transition theorists that more effort and more time is required in order to make the Russian economy function more like a developed Western one.

But can we assume Russia will ever resemble a developed Western society? The 'varieties of capitalism' literature (such as Hall and Soskice 2001; Maurice and Sorge 2000; DiMaggio and Powell 1991; Whitley 1999) would question the logic of inevitable transition towards a global society. Candland and Sil (2001) argue that the 'idea of globalization is meaningful for systematically capturing and comparing the dilemmas facing workers, unions, firms, and managers around the world' (2001: 14), yet 'everywhere we see similar kinds of economic and technological pressures working themselves out in very different ways'. (2001: 15). Gustafson's work (1999) resonates with this literature in talking of 'Capitalism Russian Style'. Rather than assuming, as transition theorists do, that Russian development will eventually result in similar social formations to the G7 countries, it is arguable that the country (as with all others) will exhibit unique features of its own, which are not temporary transitional features, but enduring national traditions. We are witnessing the emergence of the Russian model of capitalism, alongside the already established Scandinavian, Japanese and Anglo-Saxon models to name just three. All possess different forms of local dynamics and processes which refuse to meld into a globalized homogeneity of forms.

The concept of divergent capitalism is very useful. But which of these local dynamics is the most relevant in explaining the differing range of options and constraints for businesspeople, politicians and employees? In other words, how is action and structure to be understood? This question has been addressed at length by such social theorists as Giddens and Bourdieu. There is no room to go into detailed theoretical debates in this book, but it is hoped that by the end of the volume the reader will be acquainted with the rather unique configuration of globalized, Soviet-inherited or traditional social features that exist in Russia. The concluding chapter will offer some more general observations about what the experiences of Russian transformations in this book might mean for theories on postcommunism at large.

Our approach tends to fit into the third wave position, although we are sensitive to the hazards of a total subjectivist slide. To that end, we try as much as possible to ground our observations in the lived experience of globalization for Russian people. It is only by observing different aspects of Russian society in detail and then going from the specific to the general that we can attempt to build sustainable theoretical positions on Russia in the 'global era'.

The lack of coverage of the Russian experience in the mainstream globalist literature may be a reflection on the disappointingly small amounts of Western investments into Russia during this period. Cumulative foreign direct investment (FDI) into the Russian Federation stands somewhere between 10 and 20 billion US dollars (EBRD 2000; PlanEcon 1998). Nevertheless, the linkages between the nascent Russian capitalism and the broader world economic system are being examined. This is particularly true in the transition literature which endorses the Washington Consensus principles regarding the manner in which Russia could integrate itself into the world economy. Moreover, political economists have always been interested in how socialist societies, and therefore Soviet Russia, relate to capitalism (Granick 1960; Mandel 1975). More recently, Kagarlitsky (1995), Gray (1998), Gustafson (1999), Castells (2000a, 2000c) and Martin (1998), among others, all discuss Russia's complicated and partial connection to global capitalism. In recent years a large volume of literature has grown around the failure of the IMF and the World Bank's reform strategies, such as McCauley (2001), Hoffman (2002), Reddaway and Glinksy (2001) and White (2000). With titles such as *The Tragedy of Russia's Reforms*, they argue that Russia's unique Soviet inheritance made it unsuitable for the prescription of 'one size fits all' reform strategies. Instead, change will take place according to localized norms and values, within a context of established social structures (Segbers 2001).

Hence it would appear that an institutionalist framework (Maurice and Sorge 2000; DiMaggio and Powell 1991; Stark and Bruszt 1998) for understanding Russia's rather unique form of capitalism would be a better approach than neoclassical economics. Yet management studies and organization theory are areas particularly lacking in Russian studies. There is a considerable literature on Soviet and post-Soviet labour relations (Clarke 1999a, b; Siegelbaum and Walkowitz 1995; Filtzer 1994). However in the mainstream transition literature there is generally a very limited understanding of how Russian organizations function today, or how Soviet organizations functioned in the past, leading to major conceptual problems in explaining some unique Russian features (such as infrequent labour disputes despite widespread non-payment of wages and desperate working conditions). In short, the varied literatures on globalization at large, transition in general, or on Russian specifics, fail to engage with each other, and any movement towards an overall explanatory framework for understanding postsocialist Russia is painfully slow.

This book attempts to address this problem, by searching for theoretical and empirical insights into Russia's experiences. The key question of the book is this: to what extent are the regions, events, policies and economic sectors examined operating according to internal Russian logic, and to what extent are they connected and related in some way to the world economy, or 'global society'? This introductory chapter will now examine the contemporary state of play in globalization theories.

Reflections on the theories of globalization

There are many different ways of conceptualizing globalization. Some of them reflect the differences in disciplinary viewpoints. Other differences are ideological in nature. It would be difficult in a collection of this kind to find a concept of globalization that completely unifies the papers. Instead, the approach is to be regionally focused, then to come up with concepts and theories that provide critical comparisons to the global literature in all its forms.

Globalization is a confusing subject in itself, and there is very little chance that all the authors in this book could agree on some consensual definition. In the world of social science, many disciplines and individuals consider globalization differently, and this volume will reflect this. However, the contributions to this volume are all interested in understanding Russia and its regions as complex and distinctive areas with many unique features, but within a broader context of an increasingly connected world economy.

Analysts disagree on the basic theoretical tenets regarding the processes and outcomes that make up the all-pervading concept of globalization (Robertson 1992: 15–31, 165; Waters 1995: 38–64; Hutton and Giddens 2000: 1–4). It is even in doubt as to whether globalization best describes a *result* or a *process* (Urry 2000: 13). As a noun, as in Robertson's formulation (1992: 8), the word refers to an outcome, or set of outcomes. Such outcomes are typically along these lines: 'the compression of the world and the intensification of consciousness of the world as a whole' (Robertson 1992: 8). 'Globalization', as used by Giddens (1998: 31–3), is a set of processes that force and invoke change as they sweep through societies. It is 'a complex range of processes' that can 'pull away' and 'push down' on such traditional social structures as welfare states, or 'squeeze sideways' creating new horizontal linkages between regions.

There is considerable debate as to whether globalization is process or a situation, but few would disagree that globalization refers to the following kinds of issues: 'compression' of time and space, the growth of 'global consciousness', the loosening of the physical restraints of geography, trans-national interconnectedness (possibly also including growing interdependency) and cultural hybridity. There is broad agreement as to what globalization refers to, but little clarity as regards what globalization *is* or what globalization *does*. Rosenberg (2001) is one of the few analysts who gives this confusion a high profile. He argues that, if time–space compression

> were to be explained as an emergent property of a particular type of social relations, then the term 'globalisation' would not denote a theory at all – instead it would function merely as a measure of how far and in what ways this historical process had developed. And the globalisation theorists clearly intend something more than this.
>
> (2000: 2–3)

Who is claiming what? Globalization has been contributed to by theoreticians from a range of backgrounds. These include European social theorists, such as Beck (1992, 2000), Giddens (1990, 1991, 1999) and Urry (2000), economic geographers, such as Dicken (1998) and Harvey (1989), political scientists, including Held *et al.* (1999), and scholars with urban studies backgrounds, such as Castells (2000a, 2000b) and Sassen (1998). In a more politically motivated realm, environmental and anti-consumerist activists, such as Shiva (2000), Klein (2000), Monbiot (2001) and Hertz (2001), also contribute extensively to the globalization discussion. If we travel further left we find more people willing to talk in global terms. Marxists of varying outlooks, such as Hardt and Negri (2000), Altvater and Mahnkopf (1997), Jessop (1999, 2000) and Sklair (1995, 2001, 2002), have all examined globalization in some detail. Some of this examination spills over into the realms of philosophy (Hardt and Negri 2000; Bauman 1998: 34–5), and into international political economy (Germain 2000). There has been a 'global turn' in contemporary academia, as 'globalization has become the new grand narrative of the social sciences' (Hirst and Thomspon 1999: xiii).

This is not to say that global theory has overwhelmed academia to the detriment of localized studies. Ethnography continues to be a relatively popular methodology (Atkinson *et al.* 2001). Furthermore, there is a growing number of works that criticize the concept of globalization itself. One of the paths taken down this road is to argue that globalization is exaggerated, and is essentially also a *political-ideological* project (Hirst and Thompson 1999; Went 2000). In arguing that globalization is not so advanced as the mainstream would have it, such analysts claim that nation states are still to some extent in control of their own destinies, and can shape and influence the paths of economic development. Outright denials of any globalization narratives tend to be found in more polemical studies, such as Rosenberg's *The Follies of Globalisation Theory* (2001), or the chapter entitled 'The Myth of Globalisation' in Bradley *et al.*'s *Myths at Work* (2000). On the far left of the spectrum, work by Callinicos (2001), who provides a scathing critique of globalist assumptions in the chapter 'The Masters of the Universe', Lewis (1997), in the former *Living Marxism* magazine, or Meiksins Wood (1999), in the old-left *Monthly Review*, argue that globalization is an obfuscating exaggeration ('globaloney'), and if it means anything at all it is effectively a new word for Western imperialism (see also Petras and Veltmeyer 2001). The outright globalization deniers tend to engage in polemical criticism instead of empirically informed analysis.

The purpose of the book is to examine the case for globalization at work in Russia's regions. There are some clear indications of greater international involvement and interdependency in the oil and gas sectors, in the most highly developed regions such as Moscow and St Petersburg, and with regard to the ideological hegemony of neoliberalism. There are the beginnings of a 'globally oriented' elite class emerging in many of Russia's urban centres. However, Russian society, economy and polity continue to exhibit unique features that confound the globalization picture. The attempted application of neoclassical transition has not resulted in the creation of a neoclassical economy. Furthermore, global mainstream narratives make little sense in relation to many other less developed parts of the Federation.

Further complications arise here. Accompanying the globalization debates is another controversy over the nature and extent of contemporary capitalism in advanced societies. Such phrases as 'Postindustrial Society', the 'New Economy' and 'Virtual Organizations' have sprung up in recent times, throwing many of the traditional Enlightenment-modernist social science frameworks into confusion. A plethora of new terms and a new lexicon of 'flows', 'networks' and 'virtuality' have challenged, and in some academic sectors replaced, older concepts such as bounded nation states, class, ethnic and gender structures. This lexicon, in common with the globalization vocabulary, contains some hyperbole, with analysts indulging in uncritical assumptions along the lines that 'the world economy' has gone through its own 'transition from an economy based on materials to an economy based on flows of information' (Child and McGrath 2001: 1135). This is another debate entirely, but it is mentioned in order to remind ourselves that the theoretical discourse of the 'new' 'global' economy and society is still very much unsettled, shot through with assumptions and political rhetoric. Clarity is needed, and it is hoped that further research, such as that presented in Part II of this volume, and more sustained theoretical reflections, such as those developed in Part I, will allow us to come to a better understanding of Russia's experiences within the context of global capitalism.

Hence, a polemical assault on the concept of globalization is not the purpose of this text. The book is intended to test out the boundaries of the concept when it is placed in relation to a large and complex nation state that has until quite recently been radically isolated from Western capitalism and its major transformations from the 1970s onwards. If globalization is truly such an important and fast-moving part of all societies and economies, one would expect to find some strong evidence for its functioning in such a place as Russia and its numerous and often diverse sub-regions.

Russia and global theories

How far has the global debate interacted with Russia? It seems that confusion reigns. From Gray's (1998) deeply pessimistic and conservative-leaning 'social panic' perspective, to Elliot and Atkinson's (1999) journalistic anti-neoliberal tract, observers tend to lump together all kinds of events and trends and call them the effects of neoliberalism. Everything, regardless of its social origins, is hence approximated to 'the transformation of capitalism since the 1970s', surely one of the most repeated phrases ever to emerge in social science. Hence a new-right Reaganite or Thatcherite consensus is perceived to have emerged from the United States, travelled into the European Union, into the former Soviet Union, to Japan, across to Oceania, even skirting around the Pacific Rim areas of formally communist China. In the hyper-globalist approach the quite different institutional, social, political and cultural arrangements between and within these societies are ignored. The end result of the generalized demise of statism and socialism may look similar on the surface across these regions, but the processes and outcomes are often different. Or, they at least require analysis and understanding in their own terms. There is still a great deal we don't know about the empirical detail of these regions' economic sociologies.

Furthermore, all kinds of problems emerge with the application of globalization theories to the real world. There are two central difficulties. First of all, despite the talk of 'global' integration, there remain plenty of regions, cultures and peoples that have no significant connection with each other. Connections between the advanced Western societies and less developed societies are often weak. Connections between less developed societies can be even weaker. We have to look at ways of understanding how societies and economies work at local and (where applicable) international levels, and if this means to some extent limiting our scope to that of bounded nation states instead of 'global flows' then so be it. The papers presented here will contain a variety of theoretical and methodological outlooks, with some taking a 'sceptical' (Held *et al.* 2000: 5–7) view of globalization, and others a more 'transformationalist' (7–10) position. Despite this, the papers will all have in common a concern with 'grounding globalization' (Burawoy 2000) into a discussion of how relevant the concept is to different elements of Russian society.

How globalized is Russia?

As mentioned above, the decay of the Soviet economy (in the mid-1970s to the late 1980s) and the death of the Soviet Union as a political entity (finally coming in December 1991) is often attributed to globalization (Castells 2000c: 5–67). Its economy, based almost entirely on raw materials and heavy industry, such as steel production and machine building, was described as the 'most advanced 19th century economy', incapable of innovation, investment and reform (Arnason 1993). It was terminally weak in precisely the areas where globalization 'happens': the high-tech, communications and information sectors. The global economy is supposedly built on a culture of networking, of exchanging and sharing information. But Soviet planners, managers and politicians were enshrouded in a culture of secrecy and suspicion, avoiding risk and innovation. According to the first wave globalization literature, given the nature of the highly internationalized, highly competitive and highly technological economy of developed societies, it was only a matter of *when* the decrepit Soviet system would meet its end, not *if*.

However, Western twentieth-century economies also underwent considerable transformations during the Soviet period. The globalization literature strongly conveys this argument. From the first wave literature to the third wave, the picture is of all economies (Western, developing and transition) being immersed in transformation and flux. The crises in Russian industry mirrors severe difficulties with similar sectors elsewhere in the world. Autos, machine building and steel production are precisely the areas facing severe pressures in the United States, Japan and much of Western Europe. Employment relations and management systems have been profoundly altered in these sectors (Delbridge and Lowe 1998). Managers claim that it is simply not profitable to maintain employment in traditional regions, given the availability of cheaper transport and cheaper labour elsewhere. Competition from recently developed regions (particularly the Asian newly industrialized countries (NICs) and latterly China) threatens to eradicate certain former 'crown jewels' of Western national economies, such as steel production.

With the advanced countries themselves struggling, it seems beyond hope that Russian industry can reform itself to compete on an international level within a foreseeable timeframe. Domestically it has a better chance, particularly following the crash of the rouble (see Nesvetailova, this volume). Better hope for connecting Russia to the rest of the world lies in raw material exports (oil, gas and metals) or semi-processed materials derived from petrochemistry, such as polythene and magnetic tape products (see Akerman, this volume). The multi-billion-dollar question is whether the income from raw material export sales can be effectively reinvested to stimulate sustainable domestic Russian growth.

FDI was originally seen as the most likely route of bringing capital, expertise and employment into Russia. It has not worked for several reasons. For most of the 1990s Russia was actually a net *contributor* to Western economies through personal investments into Swiss bank accounts, or informal, unregulated transfers of money out of the country. With the post-1998 recovery of Russia, however, we are beginning to see some major new investment projects, such as BP's joint venture with the oil giant TNK, announced in early 2003.

More important than FDI has been the rise of the Financial Industrial Groups, and the massive recent merger and acquisition activity. Parts of the Soviet planning and vertical integration infrastructure are being reconstituted along capitalist ownership. The signs are, however, that the change of ownership has done little to affect control and management of enterprises.

A further development, and one that was perhaps the least predictable, is the importance of individual, enormously rich individual Russian investors becoming involved in transnational economic activity. In the space of a few months in 2003, some globally connected business events took place that would have been unthinkable until relatively recently. First, in May, a Russian investor named Alisher Usmanov purchased over 5 per cent of the shares of the struggling UK–Dutch steel giant Corus (Gow 2003). In July, two of Russia's largest oil companies, Yukos and Sibneft announced their intent to merge. At the same time Roman Abramovich, the largest shareholder in Sibneft, took control of London's Chelsea Football Club (and Chelsea Village hotel complex), stimulating a series of big-money football player transfers in a hitherto depressed market.

These are just three examples of Russia's connectedness to the rest of the world in a very short period of time. No one should be surprised if more such acquisitions are announced in the future. The deals certainly reveal major international connectivity, but they do so for a tiny select few. The enormous wealth of these individuals is based on sales of raw materials obtained via the crash privatizations of the early 1990s (see Bedirhanoğlu, Chapter 2, this volume). Their wealth is not derived from the transnational, digital, fast-moving and weightless world so often described in the globalist literature. A brief overview of the connections of the Russian economy to the world economy would suggest that the Russian connections to international capitalism are powerful and growing in importance, but are limited in scope, based on the actions of a handful of extremely powerful individuals. The importance of a few elites in shaping the course of national and international history is itself a long-standing Russian tradition.

Russia and globalization: gaps in the literature

Despite taking a central role in the 'transition' debates, Russia is largely left out of the specific globalization literature. There are very few references to Russia and the former Soviet Union in such texts as Harvey (1989), Hirst and Thompson (1999), Bauman (1998) Robertson (1992), Sassen (1998), Waters (1995), Urry (2000) and several others. Globalization tends to be used in reference to the advanced Western economies from which the term originated. The main source of legitimacy for neoliberal agendas was provided (at least until 1997) by the success of the NICs of Southeast Asia, and they continue to get frequent references in the globalist literature. Russia, however, is largely omitted. Aside from Gray's (1998: 133–65) conservative critique of globalization 'gone too far', Kagarlitsky's Marxist denunciation of neoliberalism (1995; Burbach *et al.* 1997: 117–37), Sklair's preliminary observations of the CIS within global systems theory (1995), and Castells' coverage of the Soviet Union's collapse (2000b: 5–67) and elite level Russian crime (2000b: 171–95), there is almost nothing in the economic globalization literature that deals with Russia. The specific East European transition literature deals with Russia directly, but rarely makes reference to the sociology, political economy, or economic geography literature on a more general level. By its very nature, the transition literature tends to reflect ethnocentric, neoliberal assumptions about the former Soviet Union territories, and how they should be behaving in order to bring about markets and democracy in the most efficient way. In that sense, the transition paradigm falls rather neatly into the first wave global literature. It argues that Russia continues to struggle with reforms well into the 2000s because the transformations have not been carried far enough, and are held back by 'non-economic forces', such as intransigent and corrupt political figures, or incompetent 'old-school Soviet' industrial managers or bureaucrats. This book rejects this view, and points instead to a number of reasons why Russian transformations will continue to confound Western policymakers.

There is a reasonable amount of work that focuses on cultural hybridization in Russia (Pilkington 1994; Ritzer 1999: 76–7, 85; Lane 1995). The imagery of Western consumerist icons arriving in Moscow and elsewhere is now something of a cliché. But in economic terms Russia, and indeed the majority of the former Soviet Union and even Eastern Europe, is conspicuously absent in globalization narratives (Martin 1998). This could well be because the performance of the Russian economy since the end of the Soviet Union has been a major disappointment in Western eyes. Castells and Sklair are unrepresentative of the globalization literature in that they even consider the implications of Russia's position within 'global change'. It is quite common to allude in passing to 'the collapse of the Soviet Union' as a 'result of globalization' (EBRD 1999; Giddens 1999; Hardt and Negri 2000: xi, 276–9; Kaldor 1999; Lockwood 2000; Schaeffer 1997: 1; Urry 2000: 41–2), but that is where the Russian references tend to stop.

So there is something of an impasse which this book tends to take a step towards addressing. It sets about doing this through a combination of theory and narrative (Part I), empirical investigation (Part II) and further conceptual reflections (Part III). Left and right perspectives on development both need to embrace *evidence* as much as possible if they are to build theoretical pathways towards understanding the nature of contemporary capitalism in the regions. There should be no room for clichés and political polemics. Neither the new-right optimism (Fukuyama 1993; EBRD 2002), nor the old-left pessimism (Bilenkin 1996; Meiksins Wood 1997) has told all, or even the most part, of the story of Russian transformations in the period 1992–2003. Castells' three-volume work on globalization is arguably one of the finest so far. His truly international perspective does further our understanding of contemporary advanced Western capitalism, and the regions that are cut off from it, but there are major problems with his often overly deterministic view of the 'power of flows' in creating inclusion and exclusion, and much of his analysis is controversial in respect of its assumption that so much of the 'Old Economy' has been replaced by the 'New Economy' (2000a: 77–215). His coverage of the collapse of the USSR economy is extensive and convincing, but not especially original, and his coverage of post-Soviet Russia somewhat patchy, focusing almost exclusively on elites. However he has included the FSU region, which is more than can be said for nearly all the other major globalization writers.

What is required is a conceptually and empirically informed new path to understand Russia and 'globalization'. From this path it is hoped that ways can be found to include Russian experiences in new theories of capitalist development in today's world. We intend to look not so much at *Global Transformations* (Held *et al.* 2000) as *Russian Transformations*, hence the title. Armed with a proper understanding of how the theory and practice of capitalism relates to Russia, we should be in a position to theorize Russia's economic position in the contemporary world. Can local research relate in a meaningful way to the abstractions of global theory? It is hoped that it can. Small-scale qualitative work *on its own* is perhaps insufficient. For example, Bradley *et al.* (2000: ch. 1) have been criticized (McGovern 2001) for using a case study of the UK Northeast to critique the idea of globalization and the breakdown of tradition. But when everything is supposedly connected to 'global flows' then ethnography is surely relevant to global discourses (Burawoy 2000). It is important that challenges to the globalist assumptions are made, in order to test the boundaries of this new grand narrative. It would be unsatisfactory if the vast literature of globalization remains cut off from qualitative experiences of life at a local level. Hay and Marsh attempt to address this problem when they state that globalization for too long has been 'a process without a subject' (2000: 6), and the third wave literature should give a higher profile to individual agency.

Introducing *Russian Transformations*

Each of the chapters addresses several central questions:

- What is the nature of Russian capitalism as evidenced in the particular regions or economic sectors?
- How well connected (or otherwise) are these regions or sectors to the international economy?
- Are there any general themes that can be drawn on in order to explain the direction of Russian capitalism at large?
- To what extent is the direction of Russian society and economy determined by international policy, the trends of global capitalism, or fundamental Russian features?
- Where does this fit into the overall, Western academic and media views of globalization?

Let us introduce the chapters in more detail. If the globalization literature so far includes such contradictions and confusions, what theoretical backgrounds *can* be drawn on? This is the main question addressed by the chapters in Part I. Pınar Bedirhanoğlu (Chapter 2) opens the section with a discussion of the key factors involved in the attempts to privatize the Russian economy in the first half of the 1990s. After a brief narrative, the chapter broadens the discussion to focus on what theoretical understandings we can derive from the 'passive revolution' of the *nomenklatura*. In what sense is this supposed 'revolution' linked to ongoing trends for increased inequalities in advanced, 'globally-integrated' economies? To what extent is the emergent neoliberal consensus to blame for the inequalities and failures of Russian capitalism? And is Russian and post-Soviet particularism the cause of the elite-dominance of the privatization processes and outcomes?

Following the reform period, the second major event in the Russian reforms was the financial crisis of 1998, an event that actually took Russian economics, briefly at least, into the media's domain in most Western societies. It was often associated with international and global crises: the 'dark side' of globalization. Gustafson claims that the crash revealed 'just how far Russia had come in integrating itself into the global marketplace' (1999: 15). Again, such a claim needs to be tested, by way of attempting to explain the 1998 crash and the recovery, with reference to processes and outcomes of globalization. Anastasia Nesvetailova's chapter (3) provides an overview of what happened in this crisis period, its political context, and the implications for Russia's future in the Putin period.

This is followed by Gregory Schwartz (Chapter 4) on the problems associated with reforming Russian industrial enterprises. He explores in depth the nature of Soviet employment and management systems, and argues that transition theories are incapable of explaining how post-Soviet industrial firms operate. The specific organizational behaviour of Russian firms and managers are, Schwartz demonstrates, perfectly logical given the unique range of constraints that they face.

Hence, Part I asks whether the privatization strategy, the 1998 crisis and the subsequent recovery, and Russian organizational forms are best seen as resulting from the effects of globalization, the effects of Russian uniqueness, a combination of both, or none of the above.

Part II deals with the empirical details of our case study regions. The Russian Federation is a patchwork of regions that vary by size and by their formal and informal relationships with the federal centre of Moscow. In fact, the capital is where our narrative begins. In an attempt to bring human subjectivity into globalization discussions, Olga Shevchenko and Yakov Schukin (Chapter 5) examine the sociology of economic life of Muscovites at the micro level. It is in Moscow where one would expect to find the largest amounts of evidence for globalization at work, but even here the evidence is of some international connectedness accompanied by much continuity of Soviet-era isolation.

Raw material exports provide the main international connection of the Russian economy to the world economy, and they have played a huge role in Russia's post-1998 economic recovery. Here is certainly an area in which Russian capitalism is integrated with the 'global' economy. Ella Akerman's study of the oil and gas sectors (Chapter 6) sheds light on the ways in which 'variable and asymmetric globalization' play a part in Russia's export connections. Nevertheless, specific regional political and economic arrangements are critical to our understanding of Russian oil and gas.

A major part of the global literature is the theme of regionalization. Regions are said to be able to directly orient themselves towards 'global flows' of capital and markets, bypassing federal central control altogether. How realistic is this picture as regards Russia's numerous and diverse regions? The book examines specific regional centres that, at some stage, have been regarded as potential 'growth poles' within the Russian Federation. There is a pair of chapters on Novosibirsk, Siberia's largest city, then a pair of chapters on two parts of an emerging centre of Russia, the ethnically defined 'autonomous republics' located around the Volga and approaching the Urals. The Novosibirsk material in Chapter 7 by Sarah Busse Spencer examines labour markets and the informal economy. We see a picture of a region that does indeed have little to do with Moscow. However, rather than the optimistic conception of Novosibirsk directly involving itself in 'world' economics, what we see is unregulated local capitalism that is oriented towards its own distinctive norms and systems. While Busse Spencer's work focuses on actors' qualitative experiences, Caleb Southworth and Leontina Hormel use quantitative data and methods to analyse the dynamics of the processes of exit from 'formal' employment in the region (Chapter 8).

The story of informality and black and grey markets is a familiar one all over Russia. The autonomous republic of Tatarstan is no exception. The neoliberal transition consensus argues that informality is a major obstacle to reform, as is state management of the economy. However, the local Tatar government is a powerful system, despite its struggles to raise taxes and create trustworthy legal arrangements, and despite generalized economic hardship, inequality and informality. Leo McCann's chapter (9) on the influence of the Tatar state in steering the Tatar economy demonstrates how there are a diversity of development 'models' (if such they can be called), which involve a combination of formal and informal processes of state control of the economy.

Chapter 10 by Caleb Southworth examines the republic of Bashkortostan (a neighbour of Tatarstan) and looks in detail at the micro-level features of industrial organization. Bashkir factories exhibit much evidence of a persistence and adaptation of command-administrative industrial relations. Employees continue to work in these plants in spite of colossal wage arrears and great uncertainty. Southworth examines why workers retain their formal employment, and how the attempts to establish neoliberal capitalism have not succeeded in creating Western-style labour markets.

Finally, Richard Sakwa in Chapter 11 provides a review of the volume and suggests steps towards new theories of Russian postsocialism, and how this might relate to the broader Western social science narrative of globalization. By focusing on Russia and its regions, specifics of the areas and sectors can be united into a broader framework of Russian development. Other texts have looked at 'transition' in a less specific way, attempting to theorize around postcommunist developments wherever they take place, in such diverse places as Poland, Estonia, Vietnam and China (Pickles and Smith 1998). So far, such attempts have not produced particularly concrete results. It is hoped that focusing just on Russia (itself a vast territory, of course), both the *diversity and the commonalities* of postsocialist development can be given a higher profile.

This introduction, together with Part I, represents the start of a discussion that goes from the general to the particular, and back again. Let us start with an analysis of the concepts of transition and neoliberalism, and what their impacts have been on Russian development at large.

Notes

1 Many thanks to Anastasia Nesvetailova, University of Liverpool, for extensive comments and suggestions on this chapter.

2 Is a 'fourth wave' emerging? If so, this could be the fast-growing anti-globalization movement literature. These texts do not deny the existence of globalization (as with Hirst and Thompson 1999, or Bradley *et al.* 2000), but they are heavily critical of globalization's effects and the policies designed by governments and non-governmental organizations (NGOs) (under lobbying pressure from multinationals) to facilitate its further expansion. Such literature would include Stiglitz (2002), Heertz (2001), Monbiot (2001) and, of course, Klein (2000). Unfortunately this book lacks the scope to go into any detail on this potential 'fourth wave'.

Part I

Historical and theoretical observations

2 The *nomenklatura*'s passive revolution in Russia in the neoliberal era

Pınar Bedirhanoğlu

Introduction

By the end of the Yeltsin period in 1999, the early Western optimism about the establishment of a liberal state and society in Russia was replaced by a more critical and cautious stance because of the rise of corruption, crime and authoritarianism in the socio-political sphere and the development of an oligopolistic market structure in the economy. This change in attitude, however, has not led to a significant sense of self-criticism within those liberal perspectives (namely, of the shock therapists and the institutionalists), which have dominated academic studies and proposed supposedly opposing policies on 'transition' during the 1990s. On the contrary, the emergence of these problems in Russia was seen as an opportunity to re-validate their assumptions on social change. For the institutionalists, shock therapy-style authoritarian interventions, which had been conducted in total disregard of the country's institutional needs and legacies, would have apparently led to nowhere but such a disastrous outcome. Economic reforms, they claimed, could have been pursued at a lower cost if complemented with additional steps to build reliable legal and judicial institutions and establish rule of law (McFaul 1995: 225–6; Breslauer *et al.* 2000: 4–5). The opposite approach of the Russian policy-makers and their advisers had resulted in Russia missing the opportunities for not only democratisation but also economic restructuring along efficiency lines and integration into the stimulating competition of the world market. On the other hand, the response of the shock therapists to these criticisms as well as their alternative explanation was simple enough: the failure had been due not to the implementation but to the non-implementation of their recipes. Hence, the irresponsible, rent-seeking Russian ruling elite becomes the sole target of blame.

This debate, which placed all the burden of 'failure' on specifically Russian dynamics, had little explanatory value. It refused to comprehend Russian social transformation as also a globally conditioned process. Against this debate, which ultimately served to preserve an idealised Western model of democracy and market economy intact, this chapter will argue that Russian social transformation in the 1990s with all its unfavourable consequences mentioned above cannot be isolated from the traumatic global restructuring of capitalism along neoliberal principles; just the contrary, it has to be examined as a by-product of this process itself.

In line with the neo-Gramscian school in IR, it is acknowledged here that the neoliberal project, which is organically shaped by the long-term economic-corporate interests of globally operating transnational capital, has been imposed on many countries since the 1980s as a 'universal truth' by the disciplinary interventions of Western financial institutions as well as the pressures created by de-regulated financial markets. The Russian transformation during the Yeltsin period cannot be isolated from this global process even though its principal task was defined as transition to market economy and the establishment of liberal democracy in the country. In practice, the 'transition' agenda turned out to be a standard neoliberal restructuring process with all its negative socio-political implications, as experienced in other countries, alongside specific consequences produced within the Russian context.

Coming to the question of the *means* through which the constitutive impact of the 'global' on Russian social transformation will be examined, this chapter focuses on the IMF, for it was the major institution that directed the flow of finance in and out of Russia in the 1990s. Hence, Russian social transformation within the neoliberal global context is explored by focusing mainly on the determining interventions of the International Monetary Fund (IMF) in this process.[1] Associating the IMF with this complex process as a whole might be considered as dealing with an incommensurate correlation at first sight, since the Fund is by definition an international financial organisation that claims to propose technical solutions to member countries' macroeconomic problems. Against this commonsensical perception, however, it is one of the important aims of this chapter to denote the political and ideological implications of the IMF policies by examining how they imposed transnational capitalist interests on Russia. Specifically, the study attempts to reveal the disciplinary mechanisms and processes used by the IMF to restructure Russian political economy along neoliberal principles. It discusses how the IMF shaped the conditions of the *nomenklatura*'s passive revolution[2] in Yeltsin's Russia.

Shock therapy as part of a passive revolutionary strategy

Although the question of how the Gorbachev-driven move towards the establishment of democratic socialism was replaced by the Yeltsin-led authoritarian process of change deserves to be examined in detail, answering this question will not be attempted here. In the late 1980s, the neoliberal reform option was only a marginal choice among others. Besides the Abalkin programme in 1989, which was an all-inclusive presentation of Gorbachev's radical democratic project, there were also other liberal reform proposals such as Shatalin's 500-days programme (August 1990) or Yavlinsky and Allison's plan for a more regionally cooperative transition (June 1991), which were both prepared in the light of Poland's shock therapy experience (Flaherty 1991: 156; Lavigne 1995: 126). Among these, Yavlinsky and Allison's proposal was important, not only because Yavlinsky himself had always been a dedicated liberal democrat in the Western sense, but also because it was a holistic project containing both economic and political concerns, which would have satisfied today's institutionalist critiques. Although in content it comprised the same set of economic policies that were later implemented by Yeltsin and Gaidar, its emphasis on institution building and socially protective policies such as rationing of consumer goods to enable people to buy at socially acceptable prices indicated its difference from the classical shock therapy programme. Its ambition was to meet two hard targets – namely the constitution of a market structure and the establishment of a bourgeois state – simultaneously in Russia. Yavlinsky and Allison hoped that the proposed social measures and concern displayed in the establishment of rule of law would have provided the state with active social support during the implementation of the economic policies despite their possible negative effects (Allison and Yavlinsky 1991).

Rather than choosing such a path, however, having enjoyed the legitimacy he acquired from the August coup, Yeltsin preferred to freeze the political situation by preserving the *status quo* and concentrated mainly on economic reforms (McFaul 1995: 226–7; Mau 1996: 68). The liberalisation of prices in January 1992 immediately caused hyperinflation, a drastic fall in living standards and a huge collapse in industrial production.[3] The hasty mass privatisations realised from 1992 to 1995 under hyperinflationary conditions constituted another failure story for the government. Despite the appreciation of the IMF and the World Bank, privatisation ultimately served to strengthen and even corrupt the established relations of production rather than transform them. Moreover, the government's attempts to fight inflation and decrease the budget deficit by imposing higher taxes and interest rates forced many newly flourishing small entrepreneurs out of business, strengthening the oligopolisation trend in the economy (Nelson and Kuzes 1995b: 123, 136).

These negative results however did not prevent Yeltsin from defending shock therapy as the right choice in his memoirs. There, in fact, he further revealed that their aims were more destructive than constructive. In his own words:

> Gaidar's reform ensured a macroeconomic shift, namely: the destruction of the old economy. It was terribly painful, done without the brilliance of a surgeon – on the contrary, with a kind of rusty scalpel, as bits of worn-out parts and machinery were torn with the flesh – but the amputation nevertheless took place.
>
> (quoted from Gordon and Pliskevich 1995: 23)

This 'end justifies the means' reasoning was shared by almost all advocates of shock therapy in the early 1990s as a necessary move to prevent well-established communist interests in Russia transforming their political power into economic power.

Against this argument, which presented the implementation of shock therapy at the expense of democratic reforms as a historical necessity, it can be claimed that Yeltsin's policies in this period were consciously formulated to eliminate any possibility of the socialisation of politics in Russia, which had been experienced during the Gorbachev years. Particularly in his first two years in office, Yeltsin effectively abolished all social initiatives that would have served to create alternative power bases to the established interests in the country. He suppressed the communist and patriotic opposition,[4] and made life difficult for the Democratic Russia Movement (*DemRossiia*). The Movement, which comprised the best-educated people of the country, such as scientists, engineers, teachers, doctors, artists, highly skilled technical workers and department heads of industrial enterprises (Garcelon 1997: 44) as well as dissidents, had always advocated a liberal democratic order in Russia, a goal which Yeltsin declared himself to be loyal to. A closer examination of Yeltsin's relationship with *DemRossiia* reveals that, apart from historical moments of close cooperation, which in fact enabled Yeltsin to strengthen his political position against the opposing interests in the parliament,[5] Yeltsin always kept his distance from the Movement, and refrained from engaging in any organic relationship with it (Brudny 1993: 164–6). In other moments, when the Movement took its mission of democratisation *too* seriously,[6] Yeltsin used various political tactics to curb the oppositional potential of *DemRossiia* and rendered it inoperative.

The apparent contradiction between the above-mentioned 'historical necessity' discourse and Yeltsin's conscious policies to dissolve any sort of democratic popular movement in the country might be resolved if these two are considered as part of a passive revolutionary strategy, which intended to realise the transition to a market economy in Russia in the form of an intra-*nomenklatura* bargaining process rather than a democratic one.[7] In this sense, rather than being an anti-*nomenklatura* move, as is usually claimed, Yeltsin-led shock therapy helped the former *nomenklatura* to consolidate around the capitalist project, the immediately available alternative in the early 1990s, which was historically proven to be the best in accommodating class exploitation. It created the most appropriate conditions for the former *nomenklatura* to transform itself into Russia's new capitalist class. In this process, also defined as primitive accumulation (Holmstrom and Smith 2000), Yeltsin's Caesarist[8] role prevented the collapse of the equilibrium established among social forces. The intervention of transnational capitalist interests, mediated most powerfully by the IMF in Russia, complemented Yeltsin's authoritarian project as well as creating some new tensions for it by insistently imposing the neoliberal agenda.

Launching shock therapy

The shock therapy programme was launched in Russia with the liberalisation of the vast majority of prices in January 1992. One day after liberalisation, Russia applied for full membership in the IMF, with which she already had a special association agreement since October 1991 (Wertman 1996: 87). In February 1992, the IMF and Russia agreed on the economic policy for 1992. After this date – particularly after Russia's full membership in the Fund in June 1992 – the economic policies implemented by the government were conducted in close association with the IMF's advisory and financial assistance, and, no less significantly, in dependence on the confidence or non-confidence signals given by the IMF to other international financial institutions – namely, the World Bank, London and Paris Clubs – international rating institutions and private investors.[9]

Besides the IMF support, the early uncontested implementation of shock therapy should be understood in relation to the strong prestige and legitimacy endowed by the August coup to Yeltsin. If the coup had not taken place, it would have been harder for the radical liberals to implement this socially destructive programme with dedication. For, despite their initial marginality, the August *putsch* provided Yeltsin and the radical liberals with the minimum necessary time until various opposing interests[10] were co-opted gradually into the regime from mid-1992 onwards. To take up the responsibility of the transition programme, a qualitatively new government, composed largely of radical liberals, was formed in Russia in November 1991 and headed by Yeltsin, who was now granted extraordinary decree powers to conduct social change (Chervyakov 1995: 240).[11] Yeltsin delegated the implementation of shock therapy to his deputy prime ministers, Yegor Gaidar, Gennady Burbulis and Alexandr Shokhin, while Anatolii Chubais became the chairman of the State Committee on Managing State Property (GKI) (Slider 1994: 370–1). It was this group of people which resolved to undertake the initial radical and hasty steps towards the declared aim of transition to a market economy in Russia.

The legitimacy and prestige provided by the August coup also granted radical liberals a temporary power of manoeuvre in the Congress, the legislative powers of which had been vastly strengthened by Gorbachev's reforms in the name of democratisation (Breslauer and Dale 1997: 306).[12] Although 87 per cent of the inherited Congress were former CPSU members, even if mostly with technocratic backgrounds (Sakwa 1990: 138; Cappelli 1993: 116), the dispersing impact of the coup prevented them from organising effective resistance against government policies for some time (Mau 1996: 67). Once they recovered from their initial shock, however, their intensive and organised attempts to control and reshape the implementation of shock therapy urged Yeltsin to search for a compromise with some of the groups in opposition. In the meantime, he also tried to overcome various deadlocks with recourse to the popular support mobilised by *DemRossiia*.

In that sense, it can be argued that the period to October 1993 was a tough one for Yeltsin. Throughout it he pushed hard for intra-*nomenklatura* conciliation by using popular support as a bargaining chip without institutionalising the latter's active involvement in politics.

The liberalisation of prices led to hyperinflationary conditions in Russia. It is true that the Gaidar government's successive attempts to stabilise the economy through higher taxes and interest rates and lower public spending produced a short-term improvement in economic indicators in technical terms (Shleifer and Treisman 2000: 41). However, in terms of their impact on the real economy, the same stabilisation policies served to destroy Russia's productive base. Industrial output in the country decreased on average by about 15 per cent each year from 1992 to 1995 (Williams 1996: 13). Opposed to the rhetoric of the market economy, these policies drove many small entrepreneurs out of business leaving the ground to the well-established state-owned enterprises, which were powerful enough to avoid tax payment (Nelson and Kuzes 1995b: 123). Furthermore, the unmanageable rise of prices led to the de-monetarisation of the Russian market due to inter-enterprise debts and wages either paid in kind or simply unpaid (McFaul 1995: 235; Burawoy 1996: 1110; Clarke 1996: 33). In short, contrary to shock therapy's declared aim to submit state enterprises to the discipline of the market, price liberalisation and the succeeding stabilisation policies brought about the subordination of the market to the requirements of the reproduction of the monopolistic state sector (Clarke 1993a: 234).

Despite these contradictory and, from a liberal point of view, unfavourable consequences of shock therapy, the IMF supported the Yeltsin reform efforts, albeit somewhat reluctantly. Under the pressure of Western governments and most notably the United States, the Fund agreed to provide Russia with a $4 billion stand-by credit after its prospective full membership[13] as part of the $24 billion aid package promised by Western governments in the G7 Summit in April 1992. Moreover, although it was an unusual practice, the IMF released $1 billion of this amount immediately in August through a first credit tranche loan on more relaxed conditions (Stone 2001: 184).[14]

The mass privatisation programme

The mass privatisation programme, which formally started in December 1992 and ended in July 1994, also had contradictory implications. Despite praise from the IMF and the World Bank, it served to strengthen and corrupt established relations of production rather than transform them. As examined in detail in various studies on Russian social transformation,[15] both the specific form and practical implementation of the privatisation programme became subject to fierce dispute between the radical liberals and the industrial interests in Russia. The process turned out to be an effective device to transform the political authority of the former *nomenklatura* into economic power. Implementation of the programme under hyperinflationary conditions exacerbated this outcome further by drawing small entrepreneurs out of the market, despite Yeltsin's populist discourse which presented voucher privatisation as an opportunity for everyone to have equal access to the ownership of state property, hence 'a unique ticket . . . to a free economy . . . with "millions of property owners" rather than "a handful of millionaires"'.[16]

Although the highlighted purpose of mass privatisations was the distribution of ownership, and in conformity with this aim the Gaidar government initially supported the idea of the sale of state assets with low prices to citizens (Clarke and Kabalina 1995: 145; Gray 1998: 145–6), the privatisation process was ultimately designed with some macroeconomic considerations (Nelson and Kuzes 1995b: 125). In contrast to the immediate efficiency purpose underlying earlier *glasnost*-era privatisations in the Soviet Union, the main intention of the post-1991 privatisations in Russia was to deal with the budget deficit problem by reducing the state's financial obligations to inefficient enterprises and bringing in revenues from their sale. The efficiency conditions were to be established later, following the subsequent redistribution process, which would have taken place when the vouchers or enterprise shares were bought by responsible owners in the secondary markets (Nelson and Kuzes 1995b: 125–6). Such redistribution, it was argued, would have paved the way for the creation of a new propertied class in Russia at the expense of established 'conservative' interests (Clarke and Kabalina 1995: 145).

As expected, industrial interests fiercely opposed the government's privatisation scheme, which threatened to destroy their authority over the productive base. Their alternative 'insider' model, which ultimately became the dominant form in Russian privatisation, proposed the sale of 51 per cent of each enterprise's shares to its employees at nominal prices, with the aim of workforce and management ownership of shares (Nelson and Kuzes 1995b: 126). Despite its unwillingness to do so, the government had to come to terms with this proposal not only due to the strength of the industrial interests, but because it failed to find buyers and ensure popular support for the radical liberal option (Clarke and Kabalina 1995: 145).

On the other hand, the radical liberals' 'defeat' by the industrial interests can be evaluated also as a concrete concession made by the former to the latter in order to reach a long-term compromise to strengthen the radical liberals' position in the parliament (Shleifer and Treisman 2000: 33).[17] For, although mass privatisation enabled the workers and managers to become major stakeholders in 70 per cent of the privatised enterprises (Slider 1994: 367; Gray 1998: 145–6), given the managers' inherited ability to control the labour collective, what really happened was that the managers became *de facto* owners of the enterprises without any formal responsibility (Mau 1996: 73). In fact, this outcome was evident to the radical liberals from the beginning. Supporting the argument that the ultimate privatisation model had been a stake provided to the industrial interests by the Yeltsin government, Shleifer and Boycko[18] in their 1993 article on Russian privatisation, argued explicitly that '[a]ny manager in Russia today can use the programme to become rich and remain in control' (Blanchard *et al.* 1993: 39).

Nevertheless, the position of the industrial *nomenklatura* in Russian political economy remained vulnerable. To continue production, they needed not only to upgrade their technological and organisational capabilities, but also to ensure the support of the state in preventing foreign competitors from freely flowing into the Russian market. However, trade and price liberalisation policies of the Gaidar government brought about not a relief but a further squeeze on industrial enterprises. While the elimination of administrative controls on imports in 1992 and the cessation of investment prospects curbed their marketing opportunities in Russia,[19] the rises in the domestic prices of primary products increased production costs, further aggravating problems of competitiveness (Sitaryan and Krasnov 1995: 526). Under these conditions and given the much easier enrichment opportunities created by hyperinflation in the spheres of exchange and finance, a corrupt process of wealth transfer from state enterprises to managers through the establishment of financial and trading intermediaries started. On the other hand, playing into the hands of the radical liberals, the privatisation process also led over time to a split in the industrial bloc, as the expectations of the profitable and relatively competitive enterprises started to differ from those of the less profitable ones. While the former shifted towards a more liberal attitude towards liberal reforms, the latter strove harder for protection and state subsidies for survival (Shleifer and Treisman 2000: 16–17).

Yeltsin's struggle for compromise with the centrist opposition

Although the implementation of shock therapy had a disastrous effect on Russian society, it had been primarily managers of the industrial enterprises and those connected to industry within the former *nomenklatura* who expressed their opposition more effectively against the government due to their inherited organised politico-economic power. Although they did not oppose the capitalist turn assumed by Yeltsin's transition programme, these groups – which can be labelled the centrist opposition – criticised the shock and anti-inflationist strategy selected on the grounds that this would result in Russia's productive base going bankrupt. The worsening problems in the economy, such as deflation, the fall in demand and accumulating inter-enterprise debts, in fact indicated the validity of such arguments, strengthening their oppositional power. Their reaction culminated in the formation of the Union of Industrialists and Entrepreneurs (RSPP). The real signs of a threat to the radical liberals appeared when the RSPP established a pro-inflationary bloc with other opposing groups against the government in spring 1992 (Mau 1996: 72–3).

The consolidation of the opposition urged Yeltsin to announce in the troubled 6th Congress that he would make some partial corrections in his economic reform policy. In conformity with this, he relieved most of the duties of his principal allies in the government, such as Burbulis and Shokhin,[20] and provided tax breaks for industry as well as subsidies for agriculture.[21] Furthermore, he incorporated some leading members of industrial, military and energy production sectors, such as Vladimir Shumeiko, Georgii Khizha and Victor Chernomyrdin, into the government in May 1992 – a move which can be interpreted in Gramscian terms as a classic piece of transformism.[22] Although it did not help Yeltsin alleviate the sharp criticisms of the opposition immediately, this initiative proved to be influential in leading to a gradual differentiation of concerns within the centrist opposition. Having secured significant export privileges for the fuel and energy sector, members of the Fuel and Energy Complex (FEC) started to incline towards cooperating with importers and to negotiate with radical liberals for a new foreign trade regime, which would enable the flow of foreign capital and technology to upgrade the extracting sector and secure privileges (Chervyakov 1995: 243–5). This enabled the FEC's gradual adaptation to the neoliberal path. This trend accelerated after Yeltsin's December 1992 appointment of Chernomyrdin, former head of Gazprom (Russia's giant natural gas monopoly), as the Prime Minister in place of Gaidar.

Nevertheless, the gradual fragmentation of the centrist opposition and the incorporation of the FEC into economic policy-making did not bring Yeltsin the relief he desired. In early 1993, Yeltsin's exigency for the centrists' support was due to the intensifying conflict in the Congress between himself, who was pushing for establishing an all-powerful Presidency, and the Supreme Soviet, headed by Khasbulatov, who was campaigning to increase the power of the parliament at the expense of the government. Having been aware of their key role for the political survival of Yeltsin, the centrists never provided him with unconditional support, but tried to use their power to influence the implementation of economic reforms as much as they could.

Hence, when Yeltsin was forced to hold a referendum[23] in April 1993 to prove people's support for reforms and strengthen his hand against the radical opposition, his primary aides were still *DemRossiia* on the one hand and the West on the other. *DemRossiia* organised street demonstrations, whereas the West provided him with an extraordinary level of financial support. Having met Yeltsin on 4 April in the United States, Clinton offered $1.623 billion in aid and loans to Russia. Under the pressure of the United States, the IMF announced that the Fund would provide Russia with $4.5 billion credits under highly relaxed conditions to solve its inflation and budget deficit problems. In addition, the United States also urged G7 countries to declare their intention to lend Russia up to $30 billion in the next five years through the IMF (Stone 2001: 187).[24]

The deadlock radical liberals faced in the Supreme Soviet was resolved by the constitutional crisis, which started with Yeltsin's unconstitutional dissolution of the parliament. Despite all the risks, the crisis miraculously ended on 4 October with the military's support for the President[25] and helped change the threatening political atmosphere into one in favour of Yeltsin in Russia.[26] The new Russian constitution, which formed an all-powerful presidency,[27] provided Yeltsin with the firm authority he had long desired, though out of the 54.8 per cent of the registered electorate 58.4 per cent voted in favour of the new constitution (White 1994: 15), which effectively meant less than 35 per cent of the total eligible votes. The Western governments tolerated Yeltsin's unconstitutional act and declared their firm support for him on the condition that he would be loyal to the principles of representative democracy. Besides this rhetoric of democracy, however, the French government spokesman Nicolas Sarcovi's public statement indicated that the best the West expected was an electoral dictatorship in the country. He declared that 'there is no other alternative than to support Boris Yeltsin, at least as long as he adheres to his decision to hold free elections'.[28]

The constitutional crisis represented a significant turning point for Yeltsin's passive revolution in Russia. Although the successive Congresses, formed after the 1993 and 1995 parliamentary elections, were as hostile as the one he had dissolved in September 1993,[29] Yeltsin's right to dissolve the parliament and issue decrees with the force of law enabled him to continue with the transition programme insistently from then on. Even though the opposition parties continued to put pressure on the government on various issues, their unwillingness to risk the dissolution of Congress forced them to come to terms with Yeltsin at the last moment rather than opposing firmly his legislative acts. Moreover, although fierce disputes persisted within the transforming dominant class over various crucial issues such as privatisation and stabilisation, compromises could become possible on a parliamentary basis. This largely eliminated the burden of occasional appeal to the masses, limiting the scope of politics. For Yeltsin, this meant that the necessity of considering the 'lumpen bourgeois' democratic demands of *DemRossiia* was finally over.

Stabilisation attempts after 1994

In terms of political struggle, the period after the formation of super-presidential rule was qualitatively different from the preceding one in Russia, for it acquired a highly intra-*nomenklatura* character due to the prevention of the socialisation of politics and the elimination of the political weapons of the parliamentary opposition. Having already met almost all the criteria to be defined as a Caesar in his first two years in office, Yeltsin, with his new extensive administrative powers, was now ready to fulfil new tasks for the transformation of the former *nomenklatura* into a capitalist ruling class. Hence, the succeeding period that lasted until the end of 1996 saw his closer collaboration with the so-called Russian oligarchs as well as with the much criticised state monopolies. However, the rest of his time in power would also prove that, under the gradually intensifying IMF pressures for neoliberal restructuring, passive revolution would in no way be an easy task at the end of the twentieth century.

Having seen Yeltsin emerge from another crisis stronger than ever and with more control over the economy, the West – through the IMF – decided to take an active part in Russian transformation starting from early 1994. The victory of the nationalists and communists in the 1993 parliamentary elections and the exit of Gaidar and Fedorov from the government in January 1994 were significant warnings that forced the West to pursue a more careful attitude towards Russia after this date.[30] In the face of the Clinton administration's intensive criticisms of the Fund, the IMF re-engaged in credit disbursement negotiations with Russia and demanded rather moderate targets, such as 7 per cent monthly inflation and a budget deficit of no more than 10 per cent of the GDP at the end of the year (Stone 2001: 190–1). As a result of these negotiations, the IMF and Russia agreed on the disbursement of the second half of the STF loan of $1.5 billion on 22 March (Wertman 1996: 89).

On the other hand, the IMF also considered Yeltsin's super-presidency as an opportunity to intensify its influence on the government's policies by shifting its negotiation strategy from the ordinary conditionality practice to a 'short-term bargaining posture' (Stone 2001: 191). This change in strategy practically transformed the IMF's supposedly 'external' impact on Russia into an 'internal' one, for thereafter the Fund started to exert a direct and visible pressure on the government's policies during its regular visits to Moscow.

While Russia's relationship with the IMF was improving, Yeltsin tried to promote a compromise with various interests in Russia by initiating a Civic Accord in February. Having promised financial stability, economic growth and reduced inflation as its ultimate target in return for their political support and supportive economic practices, the government managed to conclude a two-year reconciliation in April with more than 350 public figures – leading bankers and business people at the top of the social hierarchy – with the exception of the Agrarian Party, CPRF and Yavlinsky's Yabloko (Gill and Markwick 2000: 182–3).

What the government proposed was more than words, for the problem of inflation in Russia had long been a very lucrative business, which could not easily be given up by the commercial banks. Under conditions of hyperinflation since the start of shock therapy, they had made big profits by borrowing cheap rouble deposits from the Central Bank and investing them in foreign currencies with positive real interest rates (Schröder 1999: 965). The banks had also enjoyed the privilege of paying negative real interest rates on people's deposits as the government had assisted them by preventing foreign banks from entering the Russian market (Shleifer and Treisman 2000: 54).[31] Hence, in order to prevent the banking sector's engagement in inflationary practices the government had to promote better chances of enrichment. The promotion of short-term state securities (GKOs) with positive real interest rates to Russian financial capital (Gustafson 1999: 90) after 1994 has to be evaluated within this context, although the government presented this move as a remedy to the chronic budget deficit problem. During the implementation of the new policy, the banks were not given equal access to the GKO market as the state determined an initial twenty-five Russian banks and brokers as the authorised institutions to buy GKOs from the state and sell in the secondary markets with profits exempt from tax (Johnson 1997: 351; Schröder 1999: 965; Shleifer and Treisman 2000: 62–4).[32] This solution proved to be an effective device in bringing inflation down from a monthly high of 22 per cent in January 1994 to 8.1 per cent in May, 4.8 per cent in June, 5 per cent in July and 7.7 per cent in September[33] while creating on the other hand a gradually accumulating short term domestic debt burden for the state. Moreover, as large credits continued to be provided to the agricultural sector as well as the northern regions, the budget deficit problem persisted (Shleifer and Treisman 2000: 43).

Besides the GKOs, Chernomyrdin declared that they needed to pursue tougher credit and monetary policies to stabilise the exchange rate of the rouble.[34] The Russian government increased real interest rates and made credits scarce for the loss-making enterprises (Burawoy 1996: 1111) and introduced a rouble corridor in the summer of 1995 (Wertman 1996: 93). Although this last measure put more pressure on the Central Bank, which frequently faced the necessity of intervening in the markets by depleting its hard currency reserves, these policies finally drove inflation down to 0–5 per cent from mid-1995 to mid-1997 (Stone 2001: 201–2).

It is true that the introduction of the rouble corridor had a negative impact on the bank profits not only due to the end of the inflationary period, but also due to the fact that the CBR had sharply increased the banks' reserve requirements by between 5 and 20 per cent[35] (Gill and Markwick 2000: 217–18; Shleifer and Treisman 2000: 61). However, given the advantages provided by GKOs, only the banks that lacked state assistance had become the losers in this process, while the privileged group of banks managed to avoid the negative consequences of the policy (Schröder 1999: 965–6).

The other groups that lost due to the stabilisation policies were the export sector, whose competitiveness in the world markets had been curbed substantially by the stagnating exchange rate (Aslanova and Pashkova 1997: 158), and state industrial enterprises and farms, which used to rely on government subsidies for survival (Shleifer and Treisman 2000: 71). The rouble corridor made the production of Russian ferrous metals such as steel and aluminium more costly, while the export of crude oil became more profitable than petroleum products in time (Aslanova and Pashkova 1997: 158). As Clarke (1998b: 17, fn. 4) informs, the deteriorating export conditions for fuel, steel and iron led to a fall in their production by a third between 1990 and 1996, while electricity generation was down by 20 per cent. Despite these negative developments, however, neither the energy sector nor most of the state enterprises ended up with total failure as the government continued to support them through other policies. The energy sector, which had become the motor force of the Russian economy, was supported through various tax exemptions, while state enterprises were provided with sales credits and guaranteed gas and electricity supply even though they failed to pay their bills to Gazprom and to UES (the Russian energy monopoly) (Shleifer and Treisman 2000: 16–17, 71–3). This was made possible by the state's toleration of the monopolies' late or non-payments of tax – a policy that attracted intensifying criticisms from the IMF. It was due to this 'grand compromise' that these monopolies, most specifically Gazprom, were often labelled 'the state's second budget'.

After this brief examination, in order to answer the question of who really lost as a result of the state's stabilisation efforts, we have to turn to the working classes, since the resultant industrial stalemate without bankruptcy put them in a rather strange and insecure position vis-à-vis enterprise management. As long as the enterprises were kept at the margin of bankruptcy by the grand compromise, the workers were not laid off, but they were not paid either. Having been aware of the vulnerable relations at the factory, Yeltsin strictly vetoed the minimum wage draft law proposed by the parliament and prevented any other law on labour to acquire priority in the agenda of Russian politics from then on.[36]

Despite the costs of the government's stabilisation policies to the majority of the population, Russia's apparent success in improving its macroeconomic indicators was endorsed by the IMF on March 1995 with a stand-by agreement of $6.8 billion, the second largest loan in the Fund's history after the Mexican bailout in 1994 (Stone 2001: 193). Elimination of tax exemptions to the energy sector as a remedy to the budget deficit problem was one of the important conditions the Fund demanded in return,[37] although the tense political atmosphere before the 1995 parliamentary and 1996 presidential elections prevented the IMF from insisting the Russian government comply with this condition. However, monthly disbursement of credit tranches provided the Fund with the opportunity to discuss the performance of the Russian economy regularly with the country's top bureaucrats, as mentioned before.

The rise of financial-industrial groups in Russia

The term Russian 'financial-industrial groups' (FIGs), or more crudely Russian 'oligarchs', started to appear frequently in academia and the media after the mid-1990s, although the roots of their formation dates back to the early 1990s. The reason for their late recognition was probably the FIGs' increasingly corrupt relationship with the state, which reached its peak on the eve of the 1996 presidential elections, a situation which substantially impeded the establishment of a modern capitalist state in Russia.

When the mass privatisation process created the first small-scale FIGs in Russia as early as 1992, this was considered as a defensive development against market instability (Smitienko and Karaeva 1994: 320). However, this relatively defensive attitude of the FIGs changed into an aggressive and demanding one in time, as these groups increased their economic as well as political powers with the active support of the state. Hence, if the first round of privatisations led to their emanation, the second one, which took place through the state-initiated 'shares-for-loans' programme in mid-1995, resulted in their enormous empowerment.

The logic of the shares-for-loans programme was quite simple, though its consequences were complex and manifold. When Yeltsin authorised by a decree on 31 August 1995 the auctioning of twenty-nine state-owned lucrative enterprises to a selective list of banks, among which Vladimir Potanin's ONEKSIMbank, Mikhail Khodorkovski's Menatep and Boris Berezovsky's LogoVAZ were the most prominent, this initiative was presented to the public as the state's attempt to raise revenues for its budget deficit problem. In return for the 'loans' they had given to the state, the banks acquired management control over various state enterprises, operating in the fields of oil and other natural resources, for a temporary period. The tricky condition was that, if the state failed to repay these loans, the banks would have acquired the right to sell their shares in auctions and get their money back (Johnson 1997: 352). When, however, this happened systematically at the end of the determined dates, the shares-for-loans programme became a *de facto* privatisation process for the large-scale state enterprises. In the auctions, based on unfair conditions between 1996 and 1997, packets of shares of many state enterprises were acquired by the banks and their management, leading to outcries from those who were unable to gain from this lucrative business. At the end of this process, ONEKSIMbank had managed to acquire significant share portions in Sidanko Oil and Norilsk Nickel, Menatep in Yukos Oil, and LogoVAZ in Sibneft Oil, with the participation of Alexandr Smolenski's SBS-Agro (Johnson 1997: 352; Schröder 1999: 976–7). As might have been expected, a series of corrupt auction practices generated major conflict within the transforming dominant class. The amounts paid in return for the world's leading natural resource companies were nowhere near proportional to their real values (Gill and Markwick 2000: 218). They were practically given away for free.

The political importance of this development was that it ensured these groups' firm support for Yeltsin during the highly risky presidential elections in summer 1996. Given the fact that, besides their controlling shares in many newspapers, Menatep, LogoVAZ, Alfa-Group and SBS-Agro jointly acquired over 40 per cent of the shares of the most important Russian TV channel ORT in July 1995 (Schröder 1999: 967), it was apparent that the support provided by the FIGs to Yeltsin would be more than financial. With enormous media propaganda, directed by Chubais on the demand of the oligarchs (Johnson 1997: 349) and with financial backing of the FIGs, very low pre-election support for Yeltsin turned out to be a victory in the elections. The aftermath of the elections saw the appointments of Chubais and Nemtsov as the first deputies to prime minister, Potanin as the Deputy Prime Minister responsible for economic policy and privatisation, and Berezovsky as the Deputy Secretary of the Security Council responsible for Chechnya (Johnson 1997: 351; Gill and Markwick 2000: 195–6). The direct representation of the transforming capitalist class in the bureaucracy as well as an exchange practice in the other direction with bureaucrats acquiring positions in the FIGs continued intensively during Yeltsin's new term in office (Johnson 1997: 350; Gill and Markwick 2000: 219).

Besides the full support of the oligarchs, who benefited substantially from the election in the end, what was more striking was the scale of support provided by the West to Yeltsin and his visibly corrupt election campaign throughout 1996. The IMF's attitude towards Russia in this period was extremely tolerant despite the state's huge expenditures due to the election campaign. The Fund was very concerned about the deferred and relieved taxes of the FIGs and state monopolies as well as the continuing export taxes, but it did not raise these issues to the attention of the public in an effective way before the elections. Moreover, besides paying the last tranche of the March 1995 stand-by loan in early February 1996, the Fund agreed on a three-year Extended Financing Facility (EFF) loan of $10.2 billion, through which Russia would be able to receive $4 billion in 1996 on a monthly basis again. Although the Fund demanded Russia reduce its budget deficit by 4 per cent in 1996, to 3 per cent in 1997 and 3 per cent in 1998, and abolish export taxes,[38] it backtracked with a clear concession to the election preparations. The IMF allowed high levels of state spending in the first half of 1996 (Stone 2001: 195). This represented explicit support for Yeltsin's election campaign. On the other hand, a similarly tolerant attitude could easily be observed in the West's direct credits to the Russian government before the elections. The French government announced a $990 million credit to be used in research and development[39] and German banks extended $2.7 billion of new credits to Russia under the guarantee of the German government.[40] Additionally, with the support of the United States, Russia signed a debt-rescheduling agreement with the Paris Club in May 1996 for its foreign debt inherited from the Soviet period, and was provided with a six-year grace period from the payments on the principal amount.[41] The full implementation of the deal was made conditional, however, upon improvements in economic reforms.[42]

The attack on state monopolies: the end of the 'grand compromise'

The IMF–Russia relationship substantially changed after Yeltsin's re-election as President. Most of the issues which the Fund used to criticise regularly (though without being able to insist upon due to the vulnerability of the political situation), were brought to the government's attention in a more determined way through the disciplinary 'stick' of finance. Immediately after the elections on 24 July, the IMF delayed the disbursement of the July tranche of the EFF loan due to the government's poor tax collection performance.[43]

On the other hand, as the thirty-point programme declared by Chernomyrdin in the wake of the elections, which stated that the state would impose severe fines on enterprises with overdue tax arrears[44] indicated, the government was also intending to squeeze the monopolies and the FIGs, albeit within the limits of what was possible. Given the representation of the oligarchs in the government in person as well as the state's hitherto organic relationship with the energy monopolies, it was apparent that this would not be an easy task. The envisioned struggle was going to be one *within* the state. The financial problems which had accumulated during the election period were forcing the government to find a proper way out of the deficit plight. Due to the easy money policies pursued during the election campaign, there was a 47 per cent drop in the CBR's gold and foreign-currency reserves[45] and the uncertainty of the election environment had already risen the treasury bond interest rates to over 200 per cent.[46] Under the pressure of these problems, as well as the squeeze of the IMF, the necessity to deal with the energy monopolies' tax arrears quickly approached the top of the government's agenda. Nevertheless, the struggle to collect taxes was administered more by Yeltsin and his individual radical liberal aides than by the centrists, due to the latters' continuing links particularly with Gazprom. If Gazprom's role as the second budget of the state is recalled, it was apparent that the new tax collection agenda meant the end of the 'grand compromise'.

On the other hand, although the principal issue that concerned the IMF in the second half of the 1990s was the dissolution of the energy monopolies and the restructuring of the Russian industrial base, another chronic question, which could have attracted the Fund's serious attention only recently (Abed and Davoodi 2000), was corruption. It can be argued that a qualitatively new form of corruption had been developing since the early years of Yeltsin's radical liberal reforms in Russia, which can be largely associated with the radical liberals' attempts to overcome their marginality in the political arena.[47] As Shleifer and Treisman (2000) underline explicitly, in order to co-opt the centrist opposition into the regime the radical liberals used the state mechanism to create various new stakes since the early years of reform. As the struggle within the transforming ruling class started to intensify due to the end of the 'grand compromise' after 1996 under the pressure of the IMF, the corruptive implications of this strategy which contaminated even Yeltsin's inner circle at the top (Gill and Markwick 2000: 171) started to become public one by one.

Hence, the coming of the second round of the shares-for-loans auctions constituted an important practical reason for the heating up of FIG competition in Russia in mid-1997, while the auction for Svyazinvest, a major communications company, resulted in the sharpening of antagonisms (Johnson 1997: 355; Gill and Markwick 2000: 196–7; Shleifer and Treisman 2000: 145). The auction, which was for the sale of the company's 25 per cent plus one shares, brought Russia's two prominent oligarchs, Potanin[48] of ONEKSIMbank, who established a consortium with the inclusion of the famous speculator George Soros, and Berezovsky, who cooperated with Gusinsky of the MOST Group, face to face. The victory of the former group led to a fierce attack by Berezovsky against Chubais, whom he accused of favouring Potanin. In November 1997, media sources controlled by Berezovsky and Gusinsky revealed a corrupt book deal, of which Chubais and ONEKSIMbank group had been the two alleged culprits.[49] This was not the first corruption accusation facing Chubais.[50] The scandal forced Yeltsin to remove Chubais as Finance Minister, though he retained his posts as first deputy prime minister and the head of VChK[51] (Gill and Markwick 2000: 197; Shleifer and Treisman 2000: 145). In mid-1998 Chubais, due to his high prestige within international financial circles, was made the Deputy Prime Minister to conduct negotiations with the IMF for credit assistance to deal with the looming economic crisis.

Having seen the privatisation process discredited in the eyes of the public through the share-for-loans programme, Yeltsin officially banned it on 25 July 1997. He also met privately with the leading bankers in September 1997 'to call a truce in their overtly public battle' (Johnson 1997: 352–6). However, it became apparent later that Yeltsin's initiative was not sufficient to make Chubais forget about revenge. In December 1997, having used his authority as the head of VChK and confident of IMF support, Chubais ordered the seizure of a very profitable oil company owned by Berezovsky on the basis that it had failed to pay its taxes to the state (Shleifer and Treisman 2000: 146). The crisis, while ending with Berezovsky's ultimate compliance to pay its debt to the state, indicated that Yeltsin's power to control intra-state struggle in Russia was fading fast.

The intensification of the intra-state struggle also had implications for the IMF. The oligarchs, who started to face serious losses in their profits towards the end of 1997, due not only to the insistent demands of the IMF-backed radical liberals in the state, but also to the falling international price of oil, engaged in a public attack on the IMF and the World Bank through their media power.[52] Just to mention one example, on 18 December 1997 the Berezovsky-controlled *Nezavisimaya Gazeta*, having asked 'Why does Russia need a government of its own?', published a letter sent by the IMF Managing Director Camdessus to the Prime Minister, which proved the degree of IMF involvement in the government's decisions.[53] This indicated that the *de facto* cooperation between the oligarchs and the international financial institutions to secure Yeltsin's re-election in 1996 came to a definite end, leading Russia into various political uncertainties.

Within such a tense political atmosphere, the August 1998 default has substantially changed Russia's relationship with the IMF. Having frozen its loans to Russia after the default, the IMF has not resumed – or could not resume – lending again. If this has been on the one hand due to the IMF's persistence with demanding tough conditions to resume lending, it has been on the other hand due to the Russian state's ever more cautious attitude towards the Fund. Having been relaxed by the rise of the international price of oil after 1999, Russia under the presidency of Putin has deliberately rejected borrowing from the IMF on the grounds that, in comparison to the amount of money it lends, the IMF demands a lot from Russia.[54]

Conclusion

This chapter examined the capitalist transformation process in Russia in the 1990s as the passive revolution of the former *nomenklatura* which took place within a neoliberal global context. Having examined the Yeltsin-led capitalist transformation as an essentially authoritarian initiative which aimed to contain the threat of the socialisation of politics since the Gorbachev years, it attempted to show how this process as a whole was constituted and complicated by transnational capitalist interests, working most visibly through the IMF.

In this regard, a significant conclusion of the chapter is that, when the process of capitalist transformation was threatened by various forms of political instability, the transforming ruling class in Russia and the transnational capitalist interests collaborated with each other. At other times their clash turned the state into a terrain of an intensive – and in fact corrupt – struggle with grave implications for the process of capitalist state formation in the country. Despite antagonism between the former *nomenklatura* in Russia and the global capitalist interests mediated through the agency of Western financial institutions, the critical re-consideration of Russian capitalist transformation proposed above indicates that moments of cooperation between the two were more frequent than moments of clash.

During the first phase of the former *nomenklatura*'s passive revolution, which lasted from early 1992 to the constitutional crisis in the autumn of 1993, it can be argued that the IMF effectively supported the Yeltsin-led radical liberals in Russia, albeit from a distance. It helped them move out of their desperate political marginality. Besides Western governments' state-to-state credits, which were more than \$25 billion, the IMF, under pressure from the United States, disbursed \$4 billion and promised \$4.5 billion of credits to Russia in this period under gradually relaxed conditions. This was due to the vulnerability of the political situation in the face of the pressures posed by the uncompromising opposition of the communists and agrarian interests as well as the radical liberals' inability to secure the full support of the centrists for their programme. On the other hand, as the period saw Yeltsin's authoritarian suppression of popular opposition, including even the democratic liberal *DemRossiia* (the movement which in fact substantially helped Yeltsin's rise to, and consolidation of, power in the early 1990s), Western credits served to help fulfil this authoritarian project.

As a result of the rapid price liberalisation and privatisation processes conducted under hyperinflationary conditions as well as the inconsistent stabilisation policies, the early 1990s saw the industrial *nomenklatura* gain control of the formally privatised state enterprises, the speedy and corrupt development of the financial sector and, against the rhetoric of economic liberalism, the disappearance of small entrepreneurs who could not compete with the state-linked enterprises. Although these developments, which meant the consolidation of the economic power in the hands of the former *nomenklatura*, were not welcomed by Western observers, reformers and executives, the threat of political instability prevented them from insistently urging a neoliberal route.

In the next phase of the *nomenklatura*'s passive revolution in Russia, which was politically more secure due to Yeltsin's new super-presidency as well as his success in putting an end to the socialisation of politics, the capitalist transformation process developed more as an intra-*nomenklatura* bargain, though complicated and problematised by the interventions of global capitalist interests. The period saw Yeltsin's Caesarist attempts to manage the contradictory demands of the transforming ruling class for re-distributive state policies and of the IMF for macroeconomic stabilisation. Hence, control over inflation could be achieved by the state's providing the emergent Russian capitalists with lucrative GKO profits and the shares-for-loans programme, which resulted in the corrupt sale of the state's profitable oil companies to the Russian banks. One of the main consequences of this process was the formation of oligarchic financial-industrial groups in Russia. On the other hand, the period also witnessed the IMF's more direct intervention in state policies. In order to increase its control over the social transformation process after 1993, the IMF started to disburse credits on a monthly basis and only after intensive negotiations on the government's macroeconomic policies.

The presidential elections in 1996 constituted another significant moment of cooperation between the Russian ruling class, the economic power of which was now concentrated in the hands of the oligarchs as well as the state's giant gas, oil and electricity monopolies, and Western capitalist interests. The period saw a flood of credits from all channels to Yeltsin in order to get him re-elected rather than the communist candidate Zyuganov.

Yeltsin's re-election and the end of political uncertainty meant however the end of cooperation between Russian and Western capitalist interests. The aftermath of the elections saw the IMF place ever more intensive pressures on the state to dissolve its big monopolies, such as Gazprom and UES, as well as to collect taxes from the oligarchic enterprises, which were granted huge tax exemptions in return for their support for Yeltsin during the election campaign. It was apparent that, having secured the political future of Yeltsin for about four to five years, the IMF was now finally pushing the Russian state to a definite neoliberal path to continue with financial support.

The intensification of the dispute between the Western and Russian capitalist interests after 1996 helped make public two significant developments in the Russian capitalist transformation. It showed on the one hand that corruption had become an ordinary daily affair in the country's political economy. As the corrupt linkages between the oligarchs and the Yeltsin clique became apparent one by one, the state's legitimacy, which was already very weak, further deteriorated. On the other hand, due to the oligarchs' attacks on the IMF, which made public how the Fund dictated policies to the Russian government, the process also revealed the degree of IMF influence on the state. In the light of these revelations, it could be argued that one of the most important characteristics as well as problems of the transnationalised passive revolution in Russia has been the transformation of the state into a terrain of intensive struggle among not only Russian, but also global, capitalist interests mediated through the IMF.

In the light of these evaluations, it can be argued that the unfavourable consequences of Russian social transformation, such as authoritarianism, corruption and oligarchic market conditions, cannot be evaluated as digressions from a well-working Western capitalism. On the contrary, these problems need to be examined in relation to the traumatic restructuring of capitalism along neoliberal lines, for they have been the products of an intense struggle fought among Russian and global capitalist interests over the form and direction of social change in contemporary Russia.

Notes

1 This is not to say that the IMF was the only means through which the neoliberal agenda was imposed on Russia. Besides the agency of the other Western institutions, the disciplinary pressures created by the de-regulated financial markets imposed a structural constraint on government policies, which became gradually more bounded to these markets due to the circular budget deficit financing mechanism.

2 See note 7.

3 As a result, the living standard of the Russian people decreased by 40 per cent overnight (Rutland 1994: 152–3). Inflation skyrocketed and was calculated as 1353 per cent in 1992, 806 per cent in 1993, 302 per cent in 1994 and 140 per cent in 1995 (Williams 1996: 13).

4 Coercion used by the state against the public demonstrations of these groups has to be recalled here. In 1992, many older people and pensioners who participated in the demonstrations on 23 February (the Day of the Soviet Army), and 1 May were attacked by special forces of the police.

5 From August 1991 to October 1993, while Yeltsin and the radical liberals in the parliament were under the attack of the communist-patriotic opposition, *DemRossiia* organised three big street demonstrations to support Yeltsin, the second of which was the largest political rally since the August coup (Brudny 1993: 157, 167).

6 These were the moments when *DemRossiia* directed its criticisms against Yeltsin, claiming that he brought too many former communist officials as his staff as well as appointing them to provincial posts, raised expansionist claims against Ukraine and neglected to cooperate with the Movement after the August coup (Brudny 1993: 155–61).

7 Having borrowed the concept of 'passive revolution' from Gramsci and inspired by van der Pijl's application of it to the Soviet context (1993), this chapter proposes that the process of Russian social transformation can be comprehensively analysed as a passive revolutionary process, which of course needs to be

reconsidered within a neoliberal global context. Passive revolution in Gramsci (1971: 115) refers to the established classes' attempts to absorb an external revolutionary challenge against their rule without changing the extant power structure and by effectively eliminating the masses' participation in the process of change (Buci-Glucksmann 1979: 216; Forgacs 1988: 247). In other words, it refers to a necessary revolution in the social relations of production, conducted by the dominant classes in a controlled way in order to prevent any alternative historical contingency to emerge by people's active involvement in the process. Due to this reason, passive revolution is defined as a restrictive (Forgacs 1988: 247) or a minimal (Femia 1987: 47) form of hegemony, the integrative scope of which was confined to the upper classes only, a process with coercive implications for the rest of society.

8 Gramsci (1971: 219–20) conceptualises 'Caesarism' to refer to a specific situation, in which a great personality intervenes in the historico-political affairs of a country as an arbitrator. He considers this arbitration task crucial due to the catastrophic equilibrium reached among conflicting social forces. By preventing the continuation of conflict from leading to a radical change in the established political power structure, the Caesarist rule ultimately preserves the status quo in favour of the dominant classes as a whole.

9 As a matter of fact, this crucial role IMF started to play after 1992 in Russia had already been envisaged at the Houston G7 summit in June 1990, when the Fund was given the mission to coordinate Western institutions' involvement in the transition process in general (Polak 1997: 520).

10 Chervyakov (1995: 233) informs that, due to their privileged position in the USSR economy, the military-industrial complex (MIC), the agro-industrial complex (AIC) and the fuel and energy complex (FEC) were the most powerful and organised groups in Russia in the early 1990s.

11 This extension of authority with extraordinary decree powers was valid until 1 December 1992 (*East European Constitutional Review* (hereafter *EECR*), Vol. 1, No. 2, Summer 1992: 6; Chervyakov 1995: 242). The end of this period also meant an open confrontation between Yeltsin and the Supreme Soviet, which ended up with the September–October constitutional crisis in Russia.

12 According to the Russian constitution, which was only a slightly amended version of the latest Soviet constitution, the Congress was given the right to outlaw any presidential decree or decision as well as to remove the President from office with a two-thirds majority (Blankenagel 1993: 26–8). Because of such provisions in effect, which reflected Gorbachev's initial concerns to ensure a democratic control of the executive, Yeltsin remained highly vulnerable to the Congress despite his extraordinary decree powers granted in November 1991.

13 Russia became a full member of the IMF on 1 June 1992.

14 The IMF increased its inflation targets for Russia from a monthly 3 per cent to 7.9 per cent (Stone 2001: 185).

15 As it was one of the most important processes of reform, privatisation attracted considerable attention in almost all studies that intended to understand social transformation in Russia. Among these, Clarke (1993a), Clarke and Kabalina (1995), Nelson and Kuzes (1995a, 1995b) and Blasi *et al.* (1997) are particularly notable as concentrated pieces of research on Russian privatisation, while others such as Slider (1994: 367–73) and Sutela and Mau (1995: 70–1) provide extensive overviews.

16 *The Current Digest of the Post-Soviet Press* (hereafter *CDPSP*), Vol. XLIV, No. 33, 'Yeltsin Offers Everyone Privatization Checks', 16 September 1992: 3.

17 Shleifer and Treisman (2000: 31) argue that, besides this concession made to the MIC in general, radical liberals in the government promoted benefits for the potentially resistant ministries and the FEC as well. In this vein, the ministries

were given the veto right over the privatisation of strategic state enterprises in transportation, health, education and space exploration, whereas the FEC was convinced on the condition that the energy and raw materials sectors as well as defence would be privatised only with the approval of the whole cabinet.

18 Shleifer, a Russian-born American Harvard economist, was one of the founders of the Western-funded Russian Privatisation Center, and Boycko was the head of it (Wedel 1998: 210, 221). They are known for their close relationship with the radical liberals, most notably Chubais.

19 The liberalisation of the import regime resulted in the flow of primarily luxury foreign cars and defence equipment into Russia.

20 Burbulis continued to serve as State Secretary (Murrell 1997: 100).

21 The financial source Yeltsin was counting on to realise these engagements was the US$ 24 billion aid package mentioned before (Murrell 1997: 100).

22 Gramsci defines 'transformism' as the 'gradual but continuous absorption' of the critical and even antagonistic figures by the dominant class, a process which would bring about the 'formation of an ever more extensive ruling class' (Gramsci 1971: 58). As Femia argues, this can be achieved through various methods ranging from 'flattery to offers of employment in administration to the granting of substantial power in decision-making' (Femia 1987: 47).

23 According to the official referendum results, 64.5 per cent of the eligible voters cast their ballots. Among these, while 58.7 per cent gave confidence to Yeltsin, 53 per cent voiced their approval for the government's social and economic programme to the surprise of many experts. This, however, should not blur the fact that these numbers refer, respectively, to 37.8 and 34.1 per cent of all eligible votes (*EECR*, Vol. 2, No. 2, Spring 1993: 16).

24 *EECR*, Vol. 2, No. 2, Spring 1993: 18.

25 *EECR*, Vol. 2 and 3, No. 4 and 1, Fall 1993–Winter 1994: 17–18.

26 For a detailed examination of the crisis see Remington (1994: 63–4), Semler (1993–4) and Murrell (1997: 175–82).

27 The new constitution endowed Yeltsin with extensive decree powers and the right to dissolve the parliament if it would not approve the President's nomination to the premiership in its third reading.

28 *CDPSP*, Vol. XLV, No. 4, 'Yeltsin's Actions Win Broad World Backing', 5 October 1993: 16.

29 While in the December 1993 elections the Communist Party, Agrarians and extreme-nationalists secured a large proportion of the votes, the December 1995 parliamentary elections brought a firm victory to the Communists. However, none of the opposition parties were able to reach a two-thirds majority, which was required in order to change the Constitution (Murrell 1997: 193, 236).

30 For an overview of diverging perspectives in the West, particularly of the United States and the IMF, on the question of providing credits to Russia, see *Moscow Times* (hereafter *MT*), 'Aid Dilemma Divides West', 15 January 1994.

31 Yeltsin, by a decree in November 1993, prohibited foreign banks from opening accounts for Russian people (Shleifer and Treisman 2000: 55).

32 According to Johnson (1997: 351, fn. 33), leading Russian banks such as Sberbank, ONEKSIMbank, Menatep, MFK and Moscow National Bank earned about $1.32 billion in this new lucrative business in 1995–6.

33 From various *MT* news from 22 February to 4 October 1994.

34 *MT*, 'Chernomyrdin Makes Case for Austerity Budget' by E. Craik and L. Bershinsky, 28 October 1994.

35 This meant over $2 billion additional costs to the banks.

36 *MT*, 'Yeltsin Vetoes Minimum Wage Bill' by N. Mileusnic, 24 February 1995. Yeltsin legitimated his veto on the grounds that it was a necessary precondition for receiving a stand-by loan from the IMF.

37 During his visit in December 1994 for the negotiations of the stand-by agreement, IMF First Deputy Managing Director Stanley Fisher demanded that the government re-examine the tax exemptions given to the energy sector (*MT*, 'IMF Warns Russia to Cut 1995 Budget Deficit' by N. Stephenson, 7 December 1994).
38 *MT*, 'IMF Loan Gives Boost to Yeltsin's Pre-Poll Largess' by J. Kennett, 24 February 1996.
39 *MT*, 'IMF Head to Arrive, Talks "On Track"' by J. Kennett, 24 February 1996.
40 *MT*, 'New Loans Give Boost to Yeltsin', 7 March 1996.
41 The amount of the Soviet public debt accepted by Russia had reached $103 billion in 1996 (Tikhomirov 2001: 266).
42 *MT*, 'Analysts: Escape Clauses Mar Debt Deal' by S. Lukianov, 6 May 1996.
43 *MT*, 'IMF Delays Loan over Budget Crisis' by E. Arvedlund, 24 July 1996. The Fund used the same trick to create a pressure on the government also for the September instalment (*MT*, 'Tax Woes Prompt IMF to Hold Back Loan', 25 October 1996).
44 *MT*, 'IMF, Russia Faces Tough Post-Poll Era' by S. Lukianov, 16 July 1996.
45 *CDPSP*, Vol. XLVIII, No. 29, 'Facing Financial Crisis: What Can Be Done?', 19 July 1996: 8.
46 *MT*, 'IMF Gives July Tranche As Tax Take Looks Up' by S. Lukianov, 23 August 1996.
47 This evaluation needs to be supported by empirical research. It diverges substantially from the dominant approaches to corruption in Russia, which consider this as a problem inherited from Soviet times. The alternative argument developed here underlines the corruptive implications of the neoliberal reforms, which can be observed not only in Russia or the former Eastern Bloc countries, but also in various 'developing' countries such as Turkey. For a similar argument see also Gray (1998: 147, 154) and (Castells 2000c: 183–95).
48 Potanin was one of the oligarchs included in the government after the presidential elections. He had left his state post in March 1997 before the auction.
49 Chubais, together with the two members of his reform team, Maxim Boycko and Pyotr Mostovoi, was accused of receiving $90,000 for a book on privatisation from a publishing company owned by Potanin (*MT*, 'Analysts Say Chubais is Key to Reforms' by S. Baker-Said, 18 November 1997). Boycko was one of the authors of an article mentioned above which explicitly underlined the need to bribe conservative enterprise managers for the continuation of the privatisation process.
50 For an overview of other accusations see *MT*, 'Bear Hug of State, Business' by Jonas Bernstein, 4 July 1997.
51 Temporary Extraordinary Commission for Improving Tax and Budget Discipline.
52 Shleifer and Treisman (2000: 20) inform that, from early 1997 to early 1999, Russia's oil export and related tax revenues fell by half, bringing serious losses to the oligarchs and the state.
53 Reproduced in the *CDPSP*, Vol. XLIX, No. 51, 'NG Accuses Chubais, Premier of Sellout to IMF', 18 December 1997.
54 *MT*, 'IMF: Moscow Will Follow Fund's Advice' by A. Dolgov, 30 March 2001.

3 Globalization *po-russki*, or What really happened in August 1998?

Anastasia Nesvetailova

Introduction

Despite a recent upsurge in interest on financial crises, the Russian crisis of 1998 remains narrowly understood and under-elaborated by the majority of Western observers. This chapter seeks to critically evaluate the meaning and significance of the 1998 financial crash, putting it into the broader context of Russian political economy. Focusing on the political economy of the 1998 financial crisis, the chapter addresses the following questions. What is the relationship between the ongoing changes in global capitalism and the transformations in post-Soviet Russia? What role did national politico-economic and social factors play in mapping the future of Russian capitalism? What caused the 1998 financial crisis and what was the impact of the August collapse on the country's development? Finally, the chapter inquires into the type of capitalism that is emerging from the former socialist terrain.

Is the new system a replica of the Anglo-Saxon market-driven capitalism, as the shock therapy initially envisaged? Or can it be classified as an essentially 'Russian' model of political economy, heavily influenced by path-dependency on the command system and Soviet history? In analysing these issues, special attention is given to ways in which global politico-economic processes impact on the Russian system, and in particular, how the problem of the disarticulation between the financial and real economies influences Russia's developmental trajectory.

The chapter is organized into four parts. The first section focuses specifically on the circumstances and interpretations of the 1998 financial crisis. Whilst the majority of analysts conceptualize the 1998 default in financial and economistic terms, this essay suggests that the significance of the August crisis spread far beyond the financial realm. Hence, the second section draws lessons from the 1998 crisis and its implications for Russia's political, economic and social environment. The 1998 financial collapse came about as a turning point away from the following of Western narratives on economic growth and neoliberalism, and as a potentially positive political shift to Russia's own control of its domestic resources. The third part of the chapter reviews the key dynamics of capitalist transformations in Russia during the

1990s. Analysing the impact of global changes on the politico-economic and social structures in Russia, the essay emphasizes the significance of indigenous formations and the longevity of their impacts in shaping Russia's path towards capitalism. Among the most noteworthy changes in the crisis's aftermath was the end of the Yeltsin regime and the rise to power of Vladimir Putin. Therefore, the last part of the essay examines the phenomenon of Putin's leadership and analyses his first years in office. The chapter concludes that, at a time of uncertainty at the international arena and domestic politico-economic devastation, Putin is in a unique position to consolidate the country's wrecked socio-economic base and revive the role of the state in Russia. For a country that has suffered immensely from bold experiments with neoliberalism, the necessity of state involvement in guiding the economy and society seems to be the only reasonable option on the road to sustainable development.

The August 1998 crisis

By 1997, after four years of muddling through inflationary credit policies, Russian authorities succeeded in stabilizing the price level and the rouble. Foreign investors were thrilled with the prospects of Russia's growing markets; the IMF, having registered a firm drop in inflation, was eager to provide new funds and lure the rest of the international financial community. This seemed to be a substantial record, achieved mostly by monetary restrictions (Buchs 1999: 700). Yet, in the first quarter of 1998, the consolidated federal budget was still running a deficit of 6.1 per cent of GDP (*Russian Economic Trends*, 1998, n. 3). Under the pressure and requirements of the structural adjustment programme, as well as the memories of the hyper-inflationary years, the government in Moscow became convinced that the bond market was the only alternative to money emission in financing the budget deficit. Effectively, the central bank of Russia (CBR), by refusing to maintain the financial pyramid of domestic debt with monetary expansion, had left the government with only one way to deal with the crisis and repay the outstanding government bonds; by further decreasing non-interest budgetary expenditures (Glaziev 1998b). Faced with a choice between monetary emission or debt to finance the budget deficit, Russia opted for the latter: borrowing extensively, both at home and abroad.

Continual issuing of high-yield government short-term bonds (GKOs) and long-term bonds (OFZs) became the major source of earnings for the Ministry of Finance. Simultaneously, the major source of profits for commercial banks and investment companies was derived from trading in the GKO–OFZ auctions. The growth of the GKO market substituted domestic debt finance for money creation and was associated with a dramatic increase in domestic debt. Between 1995 and mid-1998, the stock of outstanding treasury bills jumped from 4 per cent to 17 per cent of GDP (Commander and Mummsen 2000: 17). By mid-1998, the GKO market turnover yielded over 300 billion roubles, with an existing money mass of only 370 billion roubles. If in 1994 the internal sources represented 90 per cent of the federal budget deficit financing, in 1998 the internal debt was financed almost entirely from external borrowings. The consequence of such bias towards external financing began to impinge on both individual banks' portfolios and on the country's levels of debt as a whole. With a growing portion of the debt financed through foreign borrowings, a collapse of the pyramid was inevitable, if unpredictable as to timing (Ershov 2000: 289; Duma 1999).

In late 1997, the ostensibly restored Russian economy was confronted with the danger of the Asian contagion. The Russian government turned to the IMF for additional loans to prevent domestic financial collapse. The loan package provided immediate reserves to the Central Bank that could then support the repayment of debts due, without putting pressure on the exchange rate. The package built on the government's anti-crisis programme, with a number of usual supplementary measures, calling for drastic fiscal adjustment measures to strengthen revenue performance, actions to ensure the viability of the government debt position, and a 'strengthened structural agenda' focusing on the underlying problems of the banking sector. The first step taken by the government following the deal with the IMF was to offer GKO holders the opportunity to exchange them for foreign currency bonds with longer maturities at market rate. As it happened, the IMF support was greeted by short-lived enthusiasm but failed to engender market confidence (Buchs 1999: 691). There are also suspicions that most of the IMF money was stolen on the way and never got to its intended destination (*Kommersant* 1998).

By mid-August the currency peg had become unsustainable, the foreign exchange reserves of the CBR had been exhausted, and on 17 August 1998 the Kirienko government was forced to devalue the rouble fourfold and repudiate on its outstanding domestic debt and part of its foreign debt. Schematically, there are three prevailing explanations for the 1998 crisis in Russia. The first stresses the unfortunate coincidence of events, including the Asian flu, a drop in oil prices and political instability. Another says that the crisis was essentially a result of the currency mismanagement. The third version maintains that the crisis was caused by budgetary problems – specifically, persistent deficits resulting in mounting government debt, or the GKO pyramid. Generally, the majority of observers seem to agree that everything was so rotten in Russia that the crisis was unavoidable (Popov 2001: 150–1). Let us briefly review these views.

The Russian default in a chain of the international financial contagion

The timing of the default, its immediate trigger and apparent similarities with the dynamics of the Asian crises led many to believe that the Russian 1998 crisis was the product of external effects, rather than a logical expression of internal problems. Oddly enough, the 1998 crisis was initially welcomed as a highly positive sign, 'indicating a deepening incorporation of the Russian economy into the global system' (Simonov and Kyharev 1998). Despite the absurdity of such claims, the significance of the external factors for the Russian default cannot be ignored.

First of all, global capital markets *are* characterized by information asymmetries that give rise to overshooting, sharp corrections and financial crises (Eichengreen 1999; Shiller 2000). Second, crises in emerging markets are commonplace in the modern economy. Indeed, the 'high-risk–high-return' principle constitutes the rationale for emerging market securities as an assets class in the first place (Granville 1999: 715). The Asian crisis surprised many, mostly because the main features of previous crises were by and large absent in Asia. Rather, the critical build-up of short-term debt made the economies vulnerable to a reversal. Similarly, it is being argued, Russia became subject to confidence problems, the reversal of capital flows made the collapse of the rouble inescapable, and the snowball effect subsequently hit other emerging economies. To some, the Russian financial meltdown appears as a typical example of crisis contagion: without the Asian crisis, there was no obvious reason why investors should have left Russia in great haste at that particular time (Buchs 1999: 700).

From these two standpoints, the 1998 crisis can be interpreted as a rectifying one (Gafyrov 1998). Unlike traditional fluctuations in assets prices, rectifying financial crises can happen only in emerging markets, often only once in history. As the theory suggests, they tend to occur abruptly, following long periods of sustained growth. Amid optimistic expectations of market performance, new public savings are attracted onto corporate markets; small and medium investment companies are emerging; investors are uniting into funds. Still, due to the lack of expertise and high sensitivity to price fluctuations, these new participants operate within a limited scope of securities, mostly well-known shares of big corporations. This results in a weak correlation between the market value of shares and companies' profits, indicating the immaturity of the market. At the same time, the size of brokerage companies is growing, increasing the opportunity for a tacit or explicit agreement between key participants. The market becomes increasingly unstable. The mass of small investors tend to get rid of their assets as soon as they feel the downside trend of the market, contributing to the snowball effect. Hence, rectifying crises clean the market of the mass of small brokers and investors, strengthening the positions of the leaders. The effects of the crisis can ultimately be beneficial to the long-run stability of the emerging economy. As it is believed, a rectifying crisis, not affecting the long-term processes of market development, should be regarded as the first step towards the long-term stability of a market rule (Gafyrov 1997: 58). Thus, in this vision, the 1998 crisis, triggered largely by the chain of falling dominoes in Asia, is the gauge of Russia's integration into the world market, and a promise of the coming maturity of the market economy (Gustafson 1999: 16).

Internal triggers of the 1998 default and devaluation

Notwithstanding these views of an exogenously provoked crash, there were internal causes of the financial breakdown. Difficulties inherited from the 'shortage economy', economic disruption and transitional deficit, policy mistakes and commitments to various forms of economic and social expenditure tend to prompt the fiscal crisis of a postsocialist state. Specifically in the financial sector, the CBR cut its refinancing rate back to 60 per cent, way below market interest rates. The CBR also decided to impose limits on the purchase of foreign exchange by banks, and trading was suspended on the Russian stock market. Additionally, early in August 1998 George Soros, a man Russian financial circles like to listen to, made noises about an imminent financial breakdown and called for an introduction of a currency board and a 15–25 per cent devaluation of the rouble. To increase the pressure, the major rating agencies downgraded Russia's sovereign credit rating (Buchs 1999: 691–2). Generally, apart from the external shock coming from Asia, there were several internal factors that unleashed the 1998 default:

- failure of budget revenues collection in 1998;
- policy mistakes of the new government;
- continual fall of industrial production;
- sharp deterioration of the trade balance;
- outburst of social protest by miners, teachers and students;
- Soros's speculations about an imminent devaluation.

Despite the mounting problems in the macroeconomy, some economists believe that the massive default as such was not unavoidable; that it was the poor management of the currency peg and subsequent devaluation that precipitated the debt moratorium. 'Unlike the currency crises in East Asia and Latin America, recent currency crises in transition economies were not caused by excessive private or government debt accumulation, but by excessive appreciation of the exchange rate' (Popov 2001: 154; Glaziev 2000). Blunt policy mistakes with regard to devaluation concern primarily the overly restrictive monetary policy of the CBR, which aggravated the crisis in the economy.

Far-reaching problems of the fragility of the Russian banking sector result from the liberalization of the financial market and the withdrawal of the Russian central bank from intervening in the foreign exchange operations. By early 1998, all restrictions on GKO profit realization for foreign investors had been removed. According to conventional estimates, at the time of the crisis only 30–32 per cent of market actors were foreign participants. But if one includes those assets that were employed by the foreign banks resident in Russia and operating like Russian banks, the share of foreign resources was about 50 per cent. Given the low capitalization of the Russian banking and financial sectors, it was foreign operators who provided the main support to the GKO–OFS market. Any variation from the dominant trend in prices immediately impacted upon general market indices. In consequence, Russian banks could only follow the market trend shaped by foreign sentiments (Ershov 2000: 294–5). Foreign sentiments, in turn, were not good at all in 1998, as investors were nervous about the sudden Asian collapse and prospects of other emerging markets. Out of the three regions of emerging economies – Latin America, East Asia and Eastern Europe – Russia at that time appeared by far the least favourable. It is no wonder that foreign money reached for exit immediately after Soros's speculations about devaluation.

What virtually nobody predicted was the way the Russian government handled the devaluation – declaring the default on domestic debt and part of the international debt held by banks and companies. As Popov argues, this was by no means necessary, since basically there was no debt crisis, only a currency crisis, which could have been handled by devaluing the rouble. The debt levels of the government and Russian companies were modest by international standards. Even though institutional weakness is the single most important factor contributing to the extreme magnitude of the Russian recession, it is not linked directly with the collapse of the rouble and the failure of the macroeconomic stabilization programme (Popov 2001: 145–54).

Such views, however, can be easily contested. Although Russian debt may not have been large by international standards, the mounting claims had a tremendous impact on the fragile and disrupted Russian economic system. To begin with, when the debt pyramid had outgrown the internal financing facilities, foreign participants were mostly encouraged to buy state securities; all restrictions on capital expatriation were removed. This conversion of the domestic debt into a foreign burden was a decisive policy mistake, limiting the opportunities for debt management. Russian securities and foreign exchange markets have become entirely dependent upon the actions of foreign speculators. Once the CBR's foreign exchange reserves had been exhausted, it had to devalue the rouble and ultimately declare default. As became apparent afterwards, devaluation was favoured by the majority of the industrial oligarchy, seeking to boost their competitiveness and to reduce their own domestic debt (Buchs 1999).

Apart from strategic flaws in macroeconomic policy, the Kirienko government committed serious tactical errors in declaring and managing the rouble devaluation and default. An investigation of the crisis launched by the Russian Duma (1999) revealed an illegal use of insider information by members of the government and the heads of the Russian central bank on the eve of 17 August 1998. First, the advice on devaluation was obtained by the Kirienko government without the necessary procedures of data protection. Second, there is evidence that Anotolii Chubais had consulted with top officials of the international financial institutions, including the World Bank and the IMF, on the eve of 17 August (Duma 1999). As a result, foreign players, many of whom had large commercial interests in Russian markets, had access to insider information that enabled them to exit in time and with large profits, largely at the expense of Russian participants. Conspiracy theory can not provide a comprehensive explanation of serious politico-economic problems. However, it is equally true to say that the dependence of the Yeltsin regime on Western consent determined politico-economic and social development in Russia during the 1990s. This dependence started on 19 December 1991, when the 'heroes of the Belovezh' first phoned George Bush to report about the dissolution of the Soviet Union, rather than Mikhail Gorbachev, then President of the country.[1] And it may be argued that it ended at the time of the 1998 default.

Lessons and significance of the 1998 crisis

> Russian capitalism will be to capitalism as Russian socialism was to socialism. Russia will do to markets and democracy what it did to Marxism, Christianity and the Enlightenment.
>
> (Edward Keenan, Harvard historian, cited in Gustafson 1999: 216)

So it did. August 1998 came as the crisis of the new post-Soviet way of life: it has been variously named a fiscal crisis of the state; a crisis of 'Kremlin capitalism'; a crisis of oligarchic rule; a crisis of primary accumulation. Whatever the name, the August 1998 government default on its debts has had formidable consequences. It practically erased the country's financial market, it devastated the fortunes of most of the new Russian middle layers, it knocked out romantic reformers who envisioned imminent bright prospects for a new Russia, with its Communist past long forgotten and people eager to build democracy and markets. Up until 1989, Alan Greenspan was convinced that free markets were rooted in human nature, and only tyranny prevented the rest of humankind embracing them. Commendably, in 1997, he confessed that, after 1989, he discovered that 'much of what we took for granted in our free-market system was not nature at all, but culture. The dismantling of the central planning function does not, as some had supposed, automatically establish [market capitalism]' (Gray 1998: 198; Lipton 1998). Michel Camdessus, overwhelmed with the results of Russia's reforms, echoed in 1999: 'we hadn't foreseen that the dismantling of the Communist regime would actually bring the dismantling of the state. We participated in creating the institutional vacuum, embedded in the culture of lies, shadow economy, and privileges inherited from Communism.'[2] Other former luminaries of neoliberal reform, such as Joseph Stiglitz, have made similar comments recently (Stiglitz 2002: 135).

According to an OECD report in 2000, about 35 per cent of Russia's 146 million people were living below the official poverty line compared with 21 per cent in 1997. The emerging middle class, including many owners of small businesses, had fared far worse in the short term, having lost their savings in the banking crisis. Unemployment had risen to 12 per cent. But the greatest burden of the adjustment fell on the poor, particularly pensioners whose real incomes in 2000 were about half the pre-crisis levels. Despite the recent upturn, there is little optimism in Russian industrial enterprises (see Schwartz, Chapter 4, this volume). Survival is the first priority; companies cannot continue indefinitely without investment, which is running at critically low levels. Investment is only at one-third of replacement level. Shortages are apparent in the energy sector, where growing electricity cuts loom as generation and distribution equipment ages. Ten years after the collapse of central planning, Russia is close to using up its stock of Soviet-era industrial capital (*Financial Times* 2000).

Yet, according to Mikhail Zadornov, finance minister in August 1998, Russia made the only possible correct decision at the time:

> We have managed to link up the financial and real sectors of the economy. In the last two years, the credits to the real sector have been increasing at 33–35% on average per year. [. . .] Before the 1998 default, more than 90% of bank earnings were covered by foreign exchange and securities markets. A whole new sector has emerged – a market of corporate debts of companies, now matching the size of the governmental one. We haven't had enough political will to conduct a reform of the banking sector. The major unexpected factor was the world oil price rise.
>
> (*Izvestia*, 17 August 2002)

High oil prices have been a major booster for the post-crisis Russian recovery, but dependence on exports raises doubts about the sustainability of present growth (Stiglitz 2002: 134). People's general economic expectations are of stagnation. Among the most decisive negative factors are the slowdown in investment activity and ineffective government policy. Yet Standard & Poor's A. Novikov says that 'one should not overestimate the significance of the oil factor for Russia. Its influence is confined to the budgetary sphere, the impact on the economy as a whole tends to be overestimated.' (As quoted in Tikhonov 2002). Hence, according to S&P, the Russian economy is close to entering a healthy cycle. When the critical mass of reforms create economic stability, Russians will be convinced that market development is feasible. Any optimistic promises scare people used to suffering (Tikhonov 2002).

For most Russians, August 1998 became the apogee of disillusionment with all kinds of authority in the country – of hatred for the new rich, for oligarchs, for Yeltsin and the 'Family', and for the Americans. The crisis appeared as much a crisis of fiscal and monetary policies of the Russian government as it was a crisis of the country's adaptation to the pressures of the globalizing world. In this sense, the Russian collapse confirmed the manifold contradictions of globalization, aggravating social polarization and the gap between the base of society and political leadership (Cox 1999: 27). Yeltsin would probably have thrived in any other Western country. His gift for speaking directly to and for ordinary people, his populist instincts, his naked opportunism, and his ability to outfox opponents are all similar to the qualities of other world leaders, such as Bill Clinton for example. But Yeltsin's tragedy, and Russia's, was that, after the collapse of Communism, his vast country needed a leader with vision and determination, not merely an agile political operator (*The Economist*, 8 January 2000: 25).

The crisis indicated that Russian bankers either have lost out as power brokers or have transformed themselves into raw materials producers (Åslund 1998). Opportunities for crisis management, influenced by many historical, structural and geopolitical factors, can determine the country's fortune in the global financial casino and its long-term niche in the core–periphery divide of global capitalism. Crises are dialectical in their nature; they always contain two elements within them: a danger and an opportunity. Crises are downturns in the politico-economic and social development that reveal the ongoing imbalances and contradictions of capitalism itself. But crises are also creative ruptures in the continuity of the reproduction of social relationships that lead to their restructuring in new forms (Gill 1999; O'Connor 1987: 59). In what follows, we explore whether such an opportunity for transformation exists in present-day Russia.

Globalization and capitalism *po-russki*

In the immediate period following the collapse of the Berlin Wall, the different states of Eastern Europe and the CIS embarked on different reform trajectories. But, as a general tendency, the main result of the immediate transition and the effect of global forces has been to reduce the role of the state by transferring its economic functions to private enterprises and its welfare functions to the market or the emerging civil society. The process came about via reforms from within, demands from Western donors, and the demise of state resources carried out under the guise of privatization (Sampson 2002: 301). However, the longevity of the effects of past- and path-dependency rendered the conjuncture between the global and national politico-economic transformations inherently problematic. Often invisible remnants of previous economic, political and, crucially, societal orders still shape expectations and patterns of conduct (see Stark and Bruszt 1998; Sil 2001). As a result, the actual transformations in postsocialist states deviate significantly from the pathways set out by neoliberal designers trying to erect textbook models of capitalism and democracy on what they regard as a *tabula rasa* (Hausner *et al.* 1995: 4–13).

Economic systems are products of long-term historical developments. They reflect the nation's traditions and beliefs, the evolution of property relations and the mechanisms of distribution; in short – the structure of political power. In this instance, it is important to remember that, throughout history, the ruler in Russia was above any legal norms and laws. The very idea of natural right and individual freedoms being above state authority was alien to the people's mentality and culture (Abalkin 2000: 34; Cox 1999). In this, the rudiments of Russian civilization can be traced to the influence of Christian Orthodoxy. The latter's benign norms of tolerance, submissiveness and proximity to the state, as well as the rejection of brutality of inquisitions, had a profound impact on the formation of spiritual values, morals and political skills of the people. At the same time, many of the pagan beliefs and superstitions were retained. In this sense, as Kluchevsky argued, Russia has always been a transitory country, a mediator between Europe and Asia (Abalkin 2000: 174–5). Her culture has linked her with Europe, but geopolitics, climate and environment imprinted her with the specifics and influences that pulled her closer to the East. It could be argued that the Eastern influences on Russia's development contributed to a greater embeddedness of individuals into the collective. This both constrained individual initiative and protected individuals from the impunity of the authorities. It also entailed a corporate character of social institutions, the ubiquitous reach of the state and the existence of an immense bureaucratic machine.

It has become a cliché to blame the hardships of 'transition' on the laws of 'primitive accumulation'. Protagonists of neoliberal capitalism insist that once this savage stage of accumulation Russian-style is passed, the country will evolve into mature, Western-style capitalist democracy (Yavlinsky 1998; Novodvorskaya 2000). For instance, as one Russian economist observes, the mechanism of primitive accumulation of capital in Russia resembles the classical Marxian methods of the absolute surplus value production (Plyshevskii 2000). The engine of primary accumulation – the growing command of capital over labour – manifests itself most explicitly in the depression of wages below the level of the actual cost of labour power. In 1998, indeed, the average wage of workers in Russia was only 1.98 times higher than the living minimum. Plyshevskii admits that there are certain specifics of the Russian mode of accumulation. These include a fundamental change in the institutional base of the mechanism of accumulation (privatization and state ownership); frequent and multi-level crises; and the combination of these processes with inflation. Still, generally the author believes that market reformations in Russia were conducted according to the classical Marxian scheme. They coincided with an upsurge in crime, shadow economy and half-oligarchic, half-crony principles of economic governance that were not uncommon in the early stages of, say, American 'cowboy' capitalism. Accordingly, as other similar views maintain, once the gangster stage of Russian capitalism matures into a more civilized type of political economy, the country will progress along the lines of what is traditionally perceived as democratic market capitalism.

Such hypotheses easily forget, however, that the genesis of capitalism in the West was never directed by conscious design; its processes for selecting technologies and organizational forms were governed more by routine than by rational choice (Stark 1995: 71; Burbach *et al.* 1997: 134). The 'democratic system' in Western Europe has been established and subjectively internalized for over a century. In Russia, in contrast, it is still largely alien, the outcome of a more or less opportunistic strategy to find favour with the winners of the Cold War (Elster *et al.* 1997). Today the distortion towards exporting activities in the allocation of both financial resources (direct investments, infrastructural development) and human resources (training and education in management and skills) is a characteristic of most postsocialist societies. In Russia, these two features are further endorsed by the primarily export-oriented, extractive character of the economy, with the raw materials complex being the only major vehicle of integration into world trade and finance.

A number of developments signify that the evolution of capitalism in Russia will not follow the 'civilized' mode of a democratic, market-based capitalism. On this, illuminating views come from historical sociology and anthropology. Historically, each attempt to construct capitalism in Russia was accompanied by the retained system of values inherent in pre-industrial society, and regimes of 'primary accumulation' of Russian capital invariably tended to take the form of 'primary' stealing of the state (Kagarlitsky 1999; Solnick 1998). Although Peter I strived to impose elements of Western civilization on the Russian soul, the spiritual and cultural fabric of the people stayed largely untouched, and the mentality of many millions of Russians remained anti-market. Quite in line with the long tradition of the country's radical changes, the 1991 push towards capitalism came from the top.

It is fascinating to see that, on the one hand, the interplay of national imperialism, carelessness and passivity, along with the Soviet-style slovenliness and unaccountability, had figured as a crucial impediment to the doings of romantic Western-educated reformers. And yet, on the other, it is this comparative weakness of individualism in Russia that has allowed mutual aid, kin networks and the extended family to persist to a degree unknown in many Western, and particularly Anglo-Saxon, societies (Gray 1998). Two institutions central to the Russian society – the extended family and a plot of land – are the most deeply entrenched rudiments that simultaneously help Russians cope with economic crises, and thwart the ideas of market rationality and individualistic logic from becoming popular. Throughout the CIS, earnings from dachas and private gardens account for 40–70 per cent of total household incomes (World Bank 2002). Access to connections and informal networks are key to finding a job and getting ahead (see Shevchenko and Schukin, Chapter 5, this volume), leading to highly unequal outcomes and discrimination (World Bank 2002: xiv). The principle of an extended family, in turn, when up to three generations of the family live in a single house or, worse, a tiny city flat, may inadvertently prevent new 'capitalist' ideas from infiltrating the young minds. With parents and grandparents nostalgic about the good old Soviet times, young people possibly accept the logic of individualism and competitiveness slower than their better-off neighbours in Western and even Central Europe.

The erosion of state authority and the eruption of a whole new layer of country's new rich, with big money but very few values, have frustrated the majority of Russians. The consumer consolations of the new market economy are inadequate and not available to everyone, while the sordid aspects of the new system go uncontrolled. Some of those who grumbled most in the old days now share the nostalgia of the less articulate for an age when they had fewer and less secure rights in a legal sense, yet their needs were more adequately fulfilled than is the case a decade later. And they often bring a moral dimension into their comments, regretting the shrinking of the public sector and articulating a strongly held sense that the new regimes do not respect entitlement to which they had become accustomed under socialism (Hann 2002a: 10–11; Freeland 2000).

Another source of the societal volatility is the new elite itself. As in many 'newly developing states', the Russian ruling echelons have become divided into two groups. Both rely on corruption and access to the state to ensure their control over resources and property. But they are divided by a fundamentally different approach to the use of this property. On the one side there is a bureaucratic bourgeoisie, only weakly linked to the West, lacking entrepreneurial dynamism, but striving for stability and for a social order that would guarantee them control over the use of property. On the other side there is a group of bankers and speculators, concerned only with financial rewards and giving scant regard to business ethics. All the Eastern European reforms were based on one or another formula for compromise between these two groups. But it was only in Russia that the banking and speculating group triumphed completely (Burbach *et al.* 1997). The decisive factor to help this layer succeed in the transfer of wealth and power has been the role of international financial institutions and policy advisors. When the erosion of state authority and the consequent absence of effective economic regulation led to the proliferation of mafia control over economic activity, corrupt penetration of the state, and the forging of international criminal links, apologists for liberal economics struggled to justify their policies (Stiglitz 2002: 133–65). Often the only response was to view this Hobbesian environment as an unavoidable phase of primary accumulation (Cox 1999: 22–3).

The *nomenklatura* and the bureaucracy are the pillars, the spine, of Russian history; the guarantors of social stability. Their origins date back to the time of Peter I, when the government first established a mighty military-industrial complex. Nobles, Soviet party workers, and now today's intellectual democrats, are the faithful followers of the decisions taken above. Membership of the *nomenklatura*, rather than the 'middle class', has been the guarantor of social ascent. A striking feature of the endemic corruption and the rule of oligarchy in Russia is that they both are not new at all, and can only marginally be attributed to the conduct of neoliberal reforms and the 'loans-for-shares' programme (Freeland 2000).

Back in 1970s, Soviet oil dollars paid for imported consumer goods and technologies (Kotkin 2001: 15–17). Still, the money was insufficient and the Soviet government began resorting to foreign loans: the 1970s were a time of cheap credit. As a result, Poland, Hungary, Romania and the Soviet Union came to figure among the largest debtors to the West. Corruption made bureaucracy receptive to the slogans of democracy; the new needs of the elite to exert control over the Party's holdings in the West could be fully satisfied only in an 'open society'. There was also a need for a new mechanism for the legitimization of authority. The breakdown of the Eastern bloc allowed authority to openly proclaim itself a bourgeoisie. Therefore, the years of 1989–91 were neither a turning point, nor the beginning of a new epoch, but merely a culmination of processes that had developed over the preceding decades (Kagarlitsky 1999: 127–9). The pillage of the country went ahead in close association with the restoring of capitalist relations and the subordination of Russia to the interests of the West. This does not, however, signify the birth of genuine capitalism. Rather, what is involved is a peculiar symbiosis of the traditional corporate-bureaucratic order with the power of comprador and usurer capital (Kagarlitsky 1999: 28; Kravchenko 1999).

In such a society, conducting an 'optimal' economic policy is hardly plausible: every social group, whatever it proclaims, strives not for an ideal equilibrium, or maximum efficiency, or even a triumph of justice, but for concrete results for itself (Kagarlitsky 1999: 40). In this light, globalization is by no means an external factor; its most important aspect is the hegemony of neoliberal ideology in relation to the entire bourgeois class. Most of the specialism is traditionally presented as teaching the supposedly ignorant and incompetent governments of the developing world how to run their affairs properly, as helping them to pay off debts, and as supplying them with aid through FDI, credit trenches and adjustment packages. The Washington Consensus is presented as the result of a purely intellectual learning curve: how people have learnt that 'statist' strategies do not work as well as 'free market' rentier strategies. Yet this explanation for the consensus cannot be accurate, since the old statist strategies seemed to work better in the past than the new free market strategies have worked in the contemporary period. In reality, Gowan insists, the relation between the ideal and the material are upturned: it was not the Washington Consensus idea that taught people to transform social relations; it was the material transformations of social relations that produced the power of the Washington Consensus (Gowan 1999). However, after decades of uncritical acceptance, '[t]he hegemony of the "Washington Consensus" is in decline' (Saul and Leys 1999: 24). Criticism is currently fashionable (Stiglitz 2002; Heertz 2001), but the policies remain unchanged.

While the West hurried to call the Yeltsin era 'post-Communism', in fact the decade of 1991–2000 was the last stage of Communism – its decomposition, withering away and painful reconstitution. To educated Western critiques and to most Russians, Yeltsin's regime was little more than an economic and social coup, a revolution accomplished from the top by members of the ruling bureaucratic elite (Burlatsky 2001). Having made their way to power and property, former Communists and their children, accompanied by shadow economy dealers, have built a state-monopoly, criminal kind of democracy and a market based on lies, money-grabbing and ruthless suppression of the poor and destitute (Castells 2000c: 184–7). Different in their backgrounds, the new owners are united by the lack of roots and total disrespect towards any rules and laws as well as by the lack of even minimal moral constraints. Besides, having undermined the old state economy and system of administration, the new capital in Russia was unable to create its own substitute for them (Burbach *et al.* 1997: 122–3, 135).

Contrary to reformists' expectations, the impact of the market economy plunged millions into poverty. Postsocialist regimes, increasingly constrained by international forces, have curtailed state redistribution, restored privileges to churches and other bodies, promoted private education, and generally contributed to a climate in which many citizens feel excluded from their national society (Hann 2002b: 93; Prakash 2001). Eastern Europe and the CIS are the only parts of the world where poverty rates increased during 1990–8 (Table 3.1). In the CIS, the increases in inequality have been unprecedented. In Armenia, Russia, Tajikistan and Ukraine, the level of inequality (measured by Gini coefficients) has nearly doubled (World Bank 2002: 8–9). It is also important to realize that, unlike in the Third World, in the countries of former socialism, poverty is most pervasive among those who are actually employed. The post-Communism poor are educated; in fact, poverty levels are higher among those who are more educated, and they are usually employed. Such a profile challenges the traditional theory on poverty: 'educate the poor, generate employment' (Atal 1999: 26–7). It becomes clear that, contrary to the design proclaimed by neoliberal reformers, the society that is now arising in Russia is too remote from the models in countries with highly efficient, socially oriented market economies. It is a society based on a hypertrophied property-owning stratum, on corruption, on organized crime and on dependency on foreign countries.

The detrimental results of the market reforms in Russia and other CIS states were not entirely a result of an unjustified application of a Western concept on non-Western populations and regions. The record and social

Table 3.1 Average poverty rates, 1990 and 1998 (%)

	Population living on less than $1 a day	
Regions	*1990*	*1998*
Eastern Europe and Central Asia	1.5	5.1
East Asia and Pacific	28.2	15.3
Latin America and the Caribbean	16.8	15.6
Middle East and North Africa	2.4	1.9
South Asia	43.8	40.0
Sub-Saharan Africa	47.0	46.4
Total	20.0	17.1

Source: World Bank (2002: 8).

function of the new capitalism shows that its revitalization in the 1980s was not an arbitrary imposition by the West, but that it had strong local roots. At the same time, it was clear to most observers that civil society as a notion in 'transition' discourse was wedded even more firmly in monetarism than was the case in the West. The role played by global financial capital in producing highly conflictual and divergent types of postsocialist political economies cannot be overlooked. The West has urged that those who managed to accumulate money-capital under Communism should form the core of the new domestic capitalist class (Kalb 2002: 320; Gowan 1995, 1996). But those people inevitably appear to be currency speculators, black marketeers, or corrupt government officials and tycoons in the import–export sectors, the latter particularly true for Russia.[3]

At some point this mess had to come to an end. And it did so on 17 August 1998, causing economic devastation in Russia and pulling other emerging economies, such as the Czech Republic and Brazil, into the chain of international financial contagion. Below we explore the circumstances, repercussions and politico-economic significance of the 1998 debt default.

Putin as a product of the 1998 crisis

The Russian crisis of 1998 became a turning point in the country's politico-economic development. Along with its economic repercussions, it has brought significant changes in the social sphere and political regime. The significance of the collapse of 'capitalism Russian-style' led many to rethink the issues of the global character of modern capitalism, of the validity of claims about convergence of development trajectories in the global economy, and of the future of national politico-economic systems. The crisis illustrated that globalization, including financial globalization, proceeds highly selectively, including and excluding segments of economies and societies in and out of the networks of information, wealth and power that characterize the new, dominant system. But there is more than inequality and poverty in this process of social restructuring. Fundamentally, the dynamics of universalizing 'casino capitalism' entail exclusion of people and territories that ultimately shift to the position of structural irrelevance. This widespread, multiform process of social exclusion leads to the constitution of informational capitalism. These are regions of society for which there is no escape from the pain and destruction inflicted on the human condition for those who enter these social landscapes (Castells 2000a: 165).

The Russian 1998 crisis demonstrated that the implanting of Western civilization in Russia, especially of its American version, was destined for failure. With foundations of the informal norm systems deeply rooted and firmly opposed to the attempted changes in the formal rules, the reversal was predictable. Strong notions of mutual rights and obligations that marked medieval Western Europe, and which gave rise to the 'Western way' of democracy, market economy and the rule of law, have no counterparts in Russian tradition (Hedlund 2000: 401). Russia has rejected the Western model of democracy and a market economy. Yet that does not mean that it is not developing. Its anarcho-capitalism of the Yeltsin's era does have a window of opportunity to evolve into something akin to the highly successful state-led capitalism that generated the rapid economic development of Russia in the last decades of the tsarist regime (Gray 1998: 152–65). But that, needless to say, depends crucially on the ability and will of the country's political leadership to strengthen state authority and rebuild Russia's national ideology, as well as on the skill to mobilize resources and turn from being a predominantly export-oriented appendix to the world economy into a more domestically oriented, mixed type of economic system. What is clear so far is that an administratively strong and interventionist state – one that protects Russian industry and directs resources from profitable (resource-based) sectors to unprofitable but vital sectors and regions – is an essential prerequisite to Russian welfare, since the typical costs of production will not normally be assumed by private investors with free access to the world's generally more attractive investment possibilities (Lynch 2002: 39).

For many Russians, the hope today rests with Vladimir Putin. It is understandable, after the disappointment of the feeble and wayward Yeltsin, that the new President's youthful and disciplined manner, and his plain intention to restore his country to its place in the world, should raise many Russian spirits. As Putin insists, Russia needs a proper legal framework for undertaking economic reforms that could eventually bring it justice and equity as well as material prosperity. He has encouraged tax and legal reform, and his government has also passed laws to deregulate business, to secure protection for investor's rights, and to reform the land-holding system so that individuals can hold farms and develop property. Putin has inducted some genuine reformers into his team. He has rallied Russia's entrepreneurs, small businessmen as well as magnates, to his flag. Most importantly, he has declared that the day of the 'oligarchs' is over.

Yet the doubts about Mr Putin linger. One is whether his pledge to see off the oligarchs should be taken seriously. Two of the most powerful tycoons of the Yeltsin time – Berezovsky and Gusinski – are now forced to find refuge abroad, being accused of numerous crimes, mainly to do with theft and tax evasion. At the same time, Putin's alliance with Mikhail Kasyanov, the Prime Minister, is far from reassuring. In the Russian media Kasyanov is known as a '2 per cent Misha' (2 per cent is the fee he allegedly charges for passing the necessary decrees favoured by big business). As Soros says, even if in accomplishing the transition from kleptocracy to legitimate capitalism Putin presides over an economic recovery, his state is unlikely to be built on the principles of an open society. It is more likely to be based on the demoralization, humiliation and frustration of the Russian people (*The Guardian*, 17 April 2000).

It is true that Putin has reshuffled the ministries and put his former KGB colleagues on key posts. Yet in the messy Russia, seeking an alliance when carrying out radical reforms is well justified, and Putin has proved to be a clever, pragmatic leader. It is also true that the most prominent private media channel, NTV, has been taken away from its 'papa' Gusinski and subsequently restructured. Yet NTV was also known to be a big debtor to Gazprom (itself a major contributor to the budget), so the deal can be regarded as a purely economic measure as much as it seemed a crude political step. It is true, too, that the war with Chechnya has been a sore point throughout Putin's presidency. Yet even the most severe Western criticisms of the campaign have been muted since 11 September 2001 and its aftermath.

Russians love Putin.[4] An exact opposite to Yeltsin – young, tough and charming – he belongs to a new generation: university educated, he speaks German and is learning English, and has worked in a foreign country. He did not graduate from a party school and was not heavily intoxicated by ideology (Burlatsky 2001). Putin aims to restore order in state administration, to eliminate corruption and create conditions of normal life for the people. Despite some mistakes that are mostly connected with his style of behaviour and attitude to the mass media, he thoroughly thinks over all his actions and their mechanisms. Unlike his conflictive predecessor, Putin seems to be a man of harmony. He seeks support from other institutions of power and often finds sophisticated methods to reach his goals, but the discernible elements of corporatism are by no means signs of 'authoritarianism' that seems to distress so many observers. If the West tolerated the ugly and arrogant rule by the Family, it should be able to tolerate Putin's 'guided democracy' for some time.

Putin views the economy as a critical issue of national security and, along with the criminalization of society and the threat of terrorism, he regards the multidimensional economic crisis as a threat to the very existence of Russian statehood. The political, economic and social crises that have overwhelmed the country since the early 1990s persist and, despite Russia's economic recovery over the past two years, a lot of problems remain unsolved. Spectacular growth rates in 2000–1 are largely accounted for by the post-1998 rouble devaluation and by boosted oil exports. Yet, at the same time, the country still faces deep-rooted structural and institutional problems: barter and non-payments in the industrial sector, immense capital flight out of the country, shortage of investment funds, severe social polarization and notorious multi-level corruption. Mainly for these manifestations of economic degradation, Putin sees the danger of Russia turning into a 'lost state'. To him, national wealth is a symbol, but also a precondition, a means and a result of the inner and outer state power. Before it can have a modern economy Russia must have a modern state. This is what Mr Putin seems to be trying to build up from the privatized fragments of the totalitarian apparatus he has inherited (Gray 2000; Fruchtmann 2001).[5]

Coordination in all modern economies is based on a combination of market, state, competitive and cooperative economic institutions. And for Russia there is no alternative to strengthening the role of the state and aiming at a 'regulated market economy'. A possible scenario for stability is a system of a limited market economy, a regulatory state and cooperative economic institutions in which management has an important place and in which ownership is in the hands of interconnected state and private businesses and financial institutions. This kind of state-led capitalism might ensure accumulation. Not only will the state directly channel economic rents earned from export-oriented industries, such as precious metals and energy, but also private and semi-private companies will indirectly be guided through state institutions and banks (Lane 2000: 502). The core of such a system is an active state investment policy focused on the development of science and high technology, with an annual growth of investment of up to 15 per cent, an exchange rate policy securing the protection of Russian industry, and a system of indicative planning, making possible an annual rate of growth of the economy of at least 7 per cent (Glaziev 2001).

There are many developments in today's Russia, which suggest that a kind of cooperative state-led capitalist development is a feasible development option. First, Russia's economic model is reminiscent of Japan's *keiretsu* or South Korea's *chaebol*. Like Asian conglomerates, Russian FIGs leveraged their political connections so that powerful 'clans' have emerged both in the centre and the regions (Sakwa 2000: 200). Second, there is the role of financial institutions and the interlocking ownership of holding and subsidiary companies. In 1994–9 Russian banks and financial institutions, along with government holdings, have become the leading institutional owners.[6] Third is the role of the power of management in the control of companies. The management interests, inherited from the state socialist system, are far more confident in pursuing the hegemonic role. Besides, the decade of reforms did produce a layer of middle-level professionals, whose positions are too low within the hierarchy for them to be interested in engaging in corrupt elite liaisons, but whose salaries are high enough for them to be concerned with preserving a politico-economic system that guarantees a fair living. Finally, there is a political and ideological factor – the orientation inherited from socialism is a corporate one.

The paradox of the state in Russia is that, despite its deficiencies and flaws, there is still no substitute for, or even complement to, state power. The country's institutional structure is unable to make efficient use of either foreign loans or its enormous domestic resources; any non-governmental alternative to a state-led system tends to assume a pathological character of criminal anarchy. Therefore, the state is assumed to have a legitimate role in promoting employment and comprehensive welfare. At the same time, for cooperative capitalism to succeed its leadership must be integrated into an elite consensus. In opposition are successful companies in export industries that are associated with radical market reformers in the government and external powers, such as the IMF. In this context, external political actors may still be a major constraint to the direction of economic change (Sakwa 2000: 200–8; Lane 2000: 499–502).

The country's misfortune is that the collapse of Communism coincided with market triumphalism in the West. The policies that were foisted on it had little to do with Russia's needs and everything to do with the neoliberal hubris that had gripped Western governments. It never made any sense to imagine that the Russian economy – largely a military-industrial rustbelt – could be made over into an Anglo-Saxon free market. Russia has wasted a decade following worthless Western advice. As a consequence, today it has very few options open to it, none of which seem comforting to Western observers (Gray 2000).

Concluding remarks

Therefore, what Russia needs above all is political stability, hopefully secured by a democratic order, and a coherent economic policy that will promote the country's integration into the global economy. Realistically, Russia is unlikely to emerge as a 'great power', but success in attaining a sustainable growth of up to 4–5 per cent a year would undoubtedly represent a great achievement (Cooper 2001; Sakwa 2000). A successful reconstruction will have to start with a social contract, which includes accountable government and participation by the elected representatives of the Russian people. For this to happen, the ruler must shoulder the responsibility of introducing and enforcing the rule of law. This is something very different from translating American laws into Russian. It requires a cultural transformation of quite some magnitude. Only then will other changes be possible. Also, a majority of the population must somehow be convinced not only that acting according to a set of given rules is preferable to 'fixing' things in the old familiar ways. The latter forms a perhaps greater challenge than the former (Hedlund 2000: 404–5).

Thus, for Russia, the main lesson to be drawn from the devastation of the 1990s is the necessity of state ownership as a strategic alternative to neoliberalism. If Gorbachev's semi-liberal version of Communism aided the maturing of forces oriented towards an open transition to capitalist values, the 1998 financial crisis set the way for society to return to collectivist and statist ideas. This vision is now supported by a growing number of people of the former Soviet Union: indeed, it was nationalization that enabled the old Soviet system in its best times to grow extremely fast and develop modern technologies (Burbach *et al.* 1997: 136). Any maximalism in re-prioritizing state involvement in the economy is as dangerous as free-market fundamentalism. Yet the experience of the 1990s in Russia makes it clear that the country will benefit from a mixed economy system, reminiscent of Lenin's new economic policy of the 1920s, in which free entrepreneurship in small and medium-scale sectors will be complimented by the state regulation of core strategic sectors.

So, does this mean that Russia finally has a chance? Sceptics say no, warning that the recent economic recovery is very short-term and, once it has ended, Putin's indecisiveness in implementing serious economic restructuring will throw the country back to the hopeless position of an extractive economy.[7] Optimists say that the country has had its share of radicalism, and it is the time for a balanced and fundamental reconstitution of the state, the economy and society. A task as immense as this one by definition cannot be anything other than gradual and carefully thought over. Putin is not inclined to follow the first advice he gets or the last word he hears; he is reluctant to rush into privatizing strategic monopoly producers and repeat the mistakes of Gaidar and Chubais; he has emphasized that Russia's integration into the world economy (joining the WTO, relations with the IMF and World Bank) should proceed on the conditions acceptable to Russia. It is very tempting to think that Putin, even if unable to stage a spectacular economic recovery, is at least in a firm position to consolidate the wrecked Russian socio-economic base. This will be a good enough start. At the same time, as Gray (1998: 165) has aptly put it, if there is a risk that Russia may become a Weimar state, it is only enhanced by the Western policies which treat it as one.

Notes

1 The heads of Russia (Yeltsin), Ukraine (Kravchyk) and Belarus (Shushkevitch) gathered in the Belovezh woods in the southwest of Belarus to sign a Treaty on the formation of the CIS. The Treaty *de jure* annulled the legitimacy of the Soviet Union.

2 Interview given to *Liberation*, reprinted in *Nezavisimaja Gazeta*, 1 September 1999.

3 In 1992, when the state price of oil in Russia was 1 per cent of the world market price, domestic prices of other commodities were about 10 per cent of world prices. Managers of state companies bought oil, metals and other commodities from the state enterprises they controlled on their private accounts, acquired export licences and quotas from corrupt officials, arranged political protection for themselves, and then sold the commodities abroad at world prices. The total export rents were no less than $24 billion in the peak year of 1992, or 30 per cent of GDP, since the exchange rate was very low that year. The resulting private revenues were accumulated abroad, leading to massive capital flight. In 2001, Russia's capital account was still dominated by a big outflow of $26.8 billion (Åslund and Dmitriev 1999; *Financial Times*; 17 May 2002). Clearly, entrepreneurial spirits do exist, but of a somewhat criminal kind. What made things worse was a notorious neglect of the proliferation of crime and theft in the part of the Western advisory bodies. In effect, American and European economic experts supported the legitimization of criminal economy: *The Economist* was thorough in encouraging Russian government to legitimize the sum of capital accumulated in the early years of the reform process and to guarantee property rights, and reduce influence in the economy (*The Economist*, 9 July 1994, pp. 21–2).

4 According to latest opinion polls, approximately 70 per cent of Russians approve Putin's activity (http://english.pravda.ru/main/2000/11/29/1198.html/print).

5 Russia at the turn of the Millennium, available at http://www.pravitelstvo.gov.ru/government/minister/article-vvpl_txt.html.

6 Although subsequently we have some major growth of foreign shareholdings in large oil companies, most notably BP's multi-billion dollar investment in TNK in 2003.
7 IMF forecasts for GDP growth (which tend to be optimistic) for 2003 at the time of writing stand at 4 per cent, and 3.5 per cent for 2004, as compared with world GDP growth of 3.2 per cent for 2003 and 4.1 per cent for 2004 (*Moscow Times*, 10 April 2003, p. 5), available at http://www.moscowtimes.ru/stories/2003/04/10/041.html.

4 The social organisation of the Russian industrial enterprise in the period of transition

Gregory Schwartz

Introduction

The restructuring of industrial enterprises in Russia has ubiquitously been seen as the key to the transition to capitalism. On the eve of the collapse of the Soviet Union, the leading international financial institutions in an extensive study concluded that the specific nature, functions and institutional character of Soviet enterprises made them 'one of the principal barriers to economic progress in the Soviet system' (IMF *et al.* 1991). The importance attached to the management and institutional character of large firms in an advanced industrial society should not surprise us, given the importance of enterprise management reform and its effect on the shape of the institutional environment in the experience of global restructuring of capitalism. Yet, the results of enterprise restructuring have matched neither the hopes of radical reformers nor the fears of their critics, and insofar as Russia's experience has been conceived of explicitly within the framework of the global economic restructuring, the apparent absence of workplace transformation along the lines anticipated by various commentators appears as originating from individual or institutional barriers to reforms.

Thus, in the aftermath of price liberalisation and mass privatisation, which were meant to bring enterprises and workers in line with market discipline, the unusually high employment levels in relation to industrial output were seen by various World Bank economists as testament of the failure to create a flexible labour market, singling out enterprise corporate governance as the root cause of the problem (Commander and Tolstopiatenko 1996; Commander *et al.* 1996a, 1996b; Schaffer 1995).[1] The organisation of enterprise finances (which has included the use of productive funds towards employee welfare benefits) has been seen as a stumbling block in the formation of state economic policy, and municipal and regional government reforms in Russia (Commander and Jackman 1993; Commander *et al.* 1996c; Freinkman and Starodubrovskaya 1996; see also Leksin and Shvetsov 1999; Vinogradova 1999). Demonetisation, the emergence of barter, inter-enterprise debt and problems of tax collection (Gaddy and Ickes 1998; Poser 1998a) have been linked to the specific relationship between enterprises and government, noting that the failure of enterprise restructuring has contributed to the vulnerability and corruptibility of local and regional officials, which has prevented effective fiscal federalism (Frienkman and Haney 1997; Gaddy and Ickes 1998; Poser 1998b; Wallich 1996).

Despite the difference in emphasis and focus, all sides have tended to rely on the common foundation of neo-classical economics, according to which the twin processes of privatisation and the development of the market should lead to the transition to an efficient and dynamic capitalist economy (Åslund 1995). As a result, they have stressed the apparent irrationality of Russian managers and the failure of enterprise reform, the root causes of which have been the weakness of the state, the cowardice of the bureaucrats, or the obstinacy of the workers.

This chapter will argue that the idea that the inertia of the existing system is a barrier to radical change is not borne out by the facts. There has been an extraordinary diversity, flexibility and originality of managerial strategies for adaptation to the pressures and opportunities created by the collapse of the Soviet system. The Russian economy since 1992 has seen a staggering amount of change, at a pace far more rapid than one could observe in any capitalist economy. There have been enormous fluctuations in relative prices, very substantial changes in the structure of production, enormous redistributions of income and wealth, massive fluctuations in the supply of money and in the terms of bank credit, rapid shifts in government fiscal and credit policies and practices, very substantial regional price differences and sectoral profit differences, large movements of labour and changes in relative wages. Russian enterprises have been responding vigorously and very rationally to the changes and the stimuli of the market. Unfortunately, none of these responses has tended to correspond in any obvious way to the neo-classical model of how things should proceed. It cannot be stressed too strongly that this failure to respond according to the dictates of the neo-classical model is an indicator of the failure of the model, not of the failure of reality, and it is the model and not reality that we have to adjust.

The starting point of our analysis is that the dynamics of change at industrial enterprises in Russia represent the evolutionary development of the existing system under the impact of the development of market structures, and that such an understanding involves the incorporation of the social character of organisation of production. The role of the enterprise in the social, political and economic life of Soviet society went considerably beyond that of capitalist firms. The organisation of production at the enterprise did not constitute the application of laws of marginal utility aimed at the pursuit of financial gain, but represented the productive dimension of a larger political project. The characteristic expression of the system as being socialist emanated from the centrality of industrial labour and the working class in both ideology and substance of economic policy, thereby placing the enterprise 'labour collective' as the nodal point through which social integration and control of the masses could be exercised while providing the legitimacy of the regime as representing the interests of the working class. The form of 'relations in production' (Burawoy 1985) was crucially shaped by the imperatives of this project, so that the enterprise was characterised by a specific social form of organisation which acquired a degree of complexity and durability that enabled the system of production to be sustained and reformed, but which would be relatively difficult to dismantle without provoking major struggles and involving considerable resources from different sections in society.

Thus, from the perspective of the social organisation of the enterprise, legal and political changes would be insufficient for achieving the aims of transition. Rather, the transformation of the institutional character, functions and relationships of Russian industrial enterprises to wider society presupposes the transformation of the social relations of production at the level of the enterprise. The absence of such a transformation cannot be seen as a failure and the behaviour of social actors as irrational, but reflects the form and extent of struggles over the redefinition of the social organisation of production in the Russian industrial enterprise. As this chapter will show, far from being undermined by the transition to the market economy, the specific social character of organisation of industrial enterprises has been reinforced, as enterprise Directors have struggled to reproduce the enterprise as the basis of production, and to preserve their position of control within the new environment of external constraints.[2]

The following account falls into three sections. The first section will look at the organisation of production at the Soviet industrial enterprise in an attempt to illustrate the enduring systemic features which had helped the Soviet system to adapt to changes and persist in the face of various contradictions. It will pose the question of what was promised by the transition to a market economy and the implications for the unfolding problems of the Soviet system of production. The second section will discuss the process of transition and reorganisation of production, demonstrating the significance of the specific social organisation of the enterprise for facilitating a degree of permanence despite considerable changes in the external environment in which the enterprise has had to operate. The section will also explore the growing rhetorical and structural importance which has been attached to the form of enterprise organisation as a 'labour collective' in helping the enterprises to overcome many of the difficulties associated with transition to the market. The concluding section will asses the significance of the continuity and change in the organisational form of the Russian enterprise and attempt to cast light on future prospects.

The Soviet enterprise

The Soviet enterprise differed significantly from a capitalist enterprise in that it produced not for the market but for the plan. This meant that its activity was not dictated by the need to accumulate capital, but by the need to deliver a specific set of products on the basis of a specific quantity of labour power and specific productive resources. Like a capitalist enterprise, it produced within the constraints of a growth-oriented economy. However, it differed from the latter in that it was subordinated to the demand for the growth of physical output handed down from the Politburo of the Communist Party, which controlled the distribution of resources and appropriation of the surplus, but which bore no necessary relation to the productive potential of the enterprises. The problem of disproportionalities and shortages to which this gave rise was not, however, merely an expression of the irrationality of the system (Gregory 1990), but was also a mechanism of control over the enterprise by the Party-state (Clarke 1993b: 10–12). The dependence of the enterprise on the Party-state involved it in a process of bargaining with the respective ministry within the framework of decision-making dominated not by economic rationality, but by political power and political priorities, predominantly the demands of the military and the international arms race, to which the system as a whole was subordinated.

The result of production and circulation being subordinated to the appropriation of specified products by the state was that economic transactions had an essentially non-monetary character and money played no regulatory role in the Soviet system of social reproduction.

> Although the transfer of products between enterprises took on the form of purchase and sale, in the sense that monetary balances were adjusted correspondingly, such transactions were only nominal since all transfers were, in principle, directed by the plan, and the 'money' in question was strictly money of account, which could not be converted into cash.
>
> (Clarke 1993b: 10)

Only wage payment involved cash and could function as purchasing power, but the enterprise was strictly limited in the amount it could pay out as wages, since wage funds were set within the limits of the plan, while workers were limited in what they could buy by the woeful availability of goods and services. While work was remunerated through the wage, formally wages were not set in the labour market in accordance with the supply and demand for labour, but were determined and stipulated in meticulous detail by the plan. Informally, the enterprise was forced to manipulate the existing requirements, setting wages and reward systems internally with an eye on labour market pressures generated by the disproportionalities and shortages. Since the allocation of labour power, unlike the allocation of supplies and materials by the ministries, was based on the enterprise's own ability to attract, retain and compel workers to perform with the limited resources and powers available to it, the reproduction of labour power was not achieved so much through the purchase of commodities by the workers, as through the allocation of goods and services by the enterprise. The enterprise was, therefore, not simply a unit of production, but also played a direct role in securing the reproduction of the labour force through the large number of social and welfare functions attached to it, and of Soviet society as a whole through its monitoring of every aspect of the lives of all its employees. The resolution of many production problems and decision-making regarding key organisational issues was, therefore, geared towards the reproduction of the social organisation of the enterprise, which functioned as the basis of the reproduction of the Soviet system.

Workers' control and the control of workers

While the enterprise was constrained in terms of what, how much and with what resources it produced, it was relatively free in the way in which this was to be achieved, and had very little opportunity or incentives to change the organisation and methods of production. Within the system of management, labour was subordinated to the demands of meeting plan targets, which placed priority on output volume with little regard for quality. Soviet managers had little interest in controlling how workers produced, except to the extent that this was necessary to control how much they produced, colluding with workers in securing easy targets and soft norms, padding the labour force, using authoritarian methods to force workers to meet the targets, but otherwise leaving the workers to do the job as best they could (see Filtzer 1994). Poor quality output was ubiquitously reflected in the system-wide character of production, causing pervasive waste, shortages, unreliability and irregularity of supplies. However, rather than trying to resolve the problems of production, the line managers' main tasks included 'chasing supplies, resolving conflicts, fixing breakdowns and monitoring performance in relation to targets' (Clarke 1993b: 17):

> On the one hand, . . . it is the supply of parts and materials, rather than the recalcitrance of the workforce, that is the principal barrier to achieving plan targets, so that the priority of the administration is to secure supplies. On the other hand, it is much easier for the administration to fight for a looser plan with the Ministry (and for the shop chief to fight for more resources), to fiddle the figures, or to force the workers to intensify their labour, than it is to take direct control of the process of production.
>
> (Clarke 1993b: 16)

Managers were forced systematically to make concessions to the workers to enlist their co-operation in order to achieve plan targets in the context of technologically uneven and poorly coordinated production, which meant that pilfering, absenteeism, alcoholism and production slowdowns would often be tolerated (see Arnot 1988). All of this made individual workers appear powerful, in the sense that they had been given a high degree of responsibility for ensuring that they achieve the tasks assigned to them, but it rendered workers as a whole weak, in the sense that they had no way of changing how much they produced or how hard they worked, since their pay was governed by piece wages that divided them along a variety of hierarchical lines (see below), and they had no means of collective resistance.

Employment decision-making

The focus on meeting the demands of the plan within the framework of incentives and constraints placed on the enterprise was not only reflected in the poor quality of the output and the systemic irregularity of production and shortages this caused, but also in the severe labour shortages that it fostered. The solution to this problem was for the enterprise to seek a sufficiently large labour force to tackle the problems of production, giving rise to the notorious overstaffing. The most common interpretation sees this as a problem of labour hoarding and an expression of the ultimate irrationality of the Soviet system (see Hanson 1986). But the common practice of seeking a sufficient labour force to meet the demands of the plan in the context of fluctuations does not imply that 'enterprises and organisations hoarded large labour reserves which could be freed for more effective use without cost, but only . . . that there was very considerable scope for increasing labour productivity through managerial reforms and more rational investment programmes' (Clarke 1999a: 22). Such systematic reforms as changes in the investment programme, including the scrapping of outdated plant and the mechanisation of auxiliary labour, a modernisation in the system of management and improvements in the reliability of supplies would have enabled them to meet the demands of the plan with a considerably smaller workforce (Otsu 1992: 19–20, 151–60).

In the absence of such improvements, enterprise management sought as large a workforce as possible in order that workers could be deployed when materials would become available for a limited time, or when the machinery would be back in order. The low level of mechanisation of auxiliary tasks, and the absence of incentives or opportunities to mechanise them, meant that enterprises were forced to deploy the cheap labour of auxiliary workers. But the employment of auxiliary workers in low-paid, unskilled, very labour-intensive, low-productivity tasks also reinforced the social structure of the enterprise:

> the size of the wage fund available to the enterprise depended on the number and grading of the workers it was allowed to employ. The more workers the enterprise could carry on its pay-roll whose wages could be kept down without loss to production, the more it would have available to pay higher wages and bonuses [to enhance the earnings of more valuable workers].
>
> (Clarke 1993b: 22)

The overstaffing was also encouraged by the substantial social infrastructure built around enterprises, involving social responsibilities for the labour force, the pensioners of the former organisation and the surrounding community. Most work in this sphere was labour-intensive, and there is little evidence that it would be severed even during enterprise closure, given the importance of the role played by the social functions of the enterprise for facilitating social stability and social peace.

Employment stability was important to overcome the problems associated with the shortages of supplies and raw materials, and to compensate for the absence of the necessary technology. The norm was for the worker to obtain appropriate training, find a suitable workplace and then to remain in the same enterprise for their entire working life, and this ideal was achieved to a considerable degree, despite the authorities often bemoaning the problems of labour turnover (see Lane 1986). Although stable employment was seen as vital by the Party, since it facilitated social integration and social control, it was also vital for the workers, since the depressing conditions of Soviet housing and the lack of adequate leisure facilities meant that 'the workplace was their second home and their workmates a second family' (Clarke and Donova 1999: 213). But, above all, it was vital for the enterprise management, since stable employment encouraged the formation of job-specific and enterprise-specific skills, while the opportunity of promotion, and the benefits associated with it, provided an essential lever of informal control within the enterprise.

The norm of stability was reinforced by a number of substantial incentives to stay in one workplace. The criminalisation of unemployment and personal labour activity provided important formal levers for getting the majority of the working-age population into enterprises. But labour mobility could also be kept in check by a number of substantial informal incentives to stay in one enterprise, such as the fact that many entitlements were allocated through the enterprise on the basis of seniority or personal relations with line managers, and were in general not transferable between enterprises. Many workers had job-specific skills and if there was not another enterprise in their town in the same line of business they could only apply their skills in their current workplace. The peculiarities of the social structure of the workplace and the technical characteristics of the equipment meant that there were also considerable enterprise-specific social and technical skills to be acquired as a condition for effective working (Alasheev 1995).

The strict confinement of wage funds within the limits of the plan and the stipulation of occupational hierarchies within the bureaucratic manpower framework meant that fulfilling the demands of the plan depended on internally mobilised resources and competencies. While the external labour market could be seen as 'competitive', in the sense that very few barriers to labour mobility existed,

> the prevalence of job-specific and enterprise-specific skills, the importance of on-the-job and in-house training, the formalism of the system of

> accreditation, the rigidity of job hierarchies, the pervasiveness of administrative and customary regulation, the stability of production and the stagnation of technology meant that accession to the more prestigious and better-paid jobs was primarily through internal transfer and promotion.
> (Clarke and Donova 1999: 214–15)

The fact that enterprises had a limited range of incentives at their disposal with which to attract the most skilled and experienced workers put pressure on line managers to rely heavily on informal methods in the allocation of work and pay, assignment of skill grades and professional categories and discretionary provision of enterprise welfare benefits. This, in turn, gave rise to a specific social segmentation of the workforce, which closely follows the characteristics identified by the 'dual labour market' hypothesis (Doeringer and Piore 1985).

On the one hand, line managers sought to cultivate a core of the workforce whose competence, commitment and loyalty could be counted on to overcome the problems of production in meeting plan targets. They were the 'universal soldiers' who provided the functional flexibility needed to complete the assignments in the context of unpredictability, and it was largely on their shoulders that much of the production was sustained. 'The strategic significance of this stratum was not determined simply by its technical role in production, but rather by the fact that production was organised socially around this crucial stratum' (Clarke 1993b: 21). This core of the workers, known as *kadrovye*, were the *de facto* enterprise elite and their importance was expressed in many symbolic statuses, such as leading workers, innovators and shock-workers. Many of them would be recruited into the Party, used as role models for the entire collective and be the ideal candidates for various promotions, including eventually to the post of the enterprise director. These were chiefly workers in main production and their long tenure, qualifications and acquired skills, good discipline and a record of voluntary 'social' or political activity placed them at the top of the hierarchy of workers, providing relatively good pay and extensive privileges and making it very unlikely that they would lose their standing, except for the grossest violations of discipline.[3]

On the other hand, there was a need for enterprises to retain a disposable reserve of labour within the enterprise. The existence of this layer of workers is conventionally explained by the uneven demands of production in the face of irregular supplies, so that there would be full labour utilisation at peak production periods. However, while some of these workers could be brought in to help in the 'storming' that regularly took place at the end of planning periods, most of them were barely qualified for production and the intensification of the pace of production was achieved through the intensification of the labour of the core workers. Most of these 'peripheral' workers were involved in loading and materials handling as well as agricultural, building, street cleaning and other auxiliary labour which the enterprise was responsible for carrying out with its own resources under the direction of local Party organs. While these workers caused the most trouble through high labour turnover, drunkenness, theft and other 'discipline violations', their employment allowed managers to avoid the redeployment of production workers in duties which could be both wasteful and disruptive of production. But their presence was mainly used by the enterprise management as a means of social control over other workers: with dismissals being constrained by the substantial employment rights and labour shortages, the threat of being transferred to less skilled, and thus less well-paid, work on a temporary or a permanent basis provided an important mechanism of control.

The wage system and the nature of reward management

The Soviet system of wage allocation was highly centralised, with the wage structure, pay scales, skill differentials and premiums drafted by the planning organs and ministries in Moscow, and were substantially uniform across industries. The branch or general 'tariff handbook' stipulated piece-rates in accordance with the industry, occupation, category of employment and grade, and basic wages would be related to the piece-rate through output quotas, or 'norms'. Soviet authorities attempted to construct a predictable wage system, pursuing policies aimed at constraining the growth of the wage fund within the limits of productivity growth. However, although wage stipulations were made by the appropriate scientific institutes in Moscow, the actual manner in which earnings were established was through intense bargaining between enterprises (or branches) and the respective ministries, often forcing the planners to redraft the stipulated figures and to meddle in inputs so as to meet the plan in the context of adjustments to production costs:

> In theory, the wage fund is determined by multiplying the number of employees necessary for the fulfilment of the predetermined production norms (the figures being calculated for all the branches of the economy and according to the different types of employment, with the aid of the existing data regarding labour inputs and technological factors) and is called the 'planned wages fund'. In reality the 'actual wages fund', despite the projected equivalence with the 'planned wage fund', seldom corresponded to it, which shows the extent of the actual payments. The difference arises from the fact that the 'actual fund' often includes overtime and supplementary pay, as well as a range of bonuses for the over-fulfilment of set norms.
>
> (Otsu 1992: 187)

As managers cajoled workers in order to secure their co-operation in meeting production targets within the framework of defective supplies, breakdowns, interruptions of production and endemic labour shortages, they were also under pressure to provide them, especially the *kadrovye* workers whose effort was central, with better wages, which made the development of a standardised and predictable system of wage calculation all the more difficult. The cultivation of skilled and reliable workers, to whom certain managerial functions could safely be delegated, was also important if managers were to secure production while chasing supplies and negotiating with various departments and individuals. Better wage provision and the allocation of more lucrative work was a practical necessity to guarantee that such workers would be recruited, rewarded and retained. Thus, the managerial response to an otherwise rigid payment system was to ignore, circumvent and systematically manipulate established policies, creating a detachment between the centrally established tariffs for workers in specified occupations and the actual take-home pay. The system of reward and work allocation was highly informal and relied to a very large degree upon mechanisms established through the personal relationship between the worker and those with the ability to control her or his earnings (Filtzer 1986: 230–2). Workers were highly dependent on informal relations with their superiors in order to secure their own subsistence, and this cemented managerial practices as an essential ingredient in the stability of the system and was, therefore, extremely difficult to eradicate.

Piece-wages were the rational means of compelling workers to produce in line with the demands of the plan, and they constituted the chief form of remuneration of more than 90 per cent of the industrial workforce (see Kirsch 1972). 'Wages were in principle to be regulated by assigning each worker and each job to one of the . . . skill grades; the pay of each skill grade was fixed by a "so called" *setka*, which specified what each grade was to receive relative to the lowest' (Filtzer 1986: 211). The tariff represented the hourly pay for the determined norm and, like skill grades, was centrally established by the authorities. The payment of incentives and premiums was generally related to individual fulfilment of norms and the individual 'piece-rate-plus-premium' (*sdel'no premial'naya*) pay was the dominant form of payment for industrial workers. This more lucrative form of payment was a must for main production workers, whose motivation was the key to delivering planned targets, and was regularly used to tie the lower, time-based, pay of the *kadrovye* auxiliary workers to the piece-rates for equivalent skill levels. Though collective forms of payment were experimented with increasingly from the 1970s, they were problematic, not least because workers' collective responsibility for production and for earning the wage fund of their work group (or brigade) could provoke collective forms of resistance and undermine the differentiation managers sought.

However, while the handbook and the skill scales were centrally determined, the determination of production norms took place at the level of the enterprise or shop. As a result, norms were relatively open to manipulation by managers who would try to keep them as low as possible in order to enable the workers to fulfil and over-fulfil their plan easily and to provide them with the corresponding premiums and bonuses as a component of incentive pay (Granick 1960: 207–18; Kirsch 1972: 44–66). The determination of skills was, likewise, established at the level of the enterprise and usually relied heavily on the evaluation of the line managers or foremen. The decentralised skill setting allowed anomalous real differentiation between jobs and professions to emerge, while norm over-fulfilment had lost any relationship with the growth in the output sought by the authorities. The distortion of the calculation of norms, skills and piece-rates and bonuses created a situation 'where there was no longer any coherent correspondence between earnings and a worker's performance' (Filtzer 1994: 58). 'Management and workers developed a system for the regularisation of such overpayments' (Filtzer 1986: 230), and norms and bonuses were kept at a relatively stable level, making it the key to managerial authority in face of the limited incentives available to them.

The use of payment by results entailed several well-known problems, such as the difficulty of monitoring quality, a mismatch between skills and jobs, the potential for conflict, high bureaucratic costs and so on (see Brown 1963; Cannell and Wood 1992). But the specific problem of using piece-wages in the context of the Soviet production process was that it undermined the principles of unlimited effort implied by piece-rates. The irregularity of the production cycle caused by materials shortages, breakdowns and so on, made the calculating of output and norm fulfilment difficult and some categories of workers, especially those with enterprise-specific skills or whose skills were in short supply, would be paid despite these problems so as to prevent turnover and quits which could prevent the enterprise's ability to fulfil production targets. The wages of others, derived from the same fixed wage fund, would be reduced in order to compensate for the advantages gained by *kadrovye* workers. With the wage funds stipulated centrally, norms and bonus allocations made locally, and the production process dominated by instability, informal bargaining and manipulation was not just an anomaly or a possibility, but a practical necessity if conflict was to be avoided, earnings kept relatively stable and production targets met.

Sotskultbyt ***and the management of the 'labour collective'***

Alongside wages, premiums and incentive payments, there was a variety of welfare benefits formally and informally allocated by line managers. Enterprises regularly provided housing, transportation, resort holiday vouchers, children's summer camp vacations, childcare and pre-school education, healthcare, shortage goods and food from enterprise-supported collective farms (see Kabalina and Sidorina 1999; Lane and O'Dell 1978; McAuley 1979; Nove 1964). The provision of *sotskultbyt*, or items of social, cultural and everyday need, emerged as a consequence of makeshift measures arising out of rapid industrialisation and post-war reconstruction in the absence of municipal authorities. Above all, it reflected the principles of Soviet ideology, in that the enterprise 'labour collective' was seen as the most concrete representation of working class collectivism and the greatest achievement of socialist labour. However, it also reflected the political needs of the regime, in that the enterprise was institutionally the locus of control and integration of the population into the system (Kabalina 1998).

The absence of money as a universal equivalent made access to goods more vital than the possession of the means of payment. Workers, who had no other way of obtaining such things as housing and many basic necessities, were, therefore, highly dependent on their workplace for such access. Though intended for the entire workforce, enterprise welfare provision was ubiquitously inadequate, with long housing waiting lists, competition for kindergarten places, holiday vouchers and a variety of goods being in short supply as a result of system-wide shortages. As a result, provision was effectively discretionary and managers relied on the established norms and shop-floor hierarchies as the discretionary framework for the allocation of benefits. Soviet workers 'were bound to the system through social provision within the labour collective. But the form of this social provision divided workers' (Ashwin 1999: 12). They were required to cultivate individual relationships with authority figures in order to improve their lot, so that 'the most effective way for them to meet their needs was to behave as individuals rather than to organise as a collective' (Ashwin 1999: 12):

> The ideological representation [of the Soviet enterprise as a 'labour collective'] was one in which production was subordinated to the needs of the labour collective. . . . This meant that the achievements of an enterprise were not measured in money, nor in tons produced, but in the size, education and skill composition of the labour force, the number of houses built, kindergartens supported, which dominated the iconography of the Soviet enterprise and of the achievements of socialism. . . . The reality was that the needs of the labour collective were subordinated to the production and appropriation of a surplus product, and were determined by the need to secure the expanded reproduction of the collective labourer as an object of exploitation.
>
> (Clarke 1993b: 25–6)

Thus enterprise welfare facilities were not only benefits and items of collective consumption, but played an important role in controlling the lives of employees, regulating their leisure activity, integrating them into the labour collective and providing the basis of social order and social peace. Moral control depended on encouraging or forcing everybody to participate in political, sporting and cultural events, and a strict code of discipline was usually exerted on the workforce in participating in such collective activities.

From the perspective of the liberal economist, the organisation of the Soviet enterprise was completely irrational, not only imposing extreme rigidities on managerial functions, but also being one of the major barriers to the development of efficiency and wealth of the Soviet economy. However, the Soviet conception of the enterprise differed from the capitalist view of the enterprise as the physical form of money capital to which a minimum number of employees could be attached for as long as they could be profitably employed. Rather, it was a conception which saw the enterprise as a social organism, which had to obtain appropriate resources, mobilise its workforce towards specific ends and be able to secure its reproduction in the face of serious external constraints. The character of the Soviet enterprise as a 'labour collective' went beyond meeting the needs of its employees and the aims of production. It was the basic social unit of society, 'of social and cultural reproduction of the norms and values of Soviet society, providing the structure of everyday life of local communities' (Ashwin 1999: 15).

The Russian industrial enterprise in transition

The basis of the Soviet system of surplus appropriation was the centralised control of supplies, through which the dependence of enterprises was maintained. By the early 1980s it was becoming increasingly clear that the ability to extract the surplus product was being undermined and the proposed reforms 'attempted to replace the direct appropriation of use-values by the state through the system of planning with a fiscal appropriation of the surplus by the state in the form of money', as enterprises were to be given the independence to pursue their own ends (Clarke 1993b: 43). Gorbachev's *perestroika* followed the pattern of previous attempts at reform, in that the transformation of the conditions of surplus production was sought through the transformation of the mode of surplus appropriation. However, the fundamental problem faced by the Soviet system with the introduction of *perestroika* was that to make enterprises self-sufficient was to undermine the reproduction of the system through the removal of the element of coordination of the economy.

The Soviet system was undermined by the erosion of the state's monopoly over distribution through the expansion of market relations. The use of market relations, far from being an external solvent, had developed within the Soviet system, as enterprises sought to overcome the deficiencies of planned distribution. These were merely encouraged by *perestroika*, as the growing independence of enterprises offered by the system of *khozraschet* increased their reliance on trading intermediaries, and ministries began to lose their control over distribution. As the pressures on enterprises grew, and it became increasingly clear that a 'centrally planned market economy' was not purely a contradiction in terms, enterprises came to demand their full independence from their subordination to the ministerial system. Therefore, the radical reforms that culminated in price liberalisation of January 1992 were the consequence, rather than the cause, of the disintegration of the Soviet system, and marked the completion, rather than the start, of the process of transition to a market economy (Clarke 1996: 32–42). The collapse of the Soviet system towards the end of 1991 transformed the external environment in which enterprises were obliged to operate and secure their continued existence. They could no longer obtain supplies and raw materials, investment funds for development, or the money to pay wages and to maintain welfare expenditure on the basis of the centralised allocations in exchange for the delivery of planned output, but would have to earn monetary revenues from the sale of products and services to enable them to purchase the means of production.

The ensuing struggle over privatisation, represented as the struggle of the labour collective, usually personified by the enterprise Director, was aimed at securing to the enterprise the full fruits of its labour. But, while the reproduction of the enterprise was freed from administrative control, the subordination of the enterprise to the constraints of the market did not enable it to achieve the anticipated results. The largest share of the surplus was not appropriated by the enterprise in the form of profits, but by the state in the form of taxation, and by monopolistic energy and raw materials suppliers, and financial and commercial intermediaries, which arose out of the privatisation of former state functions and which owed their monopoly position to the continued support of the state and/or criminal forces. Enterprises and organisations were subordinated to the market not only by the 'anonymous forces' of the suppliers, the escalating costs of commercial credit and the commissions of commercial intermediaries, but also by the pressure of fiscal and criminal institutions, enforced by the Bankruptcy Administration and the Tax Police, and backed up by the state and private security services:

> The burden of forced exactions imposed on enterprises and organisations in the market economy was often much greater than that under which they had laboured in the Soviet system, while they had even less capacity than in the past to increase the surplus produced.
>
> (Clarke 2000)

The immediate effect of the disintegration of the Soviet system was expressed in the intensification of the traditional problems of unpredictability and unreliability faced by enterprises. Supply chains were broken, enterprises lost markets in the former Soviet Republics due to the rise of trade barriers, state orders and the demands of the military had been sharply cut back and many enterprises which had once been customers did not have the money to pay as working capital was eroded by inflation and access to credit restricted by the limited development of financial institutions and the government's attempt to contain inflation by tight monetary policy. Thus, the immediate priority of enterprise Directors was not to transform the social organisation of production and methods of management, but to secure the sources of supply, open up markets and get sufficient credit to sustain production, using the traditional skills and connections of the Soviet enterprise Director. Enterprises resisted the incursions of the state and new financial and commercial intermediaries by leaving bills unpaid, and adjusted to the pressures of the market by evading its constraints by creating their own credit in the form of inter-enterprise debt. The pressures from tight credit and bankruptcy procedures proposed by the neo-liberal reformers were eventually relaxed as the government was forced to concede to the risks of precipitating a devastating chain of closures, further reducing the incentives for enterprises to pursue fundamental changes in the social organisation of production.

The nature of enterprise privatisation also considerably softened the subordination of production to the logic of the market (Clarke *et al.* 1994). On the one hand, the majority of the shares of most enterprises were put in the hands of the labour collective and control was effectively exercised by the enterprise Director, so that there was no pressure put on the enterprise from outside shareholders to pay dividends and the share-owning workers could be told that most or all of the profits were squeezed out by the state, capitalist and criminal forces, and the need simply to maintain production. On the other hand, the constraints on turning a profit were eased by the fact that the valuation of enterprises for privatisation effectively excluded the value of their existing land, fixed assets and stocks, so that they had only to cover their current costs out of their revenues. Combined with constant inflation and the absence of inflation-accounting which could keep in check the increases in the price for energy and raw materials, the difficulty faced by enterprises initially appeared to be a problem of liquidity rather than profitability.[4] The priority of Directors was not to restructure the organisation of production with a view to cutting costs, but to secure credits and to maintain production.

As the pressure of the market increased and enterprises came up against the threat of bankruptcy, new lines of conflict within the enterprise opened up. While the financial and marketing services sought to satisfy the demands of the creditors and to balance the accounts, which implied producing goods and services of a quality and at a cost that could be sold at a profit, production managers sought to maintain full production capacity, which implied that it was the job of the new marketing departments to sell all that was produced and the job of the finance department to find the means to buy the supplies and equipment and to pay the workers, for which they could appeal to their workers for support around their common interest in maintaining wages and employment. The priority of the Directors has been to retain their position of power within the enterprise, and it has often fallen on them to reconcile the conflicting demands within the enterprise. Even if they are primarily 'rent-seekers', it is their position as Director that gives them social status and a political platform and enables them to enrich themselves by tapping various income flows. It is extremely difficult even for the legal owner of the enterprise, particularly in the context of poor economic performance and without a visible strategy of recovery for the enterprise, to displace an enterprise Director if he has the support of his management team, his labour force and the local or regional administration. The priority of enterprise Directors in the period of reforms was, therefore, not the maximisation of profits, much less the restructuring of the organisation of production, but the avoidance of internal conflict and the survival of the enterprise as a productive social organisation.

Rather than risk confrontation with workers and line managers, Directors continued to manage production passively, even if that meant cutting production levels in response to falling sales and shortages of supplies, allowing inflation to erode the real value of wages, delaying the payment of wages indefinitely when money was scarce and allowing employment to fall by natural wastage (Clarke 1999a: ch. 2). However, adopting the line of least resistance has not been without its pitfalls and the management has relied heavily on the existing social structure of the enterprise to both sustain production in the face of possible disintegration posed by the market and avoid conflict which could undermine production in such conditions.

Employment decision-making

The conservatism of enterprise management in the social organisation of production has made an important impact on the nature of employment restructuring. The expectation raised by the disintegration of the Soviet system was that the market would force enterprises to change their employment practices, primarily by shedding up to 50 per cent of the labour force which was supposedly surplus to requirements in the short to medium term. However, adjustments to the freeing of prices and wages from state control, the disintegration of the system and output decline were not met by enterprises in the form of compulsory redundancies. While industrial output has halved since 1992 (Goskomstat 1999b, 2000a, 2001a), compulsory redundancies have been relatively low and there has been considerable frictional unemployment, resulting primarily from the reallocation of labour between different sectors. However, while more than 65 per cent of quits between 1990 and 2000 have been voluntary (Goskomstat 1996: 64, 1998: 196, 2000b: 131), the figures disguise the fact that employment reduction has taken the form of natural wastage, being provoked by low wages, non-payment or arrears, and workers being put on short-time at nominal pay (see Standing 1996).

While increased production costs, the disintegration of economic ties, and regular incursions by tax authorities and financial and criminal structures may have forced the enterprise Directors to use their traditional connections and lobbying skills to secure subsidies and credit, to open up new markets and new sources of supply, and to maintain reserves of money by defaulting on payments due to suppliers, they have also provided an incentive to reduce labour costs. While wages comprised about 12 per cent of the total costs of production in 1999 (Goskomstat 2001b: 313), they account for the greater part of the payments which have to be made in cash. However, achieving wage cuts through a radical transformation of the social organisation of production, including staffing levels, management methods and the intensity of labour, has often been hindered by the arduousness of the task. Confrontation with the workforce risks unleashing conflicts which can threaten management control and spill over beyond the enterprise. Eliciting the co-operation of line managers by the enterprise Director in order to stem the interests of line managers for maintaining production capacity and corresponding pay, and line managers the co-operation of their core workers, is a task which is made extremely difficult by the fact that few resources are available to see the process through.

The enterprise Directors have followed the line of least resistance by allowing wages to be eroded over time as a consequence of persistent inflation, failing to pay wages or extending wage delays, allowing their real value to decline in arrears. Thus, over the period of 1992–7 real wages declined by more than 50 per cent, while following the 1998 currency devaluation they plunged by a further 13 per cent and in 1999 by 20 per cent in relation to the previous year, recovering slightly only in 2000 and increasing gradually over the next two years (Goskomstat 1998, 2000c: 203, 2000d: 119, 2001b: 313). The inflation has also undermined the wage floor provided by the minimum wage, so that in 2000 the minimum wage made up a derisory 3 per cent of the average wage and about 8 per cent of the official subsistence minimum (Goskomstat 2001a: 202–5).

The combination of institutional factors, such as the softness of bankruptcy procedures, the absence of an effective wage floor and the marginal role of trade unions, has increased wage flexibility, allowing the erosion of wages at the decaying enterprises to co-exist with higher wages at plants which have fared better (see Clarke 2002a). The increase in wage inequality between enterprises has, in turn, provoked higher rates of labour turnover, which have been generalised beyond the traditionally least 'disciplined' sectors of the workforce. Putting staff in ancillary departments and Soviet-era social and welfare infrastructure, as well as certain auxiliary workers on administrative leave, or lengthening the delay of wages, led to a gradual outflow of these workers from enterprises. While allowing employees to 'drop off' in this fashion could provide enterprises with considerable savings, in the first instance through wage delays (Earle and Sabirianova 2002), but also by being absolved from providing the compulsory redundancy payments, the fundamental problem with encouraging employment reduction through natural wastage has been the lack of control over the process, with the result that the more experienced workers with enterprise-specific skills, who formed the backbone of the workforce and were traditionally relied upon to shoulder most of the work, would quit, leaving behind the 'peripheral' workers on whom it was difficult to count to meet even the reduced demand:

> The loss of stability of earnings and security of employment also undermined the 'manageability' of the labour force as workers had less reason

> to want to remain in their jobs and received fewer benefits from displays of loyalty and commitment, while line managers were losing their traditional levers of control over the workforce.
>
> (Clarke 1999a: 85)

While the problem of meeting strict production demands has been dissolved by the collapse of demand, and unemployment had reached 12.9 per cent by 1998 (Goskomstat 2000c), there have been shortages of skilled and experienced workers (Clarke 1999a: ch. 3; Schwartz 2003a). Enterprises could try to attract skilled workers, but this hinged on providing reasonable wages, which has been limited only to a handful of employers. Often, the strategy has involved attempts to sustain informally the earnings of the best qualified and most loyal workers, and workers with indispensable enterprise-specific skills. This has increased worker polarisation and has reinforced the core–periphery segmentation, but it has also given greater discretionary powers to line managers and has fostered greater dependence of workers on the good relations with their superiors, which has strengthened the managers' ability to manage and has been instrumental in preserving the traditional social structure of the enterprise.

Maintaining a sufficiently large workforce has been important for obtaining adequate labour during the expected upturn in production and overcoming the irregularity of supplies and unreliability of supply and sales networks, all of which has continued to give the impression of labour hoarding or overstaffing. Though most enterprises have relied on the networks of friends and family in order to fill the ranks of the workforce, many enterprises have had to keep an 'open door' policy of hiring people off the street and some have had to resort to using the Federal Employment Service, which seldom provides a stable workforce, but one that is not only unskilled or 'unsuitable', but also the least disciplined, or churning while on the lookout for better work (Clarke 1999b: ch. 4). The lack of money available for reinvestment in new plants, and the difficulties and risks of attracting outside investment (for fear of loss of control), has meant the need to secure the conditions for proper working in the context of absence or instability of outside technical services and the replacement of some mechanised tasks with manual labour (Koumakhov and Najman 2001; Schwartz 2003a).

Wages and reward management

The introduction of market reforms set wages free from administrative control. Enterprises were no longer constrained by the tight schedules of the plan and could devise wage systems and distribution consistent with the demands of the market. The payment systems would reflect greater managerial power and more consideration for quality and cost-efficiency through the achievement of uniformity and stability of earnings and the replacement of effort with performance as the basis for rewards. The introduction of better technical and organisational control over labour, and the bringing about of the threat of unemployment for some and the promise of increased wages for others could stem the characteristic Soviet cycle of wage bargaining which resulted from the constraints placed on wage funds by the Plan. However, while the dramatic decline in output has largely dissolved the problem of output volumes and considerations of quality now weigh more heavily in production decision-making, the disintegration of the system and the unpredictability which have traditionally been the harbingers of wage bargaining and wage segmentation, have actually increased.

The basic features of the Soviet wage system have been retained at most enterprises, allowing for continued reliance on piece-wages and incentive pay tied to the results of production.[5] While enterprises have retained much of the formal egalitarianism of wage provision and the differences in the wages paid to different individuals at different points on the wage ladder within individual firms are not significantly different between different kinds of enterprises (*Tsentr issledovanii rynka truda* 2001), this disguises the fact that line managers have continued to see the wage system as a soft framework of discretionary pay allocation in relation to the existing hierarchy of the workforce and the needs of production, which has been necessary to maintain their own control over the precarious situation on the shop floor. Formal changes may have been introduced by the administration in the course of tackling the difficulties of production over the decade, but these have often generated implementation only in name, much of the practice being a distortion and adaptation of the newly devised framework to the needs of line managers who have been under pressure to meet the demands of production.

Changes in the environment in which enterprises have had to operate and secure their reproduction have imposed new constraints on enterprises, modifying the terms of the effort–reward bargain between managers and workers. However, in the absence of organisational changes or technical improvements, both of which have been constrained by the choices of enterprises to pursue survival rather than reforms, employers have divested economic uncertainty to the shop floor, increasing the share of bonuses constituting workers' earnings and making take-home pay more vulnerable to the external environment. In response to low morale and low motivation caused by wage fluctuation, line managers have reacted with various attempts to sustain the expected wage levels of *kadrovye* workers and use greater discretion and wage differentiation as a way of making an essential contribution to enterprise survival.

The conditions of production which precipitated many practices in reward management in the past, have become constrained by the greater pressure experienced by the line managers in terms of the irregularity of supplies, lack of capital investment and a poor state of technology, to which the transition has added unpredictability, shortages of qualified personnel and technological degradation. However, while the problems have become more acute, the relations in production have been more difficult to change and managers have had to operate in the realm of production by relying on familiar practices, even if this has meant a decline in the earnings of some workers, poor morale and growing resentment in the ranks of the workforce as a whole.

Low wages are both the product and the cause of the lack of fundamental reform of the social organisation of production, as alteration of the traditional differentials will almost certainly translate into open conflict within the workforce, while radical alterations of on-the-job and professional differentials implied by such reforms would almost certainly endanger traditional hierarchies within shops, undermining production efforts in the immediate term. Moreover, so long as wages remain low, and wage arrears and non-payment pose a threat, managers are constantly obliged to defuse conflicts over these issues, which is chiefly achieved by dividing and fragmenting workers.

Individualised wage bargaining within the framework of traditional wage systems has provided the line of least resistance in shop-floor labour relations, as line managers have tried to rely on the existing social divisions within the workforce to legitimate segregation. While this has contributed to some stability of labour relations in order to carry on work under increasingly strained conditions, there have been limits to the extent to which line managers or employers generally can meet the needs of their workforces, as rampant inflation has, until recently, constantly eroded the purchasing power of wages and there was a generalised downward pressure on earnings.

Sotskultbyt *and the relevance of the 'labour collective'*

The absence of constraints to pursue changes in the social organisation of production has made an important impact on the nature of the traditional social function of the enterprise. The collapse in demand and the problems of production caused by the absence of credit and liquidity has meant that enterprises have been short of money to provide cash which would enable employees to obtain their own housing, private childcare, medicines and so on. Employers have been absolved from the risky and potentially disruptive process of regrading and reclassifying different sectors of the workforce in order to provide better wages for some and forcing redundancies on others. They have also adopted the line of least resistance in terms of reorganising production, given the virtual non-existence of a wage floor and the absence of trade unions capable of defending their members' interests. However, while it has been easier to manage through gradual wage reductions and the continuing capitalisation on past capacity, the end of government-sponsored wage premiums and 'social funds' has meant that many enterprises have had even fewer levers of control over labour than in the past, while their wage-funds had been considerably more constrained than even in the Soviet period.

The problems of low morale and poor 'labour discipline' (see Morrison 2003), to which low wages and instability of employment give rise, have meant that many enterprises have been facing considerably more significant problems of motivation than during the Soviet period. While many enterprises were busy divesting social assets or failing to invest in their maintenance, there has been a dearth of alternative leisure and recreational facilities, while the few new monetised services have been prohibitive to most workers, whose earnings have been well below the level necessary to be able to enjoy them. The combination of the disintegration of many institutions in post-Soviet society and the absence of many basic public services has been causing a deterioration of public health, particularly in the incidence of alcoholism and in a drastic decrease in life expectancy (Zohoori *et al.* 1998). Many employers and trade unions have lamented the loss of the moral functions of the enterprise, mainly in their capacity to transmit and enforce values and order.

As real wages fell, lay-offs increased and wages remained unpaid, management relied even more heavily on the goodwill of their workers to ensure the survival of the enterprise than they had in the Soviet system, making it even more dangerous to try to transform the social organisation of production radically. As a result, many enterprises have retained the basic features of the Soviet wage system and have tried (with various degrees of success) to retain access to welfare benefits, replace traditional benefits with a variety of newly devised pecuniary rewards (such as short-term loans and material assistance) and use traditional methods of moralising workers as a way of attracting and retaining, rewarding and disciplining the workforce, and facilitating social integration and social peace through difficult and unpredictable times (Smirnov 1999: 13–16; see also Vinogradova 1997, 1998).

The traditional system of welfare provision has seen a variety of changes in terms of the substance of the welfare benefits provided. Nevertheless, the nature and functions of such provision continue to be an important element in labour management. On the other hand, to view them as purely instrumental on the part of management in their efforts to overcome labour market constraints or undermine workers' power as a component of paternalism understates their continuing social significance in reinforcing the ideology and substance of the labour collective as a social organism united against external constraints and with the purpose of the development of the human potential of those employed at the enterprise, as well as those who worked and those who have yet to work there.

Rather, the continuing relevance of welfare provision lies in the persistence of the particular production relations at the level of the enterprise. Welfare benefits in the Russian enterprise are neither adequate nor could be said to represent a premium on wages which is somehow linked to productivity (see Morrison and Schwartz 2003). In contrast to the Soviet period, their quality has declined considerably, and this has made provision all the more discretionary and (in the absence of the Communist Party as the station of last resort for grievance settlements) much more individualised. As a result, workers have become much more dependent on their relationships with shop managers and enterprise authorities, and this dependence has reinforced their atomisation and inability to organise effectively.

From the perspective of line managers, the existing welfare benefits do not represent an adequate solution, though they represent a set of ready-made, reliable antidotes, which reinforce the existing hierarchical structure and their authority. Trade unions are highly dependent on the continuing survival of their enterprises and are deeply implicated in labour management through the administration and management of enterprise welfare. All of this makes the unions ineffective as representatives of the workers, but it also provides no incentive for the employers to seek alternative solutions to labour management, so that it is less problematic, less destabilising and much more economical to offer inferior benefits within the framework of paternalist control, while capitalising on past capacity through a combination of deteriorating wages and terms of employment.

Conclusion: recasting the labour collective

While the initial neo-liberal rhetoric of privatisation found an unlikely ally in the enterprise Director, the subjection of enterprises to market forces dashed the hopes of securing the profits which seemed imminent with the demise of the administrative appropriation of surplus. Privatisation and the development of a market economy, which has outwardly appeared to be a fully fledged capitalist economy (Åslund 1995), has not brought about reforms in the form of social organisation of production at Russian industrial enterprises. The subordination of enterprises and organisations to the market has been largely purely formal, with the management structure still oriented to the achievement of production targets with little regard for costs, the core of the management team still being comprised of the Director, chief engineer and shop chiefs, and the economic, finance and personnel departments still being peripheral services whose only function has been to collate figures and prepare reports.

Far from forcing changes in the social structure of the enterprise, the subordination of the enterprise to the market has reinforced many traditional problems of production, which have only worsened by the increase of raw materials and energy costs brought about by price liberalisation, and the breakdown of long-established economic links and the collapse of demand for enterprise products. Unpredictability, irregularity of supplies and unreliability of supply networks, along with the need to secure the conditions for proper working in the absence or instability of outside technical services, have reinforced the traditional concerns over employment decision-making and the questions of pay and reward management.

Likewise, while wages have been freed from administrative control and enterprises could introduce better control over labour by bringing about the threat of unemployment for some and the promise of increased earnings for others, the unpredictability has restricted enterprise wage funds to a greater degree than during the Soviet period, bringing about long waves of wage delays, non-payment, short-time work and administrative leave, which has contributed to quits, labour turnover, the ossification of enterprise skills and poor morale, while the poor control over hiring, training and development has exacerbated the problem every step of the way.

The salvation for the privatised industrial enterprises has been the absence of a vast development of new sectors of employment, which is partly explained by the concessions made by municipal, regional and federal authorities in the face of the threat of the majority of enterprises on the verge of bankruptcy precipitating complete economic collapse. The result has been the confinement of the majority of the workforce to the decaying enterprises with difficult and hazardous working conditions on meagre wages, while the absence of a wage floor and effective unemployment benefits creates the need to be in full-time employment in order to access social support. Given the absence of trade unions able, or willing, to represent the interests of their members and the continuing identification of trade unions as the appendages of enterprise management, it is more secure and less taxing to offer deteriorating terms of employment, low wages and inferior benefits while capitalising on past capacity. All of this has provided enterprises with a cheap, extremely flexible workforce and has taken away from them the incentives to restructure.

Enterprises have no real motivation to transform the social organisation of production. By the same token, the precariousness of the production environment which the survival strategies of enterprises have produced has forced managers to rely on the goodwill and willingness of their workers to carry out production through what are presented as difficult times. Workers have tended to respond in traditional ways, bargaining with managers for individual amelioration or improvement or using their personal connections to find a better job elsewhere while looking to their managers to represent their collective interests. However difficult the situation might become, workers have passively suffered falling real wages, lay-offs, short-time working and the extended non-payment of wages (see Clarke 1998), so long as they have believed that their managers were doing the best that they could for them, and line managers and enterprise Directors have gone out of their way to sustain that belief. Line managers share the workers' interest in ensuring continued production, often eliciting the co-operation of the workforce in the search for work, perhaps encouraging their workers to look for orders on the side or turning a blind eye to the misappropriation of enterprise resources, and enlisting the support of workers, even to the extent of encouraging them to strike, in the traditional competition for resources within the enterprise or the traditional battle to replace a failing Director. The Directors, meanwhile, have tried to deflect the anger of the employees at low pay or the failure to receive their wages by blaming the failure of the enterprise on external forces, and would try to secure the support of the labour force in their attempts to find a way out of the crisis by appealing to local, regional and national government for state support, relying on traditional methods of lobbying (Clarke 2000).

In these circumstances the ideological and substantive significance of the labour collective as a social organism concerned with its own reproduction has played a key role in sustaining the viability of the enterprise. But the more significant question posed by these developments is of the extent to which such a system can continue to persist without undermining the productive basis on which it subsists.

Notes

1 By 1998 employment in industry had fallen by more than a third, and construction and science by about half, while employment in credit and finance had increased by 90 per cent, from a very small base, and employment in trade and catering, the branch dominated by new private enterprises, increased by over half, rising up to two-thirds by 2001. The engineering industry, which had employed one in eight of the working population in 1990, shed more than half its jobs, and almost two-thirds of the jobs were lost in light industry, while employment in gas, oil, electricity generation and non-ferrous metallurgy increased significantly (Goskomstat 1999: 88). Overall unemployment levels reached 5 per cent in 1992 and stood at approximately the same level for most of the 1990s, reaching 12.9 per cent following the 1998 financial crisis and falling steadily since then (Goskomstat 2001a).

2 The question raised by the experience of reforms during the last decade is the extent to which the social organisation of industrial enterprises as 'labour collectives', geared towards self-preservation against external constraints, will continue to be relevant in the near future. Following the financial crisis and devaluation of 1998, there has been some recovery of the Russian economy. Wages and employment have been rising, wage delays and inter-enterprise debt have been falling, there has been some recovery of investment and the transfer of ownership to outside investors, not to mention the increase in the size and significance of the oil, gas and metallurgy sectors, and the positive effects these have had on the economy as a whole. But the results of the recovery do not yet provide a clear picture of the character of change and it is not yet certain whether the initial changes are sustainable. In this account, I will deal with the issue at hand only up to 2000–1. For a more in-depth discussion of the post-crisis developments, see Schwartz (2003b).

3 The priority of 'main' workers derived from both the ideological principles which stressed the pre-eminence of 'productive work' (in occupations immediately related to enterprise output) over services which, along with supervisory and administrative tasks, were seen as a drain on the wage fund, and the practical response to the imperatives of physical output which was unconstrained by other considerations, primarily that of quality.

4 In 1992, 93 per cent of industrial enterprises were 'profitable', a figure which had fallen to 51 per cent by 1998. In 1992, taxation accounted for 28 per cent of net profits, rising to 61 per cent of a relatively smaller total in 1994. In 1998, by which time net profits in the economy were negative, direct taxation of profits amounted to 3.6 per cent of GDP (Goskomstat 2001a: various pages).

5 The 2000 round of the annual Russian Labour Flexibility Survey (RLFS), covering 308 industrial enterprises in different parts of the country, revealed that 23 per cent of the firms still used the Soviet tariff scale and a further 45 per cent used it as the point of reference for their payment system (Tsentr issledovanii rynka truda 2001).

Part II

Empirical investigations

5 From socialist camp to global village?

Globalization and the imaginary landscapes of postsocialism

Olga Shevchenko and Yakov Schukin

Introduction

Globalization theories are often criticized for their overly abstract nature. Hay and Marsh (2000: 6) call globalization "a process without a subject." How is globalization experienced by Russian people? To set the stage for a discussion of the lived experience of globalization and postsocialism in today's Russia, there is no better starting place than the imagery of the iron curtain. The finite and irreversible air that surrounded this metaphor was, and is, something of an exaggeration, since the curtain was in fact porous, allowing for a modest amount of exchange and interpenetration which, in the atmosphere of information deficit, could yield surprisingly potent results.[1] Yet the scope of transnational exchange remained limited, the numbers of Soviet citizens allowed to travel abroad (mostly to Eastern Europe) was no more than a few thousand a year, and the global-internationalist thinking was largely confined to a narrow section of policy-academic elite (English 2000). In the minds of millions of Soviet citizens, the iron curtain had the immediacy of actual reality, delimiting their sources of information about the world, their sense of opportunities and the economic reality of their everyday lives.

The sense of self-imposed isolation from *zagranitsa* – a telling term designating all countries beyond the border of the Soviet Union, a dream destination for many – stands in sharp contrast to the unfolding intensification of contacts across borders, to flows of transnational migration and proliferation of international economic and political bodies which comprise the reality of postsocialist Russia. But does that mean that the inhabitants of the socialist camp suddenly found themselves in a global village? Clearly, Russia's sudden openness to the international economy and politics profoundly affected the Russian people. However, the forms and directions of this influence have to be explored.

This chapter addresses the lived experience of globalization in what is arguably the most global Russian city, Moscow. While it is true that hardly anyone in Russia can be considered unaffected by globalization (largely because of its macro-economic consequences for countries around the world), those affected by it do not constitute a coherent group, but differ widely in their experience of the process and their relation to it. Once again, the concept of a divergent, contradictory and asymmetric globalization emerges. In order to get at the experiences of globalization on different levels of involvement with global institutions, we examine in depth six case studies of individual Muscovites who in the course of the 1990s had been drawn into the "new economy" in various capacities, from accidental exposure to it as a cleaning lady in an exclusive furniture salon to conscious pursuit of a career in international management in a large British corporation. This chapter explores the specific ways in which these differently positioned actors experience globalization in their everyday life, identifying what in fact are many different "globalizations." We pay particular attention to the relationship between the economic aspects of globalization, i.e. the involvement of individuals into the open economy and the gains that such an involvement entails, and its ideational aspects – their awareness of the trends, identities and ideologies that cut across national boundaries, and their consciousness of the world at large. We stress that globalization does not always occur on both planes, and that, even when it does, the speed and intensity of these processes are out of synch with each other. Global ideologies of "one-worldism," transnationalism, participatory democracy and human rights do not always arrive hand in hand with the openness of a national economy. In fact, as we will show below, the everyday reality of postsocialist global economy can make these ideologies counterintuitive. While globalization creates new workplaces and opportunities, it often lacks legitimacy because it also destroys habitual patterns of employment and can cause disorientation and social dislocations. As a result, even those actors who economically benefit from the new and open economy may be resistant to much of its rhetoric and ideology, and adhere with renewed conviction to distinctively local sentiments.

Postsocialism and globalization

Even prior to 1989, countries of the so-called Second World were not completely disconnected from the world economy. In fact, the very breakdown of the Soviet Union can be seen as a product of global pressures to compete on the world economic arena with other world-system players (Wallerstein 1979, 1991). But even as socialist countries participated in international trade, they did so through a rigid system of specialized institutions, so-called FTOs (foreign trade organizations), precisely in an effort to isolate their internal development from external influences. When the Soviet Union collapsed, its member countries opened up on a whole new scale to the opportunities and constraints associated with global capitalism. The "old economy," which consisted of firms created a long time ago, when profit-making under the conditions of openness was not a relative consideration, was supplemented with the "new economy," i.e. firms created from the very beginning as profit-making enterprises under the conditions of economic openness. New influences were not only economic, but also ideological and cultural, channeled through media, advertising, arts and literature. Thus, post-socialist countries seem to offer one an ideal case study of the impact of globalization: what happens when a relatively autonomous entity is absorbed into a larger economic and political order.

Existing approaches to the impacts and manifestations of globalization emphasize a variety of its dimensions: globalization of production and its impact on work relations (Schaeffer 2002); new forms of labor organization and citizenship (Ong 1999); emergence of new patterns of spatial organization (Laguerre 2000; Sassen 1991); influence of global political and economic processes on the forms of contention and collective identity formation (Castells 2000b; Smith and Johnston 2002), as well as on forms of national self-imagining (Oommen 1997); transnational solidarities caused by a new awareness of global risks and of the need for their prevention (Beck 1998); the dissemination of information technologies and formation of new transnational knowledge communities (Castells 2000a); the increasing compression of time and space (Harvey 1989); the flow of ideas, individuals, images, technologies and finances across national boundaries (Appadurai 1990); and the deepening awareness of the world at large (Robertson, 1992). While each of these dimensions of globalization has been studied in detail, little was applied to the Russian context. More importantly, there has been preciously little research on how all of the above dimensions relate to/translate into one another. Some approaches, such as the world society tradition (Meyer *et al.* 1997), assume that economic and political globalization translates neatly into cultural convergence of nation-states around the globe and their ever-growing commitment to "highly rationalized and universalistic" ideology (p. 153). Others are far less categorical about the actual content, or even a possibility of one world culture, but there is little doubt that cultural transformations (of whatever character) go hand in hand with economic ones. By contrast, this chapter questions the assumption that all manifestations of globalization discussed above occur in a given society simultaneously. Instead, it sets out to explore the varying configurations of economic and cultural "globalizations," and their embeddedness in the experiences of different social groups in a given society.

To gain analytic insight into the trajectories of global change, it is important to look into particular case studies and to identify the tempo and nature of the lived experience of globalization among differently positioned individuals. There is no better place for it in Russia than Moscow. The negative consequences of globalization have been felt in Moscow as much as in other cities (closing of many enterprises and institutes, volatility of the rouble, inflation, unemployment), but there are also many ways in which one could ride the tide of globalization by exploiting the newly emerging opportunities. Moscow is a site of great concentration of capital. Headquarters and country offices or international corporations, banks, financial investment and consulting companies, and NGOs are all in place. All of the world's top financial corporations have bases here. It is not a global city in Sassen's (1991) sense – the site of production of global services and financial goods on a world scale – but it is as close as it gets in Russia. And, as in Sassen's global cities, an entire supporting infrastructure exists in Moscow to make its global operations possible, and this infrastructure on all levels is filled by working Muscovites.

The six individuals whose views and postsocialist career paths are described in this chapter are taken from a larger sample of Muscovites recurrently interviewed in the course of 1998–2000 by Olga Shevchenko as part of a larger study of everyday experiences of social change in a contemporary urban Russian setting.[2] The rationale for concentrating on these cases in depth has been that they exemplify different levels of involvement with, and experience of, global forces and institutions, from cursory and accidental to relatively consistent and comprehensive. While no individual actors can be considered "typical" for any social context at large, we feel that the cases at hand exemplify many subtleties and complexities in the postsocialist actors' relationship to globalization, and can thus be revealing of the conceptual blind spots in the globalization literature.

Taking discrete case studies of individuals' relationships to the global economy involves trade-offs. On the downside, we will not be able to gauge the profundity of changes that have taken place among various groups in the Russian population; a large representative sample would be needed to do that. However, we will use the case studies to assess the scope of variations in individuals' experience of globalization, and to shed light on the complex relationship between its economical and cultural dimensions. To use Michael Burawoy's (1998) terminology, we will approach our cases through the lens of the extended case method, in which ethnographic data is examined to refute or to build on theory. In our case, the world society approach represents the most radical of theories of global cultural change, in that it stipulates not only the centrality of the cultural component of globalization, but also its content ("highly rationalized and universalistic" ideology with an emphasis on "self-determination, responsibility, [. . .] social justice and protection of individual rights" (Meyer *et al.* 1997: 153). While most other theorists are more cautious about the convergence of local cultures into one unitary "world culture," the co-existence of some kind of cultural transformation and of global economic integration is often treated as a given. Here, we hope to contribute to advancing the cause championed by Guillen (2001), who argued for "further theoretical work to clarify the economic, political, cultural, and aesthetic dimensions of globalization and how they interact with one another" (p. 157). But, before we turn to the exploration of individual trajectories in the globalizing world, we need to understand the point of departure, i.e. the "closed" world of late socialism from which they emerged.

Remembering late socialism

We should say a couple of words about living under late socialism, since this period (1970s and 1980s) is a very important reference point in the discourse of our respondents. We should emphasize that what we are talking about here is how our respondents see late socialism *now*, not necessarily how they saw it in 1970s and 1980s. As any retrospective discourse, the discourse about life under late socialism is highly selective, and emphasizes the aspects of life that have been eroded by the more competitive and economically volatile postsocialist order. At the same time, the features of everyday life under socialism that were competitive in their own ways (struggle for resources and privileges, career advancement or access to power) are *de*-emphasized because their absence is not experienced as a loss.

Overall, the socialist period is seen as the time when the relationships between people "were good" (*horoshie otnoshenie mezhdu lud'mi*). Educated people worked at research and planning institutes (so-called *NIIs*, *Nauchno-Issledovatel'skie Instituty*), universities and other state-financed organizations. Less educated people (working class) worked at the factories which produced material goods. Both groups had intensive social lives, interacted with friends and participated in such activities as hiking, nature outings and guitar-playing/singing (sometimes within the semi-formal framework of organizations such as *KSP* – the *Bard Song Club*) in their free time. The Russian economy was seen as self-sufficient, and not dependent on the economies of other countries. Both of these groups (intelligentsia and workers) saw themselves as "working," as opposed to people who were engaged in "selling/buying activities," or "speculation." These types of activities (if not carried out by the state itself) were considered to be morally impure. Inequalities within the society are believed to have been mild. People aspired for education *not* because it would give them higher wages (in fact, workers and engineers were paid approximately the same), but because they wanted to associate with "nice," "cultured" people – to be member of the intelligentsia. Intelligentsia people would not only drink vodka (everybody did that), but they would accompany it with talks about books, movies, politics and other interesting subjects. In summer, everybody could go to the Black Sea area (Crimea or Caucasus), to the Baltic Republics or anywhere else in the former Soviet Union. Travel was cheap, and people knew that every corner of the Soviet Union was accessible to them.

What is even more important is that the Soviet Union was a "micro-world." It had its own "civilized West" (Baltic Republics), its own "Mediterranean" (Black Sea), its own "Orient" (Middle Asian Republics) and its own "frontier/wilderness region" (Siberia and the Far East). Any kind of experience one was looking for, one could get. And the relationships between different ethnic groups living in the Soviet Union were supposedly peaceful and harmonious.

While travel within the Soviet Union was generally unproblematic, people could not freely go abroad, especially to the West. Partly because of that, and partly because of the contradictory nature of information that was available about "the West" from various sources (rumors, personal accounts, films, political information), this "West" was constructed ambivalently – as the locus of consumer opulence and "normality," and as an ephemeral, unreal place. As many respondents said at different instances during interviews, they never expected that, in the course of their lives, they would ever have an option of seeing capitalism with their own eyes. Much less did they expect that to happen on the territory of their own country. Let us turn to the case studies in order to gain an in-depth view of globalization as it is felt by a selection of Muscovites.

Case studies

Vera and Nina: reluctant exposure to globalization

Vera and Nina represent the minimum level of engagement with globalization processes following the fall of socialism. People at this level have found a job in a profit-making enterprise of the "new economy," but they do not break their ties with the poorly paying, yet secure, "old economy" completely, since this provides some fringe benefits and they do not feel secure enough about the new jobs to make them the sole sources of income. This is an extremely common postsocialist experience (see Southworth, Chapter 10, this volume, for coverage of this situation in Bashkortostan).

In Nina's case, the old job is at *NII* (she works as an engineer); in Vera's case it is work at the Supreme Court (she works as a janitor). Despite the very different character of work they do, they are paid approximately the same, which indicates how skill differentials in the old economy do not neatly translate into pay differentials (which is not surprising, given that profit-making was not a consideration in the old economy).

Nina's research at the *NII* is in physics and chemistry, and the particular laboratory she works at provides environmental expertise of physical and chemical processes developed in the other laboratories of the same institute. So, this laboratory is a kind of "in-house" environmental watch-dog. Some other laboratories in this institute are doing well since they have grant money, but Nina's laboratory does not have grant money (either because they cannot get it or because they have never tried – we cannot say at this point). Nina's feelings towards her old job are ambivalent. On the one hand, she is really proud of being a physicist and an engineer. On the other hand, this pride does not lead her to seek grant money for her laboratory or to try to become integrated into the global community of physicists by some other means. So, to get involved in the new economy she had to acquire not only a new job, but a new occupation.

Before she had a job in the new economy, her vision of reality was the following: she and her colleagues are "doing science." The state forgot the people doing science, which is bad. People in the new economy do not produce anything. They just buy and sell, or administrate – which is not real work.

Then, in 1999, through her friend, she got a job in the new economy at a bakery firm that occupies the same building where *NII* is located. Worker turnover at the bakery is high, so there is a constant need to write new employment contracts. Nina's job is to take care of these two problems. Every week she writes employment contracts for new workers and obtains entry permissions for them. As one can see, this new job is entirely administrative and hence not respectable by her initial standards. However, although Nina still maintains her old job, her perception of its value has changed. As she pictures it now, her research colleagues and herself (in the old job) sit idly and do nothing, or, as she put it, "*sidat i plyut v potolok*" (sit there and spit at the ceiling). At her new job, she has to work really hard. At the same time, on an abstract level, she continues to think that administration is not real work, and is still ready to criticize politicians, businessmen and others who do not work with their own hands. Yet, she is not ready to give up her new job. That shows that the old Soviet ideal of "producing" is still alive and well, even though it comes into direct conflict with the realities of the labor market generated by globalization. In the global economy, there are fewer and fewer places which "produce" anything, and more and more places "distributing" what is produced somewhere else, but, even in the eyes of their own employees, they continue to lack legitimacy.

Vera's transition from the "old job" to a "new one" did not involve a change of occupation. She was (and still is) a cleaning lady at the Russian Supreme Court, but she combines it with a job as a cleaning lady for a private shop which sells expensive Western furniture. Many clients of this firm are affluent politicians and employees of Gazprom, the Russian gas monopoly. Vera's experience of the new economy is colored by her encountering a capitalist enterprise from the "primitive accumulation" period. Her boss is a Syrian businesswoman who treats her employees in the manner of a Dickensian small shop owner: there are no paid vacations at Vera's job, no paid sick days or holidays, the work shift lasts for 12 hours, and all conflicts are resolved in an arbitrary and dictatorial fashion. Of course the reason why Vera's boss can do it is because she pays her employees above-market wages. People who are sure that they will be able to find another job leave her, but Vera cannot do it for family reasons (see below). Such experience of the new labor market made Vera put a lot of emphasis on "decent relationships" between people, which, as she feels, are missing in the new economy.

It is important to note that both Nina and Vera are single providers for their families. Nina is a single mother with a son. Vera lives with a husband, who became disabled about five years ago and cannot work, and two sons. Vera's husband has a tiny pension. The financial situation of both families is tough.

In terms of family finance and standards of living, even minimal involvement in the "new economy" gives a boost in income. Both Nina and Vera make about $200 per month. Before they got their new jobs they were making less than $100. In Moscow prices, their current earnings are just about on the border between physical survival (not being hungry) and psychological survival (not thinking about the possibility of being hungry). They both enjoy their higher incomes, yet they also talk about the evil and moral corruption of consumerism. Interestingly enough, they spend a considerable amount of money on education for their children (buying a computer, paying for English lessons), combining it with talk about how you have to be not only educated, but aggressive, tough and mean, in order to succeed "these days." Thus, we can say that, when it comes to putting high value on education for your children, both Nina and Vera follow the norm of the "global culture," which in this case coincides with the Soviet norm. The difference is that in the Soviet era receiving higher education was not associated with obtaining a high standard of living (one could obtain it with or without education), but now it is.

When it comes to politics or some other "non-everyday" social problems, the views of Nina and Vera are very remote from Meyer *et al.*'s (1997) ideal of the global culture. In other words, the diffusion of participatory democratic rhetoric is far less noticeable in their case than the diffusion of global economic patterns and relationships. They do not see themselves as efficacious citizens whose interests are served by the state. In fact, they do not see the state as serving any kind of collective good. The picture they have is "us"(the people) vs. "them" (politicians and bureaucrats). Politicians are always corrupt; they do not care about "common people," and "we, the subjects," rather than "we, the citizens," is the perspective Vera and Nina assume. Similarly to the discourse of participatory citizenship, the discourse of individual rights – another component of Meyer's "global culture" – is conspicuously absent, both in terms of the speakers' own sense of entitlement to basic right and freedoms (such as freedom of information), and those of other social and ethnic groups (indicative in this respect are their sweeping statements concerning "blacks" (*chernye*), i.e. Azeri, Armenian and other ethnic traders who are distrusted and disliked by Muscovites of various educational backgrounds). Thus, overall, the expectations of a "highly rationalized, universalistic ideology" appear unrealistic.[3]

A weaker definition of globalization as the flow of ideas and technologies across borders, as well as the increasing consciousness of the world at large, appears to produce a different picture. To take the above-mentioned hostility to "blacks," it demonstrates not only lack of familiarity with the discourse of cultural and ethnic tolerance and human rights. It also serves as evidence of the ease with which categories of racial superiority transcend borders and get appropriated into contexts to which they, seemingly, are ill-suited, such as the juxtaposition between ethnic Slavs and the representatives of ethnic groups springing from the Caucasus region (designated, interchangeably, as blacks (*chernye*) and as Caucasians (*kavkaztsy*)).

More conspicuous signs of diffusion of transnational symbols and practices in Vera's and Nina's lives are the pieces of technology they have managed to afford due to their recently increased earnings: a VCR/TV, a fridge and a computer in the case of Nina, and a VCR and a vacuum cleaner in the case of Vera, as well as their choice of dollars as a mode of preserving savings. At the same time, as we pointed out above, Nina and Vera rhetorically separate themselves from the consumer pleasures that the new economy has made available to them, and draw heavily on the late socialist discourse of morality, culture and "good relations between people" as the opposite of what they perceive as the cold, calculating and inconsiderate ethics of the contemporary period.

Their sense of space and international relations is similarly ambivalent. They recognize the role of the dollar in the Russian economy, and are willing to trust the US government with their savings (that is, to keep their saving in dollars). As "naïve monetarists," they believe that inflation is predominantly caused by an excess of roubles in the economy, as measured by the dollar/rouble exchange rate, as opposed to internal economic forces. At the same time, despite this acute (and sometimes even exaggerated) awareness of how Russian economy depends on other economies, they do not consider this dependency a positive development. The economic ideal for Nina and Vera is still "industrialized self-sufficiency" – something like the idealized late Soviet Union when "we were doing everything ourselves." As a result, they are harshly critical regarding the current economic situation, because "they (i.e. the West) use our resources, and all we do is pump out oil." This exchange is clearly seen as uneven, and mutual economic dependency is not seen as something valuable.

In general, Nina and Vera do not have much awareness of living in one global world. The idea of globalization as a force vaguely exists in their visions of the world, but they do not connect their own job mobility with it. They do not mention the term "globalization" explicitly, but the general connotations of the phrase "all these changes" (used to describe what has happened in Russia, starting from *perestroika*) are largely negative. In fact, in their own lived experience, a shrinking of the world (in a sense of localization and contraction) has taken place rather than globalization (in a sense of expansion). The reason for this is the breakdown of the Soviet Union and the developments that followed (rise of rail tariffs, expensive tickets to go to the Crimea, new currencies, higher phone and postage rates). The global strategic realignments that took place on the international arena in the meantime had little to offer in the way of ameliorating these sharply felt complications.

Lyuba and Roman: dollars and dreams

Vera and Nina were reluctant to exchange the habitual pattern of their daily existence for other pursuits more in line with the "new economy," cautious of the risks that these occupations could pose to the stability of their earnings. Their precarious family situation (Nina as a single mother, Vera as a mother of two with a disabled husband) justified such caution, and even as these women reluctantly embraced the new opportunities, they were careful to continue adhering to their old, badly paying but "stable" jobs, at least until the new jobs proved to be a reliable source of income. In the case of Lyuba and Roman, such measures were not necessary since, in both cases, their families had other wage-earning family members whose relatively stable but low-paying jobs provided a backing for Lyuba's and Roman's explorations into the world of the new economy.

As they quickly discovered, while the value of their old employment was measured by a number of considerations: salary, schedule, tasks fulfilled, distance from home, and the like, the only relevant criterion in the postsocialist economy became *dollary*, or, as they were often called, *baksy* (bucks). In other words, both Lyuba and Roman came to realize that, in the situation of escalating inflation and periodic devaluations of the rouble, *de facto* deflation of their salary can be countered only by tying earnings to a fixed dollar sum which is converted into roubles at each paycheck according to the rate of the day. Their consequent search for employment was predicated on this requirement, and, while some employers readily accepted it, in other cases one had to negotiate and bargain.

Lyuba's work for the new economy began in 1993, when, after six years of staying home with her son, she returned to the labor market to work as a cleaning lady at a bank. Lyuba's previous position – as a head nurse in a psychiatric hospital – seemed too time-intensive at the time and paid worse than part-time cleaning at a modern office building rented by the bank. After the bank went bankrupt in a series of financial scandals of the mid-1990s, Lyuba was forced to look for a new position. At this point, she was aware of the benefits of working for a commercial structure (apart from the earnings, she still nostalgically remembers the abundant food orders which were available weekly at the first bank she worked at) and looked for a new position vaguely related to this sector. In a few months, she found another part-time cleaning job in a new bank which paid her as much as her husband, a professional policeman, earned in his full-time work as a municipal security guard. Cleaning provided her only with part of her income; the other part she earned doing odd jobs for a market research company: as a focus group hostess and recruiter, as coder and as telephone interviewer working for $2/hour. Because of the distances she has to cover between her jobs, Lyuba's working day sometimes lasts as long as 14 hours. However, she can exercise control over her schedule, has a paid vacation and is happy with her monthly income which typically hovers between $200 and $300 and is about twice as much as the money brought home by her husband.

Like Lyuba's, Roman's Soviet-era job had little to do with his subsequent career. His working biography started in the industrial sector where, for a total of 17 years, he worked first at the Khrunichev Space Equipment Plant and later at the Moscow Aviation Equipment Manufacturing Plant. In early 1991, when both the workload and the earnings at the plant started to falter under the combined pressure of disarmament, infrastructural breakdown, budget deficit and inflation, Roman took an invitation to join a private bronze-casting workshop. The job turned out to be physically hard but lucrative: Roman's starting earnings were about four times higher than his former pay at the plant, and the flow of orders was steady. Much of the workshop's success came from being in the right place at the right time. According to Roman, the bulk of commissions came from the federal administration, which, in the early 1990s, was busy furnishing itself with new national symbols (although Roman was very critical of Yeltsin and his administration, he pointed with a touch of pride that the two-headed eagles which grace the offices of the White House were cast by his workshop). Emerging financial institutions and banks provided their share of commissions as well, by ordering cast bronze columns and statues for their headquarters and offices. However, while these global actors kept the workshop going, other workshop clients were destroyed by the very same process of globalization and postsocialist restructuring. Because of the breakdown of the country-wide organizations with which the workshop was associated, salaries quickly became irregular and in 1995 Roman left, following a lead offered by a *dacha* neighbor, to work for a Yugoslav construction company which was at the time forming a permanent brigade in Moscow.

Unlike many other construction companies Roman was aware of, the Yugoslav brigade he worked for provided its employees with a semblance of welfare arrangements: they were entitled to a three-week paid vacation every year, although sick leave was unpaid. The schedule of work was intense – the permanent staff worked 10 hours a day, six days a week, but Roman considered himself lucky since the work was fairly regular and his monthly pay was higher than in other companies of similar profile (even as it went from \$500 to \$400 per month in 1998–9 because of the economic crisis). During slow periods when the company had no contracts, the management dismissed the workers with no pay; such slow periods could last for months on end, in the course of which Roman either worked on repair contracts he obtained through connections (which is what he was doing when I first met him), or else his six-person family had to rely on savings and his wife's and son's earnings, supplemented by \$300 a month they received by renting his mother-in-law's apartment.

The economic openness of the postsocialist system is clearly what made companies such as Roman's and Lyuba's possible. It is the case not only because the initial investment, as well as the bulk of the labor force in Roman's company comes from Yugoslavia, while Lyuba's employers are tied into international systems of professional association and exchange, but also because many contracts these companies work on are provided by banks, headquarters of international companies and other recently emerged actors on the postsocialist scene, or, in case of Roman, ordered by individuals who have been sufficiently successful in working the system in order to afford the expense of repairs. Even the type of repairs in which Roman's company specializes evokes the reference to the West in its title, *evroremont* (eurorepairs). The term refers to a thorough remodeling of apartments, in the course of which all plaster is knocked off the wall and the walls are practically redone all over again, as are window frames, sills, electric wiring and doors, in an effort to create "European" environment which is, in essence, a dream of the Western quality and affluence that the postsocialist imagination has generated.

Should we conclude, then, that Roman's and Lyuba's vision of the world and its boundaries has changed and that their involvement with the transnational forces (the economic ubiquity of the American dollar, international companies and its international clients) and actors (Roman's Yugoslav and Moldavian colleagues, or the clients of the marketing company whom Lyuba serves during focus groups and meetings) has made them into more globally aware persons? In a way, it is true. Both of them are acutely aware of the role the dollar plays in the Russian economy, carefully monitor all fluctuations of its rate (to the point of making it the first thing they look up in the morning, after the weather forecast), put a great stock in it by preserving their savings in hard currency and even use it as a substitute for the rouble on certain occasions (such as transactions with their children's tutors, all of which are done in dollars). They are well aware of the importance of the knowledge and information economy, and make the education of their children, particularly English and computer courses, a first priority (as Lyuba said, "There us nothing that we as parents can give our children, except for education. If we give them good education, they will earn the rest themselves."). Both greatly enjoy the consumer opportunities that their earnings allow them, and measure their success in navigating the postsocialist economy by their ability to partake in the global icons of consumption: "Although it's hard, but it's possible to live, to take kids to the theater, to McDonalds, give them the stuff they are interested in" (Lyuba). They have an interest in international and home politics and some strong opinions about it: Lyuba was highly critical of the US involvement in Yugoslavia, which she considered a violation of national sovereignty, while Roman was skeptical of the IMF and often discussed home politics with his Yugoslav and Moldavian co-workers. Professionally, too, he clearly capitalizes on the "European" origins of his company when he proposes his *evroremont* services to his clients. There are, however, aspects to Roman and Lyuba's respective outlooks that don't conform to a blueprint of a global citizen that all the above would imply.

To begin with *evroremont*, the dream image of the West as the opposite of all things Soviet and as a place of affluence and higher quality standards was part and parcel of the popular mythology throughout late socialism (Bukovskii 1981; Humphrey 1995), and its perpetuation signals not a greater opening to the world, but, quite the contrary, the continued division between the familiar surroundings and the exteriorized and imaginary world of the *zagranitsa*. Although Roman does not himself fully share this vision (his exposure to the actual living representatives of the said *zagranitsa*, his Serbian and Montenegrian colleagues complicate this image), he has little evidence to counter it. His circle of foreign contacts is too small and, moreover, he is not quite sure where they fall within the Yugoslav society. As a result, his own assessment of the European living standard is rather contradictory:

> Somehow, they seem better developed in many ways. Even if you look, let's say, at our Yugoslavs, they sometimes bring their photos to show, and the way our New Russians build large cottages, – that's the way all of them have, large plots, lawns, a good solid house, with running water, all that, and they live there. And here (*u nas*) it's only New Russians, not simple workers like them. And in Germany too, I've seen photos, all houses are so neat, whereas my dacha is just a log cabin and that's it. [. . .] But then again, in Yugoslavia, they also have a lot . . . there is a lot of poor folk that works at our [company]. Even on TV, they show all these refugees, and these guys we have, they are working, and their parents still live in the village and their houses are nothing special. [. . .] So it must be that some are doing better than others.

As one can see from this quote, the "West" blurs in Roman's eyes into one undifferentiated image, so that pieces of information about Yugoslavia and Germany come across as mutually replaceable. Without a clear framework for interpreting the bits and pieces of information that he receives from his Yugoslav colleagues and from the media, he finds himself hard pressed to form a coherent opinion, as does Lyuba when, in response to a question about the Western living standards, she says:

> Well if I've ever lived in the West, seen things with my own eyes, then I'd know. And like this, through rumors and what not. . . . So I don't really know. Maybe it wouldn't be bad if we borrowed something from them. But how would you borrow everything? I don't think everything would fit, may be some aspects. But you see, I really can't compare – I haven't lived there. [. . .] I think we are, I don't know, I guess more emotional, and they are more practical, or how should I put it. With us, emotions sometimes overshadow everything. And with them, – it's more calculating. For instance, as we live, I don't do any accounting at all, I spend what I spend, and shoot me if I know how much, whereas they probably know for sure how much money they spend monthly as a family (laughs).

The kind of undifferentiated "them" that refers to the West in the above quote relies less on actual cultural encounters or literary sources than on common stereotypes. Lyuba has no illusions to that end, and this explains her initial reluctance to comment on the issue. The rest of the world, thus, although admittedly not cut off from her as it was a decade earlier, still has an imaginary, hypothetical existence. In this respect, it is significant that both Lyuba and Roman have never traveled abroad, although they do not considered such an expenditure to be beyond their economic means (Lyuba actually considered a trip to Bulgaria with her husband, but later the couple changed their minds and went to a fishing resort on the Don river instead). For them, like for Nina and Vera, a far more significant event than the fall of the iron curtain has been the break-up of the Soviet Union, and the fact that the former "sister"-republics turned into foreign states, requiring a change of currency, custom clearance and sometimes visa paperwork for entry. This break-up, which both Roman and Lyuba consider unreasonable and disadvantageous, made them resent the 1990s as the time when their immediate milieu *shrank*, not widened. The scope of regions where they could travel effortlessly and without linguistic difficulties decreased dramatically.

Roman and Lyuba's awareness of the surrounding world is limited not only in terms of their travel plans, but also in respect to the larger forces that they see at work when they look at postsocialist Russian politics and society. While they are conscious of the existence of transnational forces and organizations, such as the World Bank and the IMF, their skepticism towards them stems precisely from the belief that their activity in Russia is completely useless. For example, instead of debating the optimal venues for these organizations' involvement in the economy, Roman adheres to the opinion that the ideal arrangement would be that of full economic self-sufficiency and commitment to the enterprises of the "old economy." In other words, despite his own personally positive experience with globalization and joint ventures, Roman believes that Russia should not buy anything from abroad, but instead concentrate its efforts on retaining the old infrastructure and producing all it needs itself (at the same time he nostalgically remembers the days when the Soviet republics exchanged goods and services, calling it "sharing" ("*delilis' vsem*"), which points again to the discussion about the violated sense of organically shared territory). Lyuba was more in favor of restructuring the old economy. However, the goal of this restructuring was not negotiation of a smoother entry into the global economy, but, similarly to Roman, a better system of economic self-sufficiency within the country. Lyuba's dislike of imported clothes and foreign foodstuffs, quite common among the Russian consumers (Humphrey 1995) is of a similar nature, since she sees the economic and political standing of the country somehow diminished by the goods that it imports.

Considering the impact which the breakdown of the Soviet Union has had on Lyuba's and Roman's sense of "their" territory, one can interpret the current preoccupation with territorial wholeness, self-sufficiency and preservations of borders as a reaction to the rapid disintegration of the Soviet Union, and such arguments have been made (Humphrey 1999). One important implication of such an enhanced sense of territorial identity is the increased attention to domestic politics, which often overshadows international developments or writes them off as insignificant. Despite Roman's and Lyuba's awareness of, and investment in, foreign currency and the global economic processes that influence the dollar rate in Russia, their perspective on this issue is intensely local. They pay very little attention to the international factors that influence the dollar rate, considering the fluctuation of the Russian currency against the dollar a matter of narrowly Russian politics. Roman's interpretation of the fiscal crisis of 1998 did not involve the Asian currency crisis, or Russia's default on its loans, but approached the "August breakdown" as an expression of political struggle in the course of which some political forces where trying to "get Kirienko,"[4] while Lyuba considered the fiscal crisis to be squarely an effort, on the part of the government, to extract money out of the population by raising consumer prices.

Finally, while global images and actors play some (although by no means defining) role in Roman's and Lyuba's worlds, Meyer's ideal of participatory rhetoric and citizenship discourse is still a long stretch from the reality of their lives. A case in point here is the personalized and antagonistic vision of the state and government which can be discerned behind the attributions of responsibility for complex economic developments solely to the malevolent power. And if the problem that Roman and Lyuba identify with post-Soviet politics is framed in far less global terms than those of participatory democracy and human rights, so is the cure, which they envision not in terms of civic control and contention, but in the notorious image of the "good ruler" ("*khoroshii khozyain*"), who is expected to restore order in the manner of a "good company boss." This image is not only unrealistic, but also completely disconnected from any global discourses in terms of which it can be realized, as well as from any kind of civic entitlement that is associated with the democratic control of the government.

Zhenya and Anton: riding the tide of globalization

Both Zhenya and Anton belong to a "new class" of Moscovites – professionals who work for large (in Anton's case multinational) corporations in Moscow. Anton grew up in the city of Ul'yanovsk and moved to Moscow after high school, to study international trade and foreign languages at a highly prestigious university, *MGIMO*. As he himself freely acknowledges, at the time of his university studies, this training was aimed at making him not only a good specialist in "international trade," but also a spy. Thus, if the Soviet Union were still there, his most likely career trajectory would have been a position with a Russian *torgovoe predtavitel'stvo* (trade agency) in the Middle East, doing some trade, but mostly "working to expand the Soviet sphere of influence in the Middle East and fighting the CIA and Mossad." Fighting the CIA and Mossad here would have been a much more important component of his career than "trade"; almost all people who were taught

English at a good level were expected to do some ideological work of promoting socialism. Ironically, many of the exact same people now are on the front line of building capitalism in Russia.

At the time of Anton's graduation, in 1992, a slow and bureaucratic career in international trade already looked bad in comparison with the many emerging opportunities in the country. After a year of working for a large Russian company, where he got to know some of the key actors and procedures in the evolving field of international business, Anton got a job with a multinational company, first as a sales representative, then as a manager and finally as a head of the business development department. This is the stage he is at right now. On several instances along the way, Anton tested himself as an independent entrepreneur – he and some other people founded a company for importing cigarettes and alcohol – but he found the business environment "too criminal and not really pleasant," so he quit. He prefers to be a manager in a "civilized" Western company. In other words, we are dealing with a "worker" in the global economy, and not "the owner" of it.

Zhenya is also a worker in the new economy, and she never had an ambition to own her own business, because of the corruption and risks she associates with it. She graduated from college as a programmer in 1987, and, after a year spent working at a state factory, she was invited by a former co-worker to join him in working for *Hermes* – one of the many banks that were created in the late 1980s–early 1990s and which collapsed shortly after privatization owing its investors large sums of money. Zhenya, who was too low in the hierarchy to benefit from the company's dealings, argues that her "conscience is absolutely clear" because she never advised anyone to invest into the company. *Hermes*'s meltdown did not catch Zhenya off guard. She left the company at the earliest warning signs of the coming trouble, and quickly found another job as a financial manager for a large Russian oil conglomerate. At the moment, she characterizes her professional responsibilities as "professionally count[ing] other people's money," i.e. organizing payment transactions and invoices, and overseeing the financial documentation for the firm.

In terms of material status, working for a corporation provides one with a standard of living comparable to that of one's peers in other countries. While in absolute numbers, the managers in Russia are paid less, this difference is compensated for by a lower cost of living. So, overall, both Anton and Zhenya are comfortable financially. Anton bought an apartment in Moscow, there are two cars in his family and he hires a nanny for his son, despite the fact that his wife is a home-maker. He completed *evroremont* in his apartment. Plus, following a Russian-Soviet tradition, he is building a dacha, which is "a long-term investment" and which is going to be "something special." Zhenya also considers herself well-off: she drives a Jeep, generously lends money to her friends for both business and personal purposes, and recently remodeled the apartment where she lives with her boyfriend and her teenage daughter. The fact that their incomes and professional skills are comparable to the ones of their foreign colleagues has an important implication for their sense of professional and class identity, especially in the case of Anton, who has a closer contact with foreign executives due to the nature of his job. He (and to a smaller extent, Zhenya) feels a much stronger affinity with the managerial class in other countries than other respondents in this chapter would with service or construction workers outside Russia. In other words, Anton's professional identity is transnational, and so are his references in which he habitually evokes his foreign colleagues and friends, their work ethics and experiences.

Zhenya is a more complex case. She knows that her qualifications can enable her to work and occupy a respectable position in any other country, and has professional contacts abroad. At the same time, she is careful to emphasize that her loyalty to her fellow Russians of various economic standing is far stronger than her identification with her foreign colleagues. Unlike Anton, who considers himself a businessman and a person with distinct and ambitious career aspirations, Zhenya emphasizes that her career and income are merely a means to achieve a comfortable routine unaffected by larger social and political tribulations. In a sense, then, her involvement in the open economy gives her a material opportunity to achieve, paradoxically, something quite opposite to the integration into the global patchwork of lifestyles, trends and ideologies. Rather, Zhenya seeks a secure foundation in order to be able to continue enjoying the things she has been enjoying for many years: the stable company of friends, the core of which has been established in the institute where she studied, stress-free provisioning for her daughter and summer vacations in the same seaside village in Latvia where she and her family has been going for years. Although she has all the means for it, Zhenya has never spent vacations outside of the former Soviet Union. Even her Internet use is confined to Runet (Russian-language Internet), so that this most global medium serves primarily as a tool of identifying local shopping deals and entertainment options in Moscow.

By contrast with Zhenya, Anton is substantially more cosmopolitan in his pursuits and interests. He is an avid traveler, and doesn't spend a year without going abroad with his family. He is passionately interested in politics, both international and domestic, and follows it on the Internet and through domestic and foreign mass media (English-language newspapers, satellite TV). Anton's interest in politics, however, has a detached character: while he considers political developments consequential for his immediate business interests and is ready to debate his position on Internet discussion boards (which he did, for example, when he defended Russia's pro-Serbia position during the bombing of Yugoslavia in 1999 on the BBC forum), he deems it naïve to expect transparency and accountability from the Russian political actors of the day. In fact, he considers the almost complete political apathy of his Russian contemporaries to be "the greatest blessing of Russia" during the "transitional" period of the 1990s, since he interprets it as a sign of genuine practicality and of preoccupation with building the social and economic infrastructure necessary for further development. In this sharp opposition between the "worthy" business of working and building networks and "unworthy" political activism, Anton is not far from Zhenya and the other Muscovites discussed in this chapter, who also demonstrate little of the rationalized participatory citizenship rhetoric global culture theorists like Meyer (Meyer *et al.* 1997) would have one expect. At the same time, he is much more familiar with the corresponding rhetorical conventions (which is what allows him to participate on an equal footing in discussing international affairs on English-language Internet sites), and does consider Western-style democracy, with the corresponding rule of law, human rights and mass participation, to be the desirable end point for Russia's development. For the here and now, however, his responses are fueled by a fundamentally local sensibility centered on providing oneself and one's family with maximal autonomy from the state, rather than on an active engagement and negotiation with the state structures in the interests of monitoring their activity.

Moreover, while the lack of transparency and accountability in political and administrative affairs is as much a source of vexation for Anton as it is for the other respondents, he also acknowledges these same features as the foundations of his competitiveness in the global arena. In other words, the inadequacies of the local political practice, cast into light by comparison with the idealized image of the West, do not automatically mean that exposure to the global standards of rationality, efficiency and transparency generate civic action to advance these principles locally. What one can see happening in Anton's case is a differently directed process. He is fully aware of transnational dependencies and of the place of the Russian economy in the process of globalization. Basically, his discourse is the discourse of the leading Russian business newspapers and journals – *Kommersant*, *Ekspert*, etc. He understands the problems of (un)competitiveness of Russian producers, the problem of barter and the role of political factors in economy, so from this perspective he is a competent member of a global business community. But his understanding of his own "niche" in the global business community makes use of the Russian idiosyncrasies. Competence in the convoluted world of the Russian largely "gray" economy is the cultural capital that makes Anton attractive to the employers, and, thus, even though hypothetically he would welcome the time when the Russian economy comes out of the shadows, he is not personally interested into speeding this process up.

Globalization and discourse

Expectation of coherence is hardly sustainable when one deals with as mutable and fragmented an entity as the human discourse. Rationality and the logical principles of inference are not the only considerations by which discourse is produced, and are often not considerations at all. The logic of practice, as Bourdieu reminds us, is "logical up to the point where to be logical would cease to be practical" (Bourdieu and Wacquant 1992: 22–3). Given this, it would be unwarranted to expect the discourse on globalization to be any more solid and inherently non-contradictory than any other discourse. What appears important for the case studies at hand, however, is that the expressions of ambivalence regarding desirability of globalization are patterned and based on the very experience of globalization as it was lived by individuals at different levels of the economic continuum.

There are several ways in which some aspects of globalization conspire to produce views and sentiments that run counter to the expectations embedded in the globalization literature, and the effects of this process differ at different levels of individuals' participation in globalization. On the more cursory level of involvement, the negative experiential aspect of globalization (exploitative work schedule, breakdown of old enterprises) outweigh the positive trends both economically and culturally. For one, while globalization creates new opportunities of work and leisure, it does so by virtue of destroying the opportunities that existed before. There is little confidence in the fact that one's skills guarantee a stable position in the future, and, hence, despite the gains obtained from this involvement, Vera and Nina are reluctant to fully endorse their new occupations and the lifestyle that they allow. Moreover, the break-up of the Soviet Union, with the geographical fragmentation and disconnections that it involved, amounted in the experience of many post-socialist subjects to a shrinking of the world and the curtailment of the imagined horizon that they considered "their own."[5] The fluidity of borders and increasing regionalization within Russia itself contributed to the sense of anxiety regarding territoriality and even, as some scholars have argued, to the growing ambivalence over transnational migration and the import of foreign products, both of which are thought of as threats to the spatial integrity of the country (Humphrey 1999).

Roman and Lyuba, whose gains from the opening of the Russian economy are more obvious (not unimportantly, to themselves as well as others), have many similar reservations. For one, while the more central players in the global economy are exposed both to the gamut of its gains and to its cultural and ideological dimension, those who benefit from it less systematically have little to draw upon for understanding the larger significance of the changes they experience, and may not even see their economic returns as consequences of globalization. The face of the new economy that they perceive is not unlike the experience that structured the responses of the nineteenth-century European working class – increasing competitiveness and exploitation, breakdown of the traditional structures of authority and social fragmentation – and the response to these pressures appears to be similar (Aminzade 1993; Calhoun 1982; Joyce 1980, 1991; Sewell 1980). In addition, contemporary Russian actors are witnessing the cutting down of social services and protection that were in place during socialism, which further justifies their nostalgic perspective.

There is, hence, very little in Vera and Nina's experience that makes them particularly susceptible to the ideologies and pathos of globalization. But, even in cases when the experience of openness is more direct, and when individuals routinely find themselves encountering foreign actors, as do Roman and Lyuba, this does not necessarily guarantee diffusion of internationalist ideology. As Roman's interaction with his Yugoslav colleagues shows, foreign actors and symbols of globalization are far from being its advocate at all times. Often they themselves are just as bewildered by the ongoing changes as are their Russian co-workers. They spend little time discussing Yugoslav politics, and in the Russian context they sympathize most with the protectionist policies advocated by the Communist leader Gennady Zyuganov, who happened to be one of the harshest critics of globalization on the post-Soviet political arena. Other international actors that Roman, Lyuba and Vera encounter in the course of their daily activity are more self-consciously supportive of globalization, but they also occupy an incommensurably higher economic standing, which makes it close to impossible to identify with them (in the case of Vera, humiliating encounters with her transnational boss in fact only solidified her resentment for international trade and the open economy).

An important part of the reluctance to endorse the increasing openness of the Russian economy has to do with the moral legitimacy that is widely enjoyed by many Soviet-era dispositions, such as disregard for open competition, a sense of educational entitlement and a redistributive ideal of social justice. The sway that these dispositions still hold is hardly surprising considering the fact that many of the resources currently used for drawing gains from the open economy (education, connections, skills, and material resources such as cars and apartments) were initially obtained under the old "closed" system. Since the advocates of globalization failed to produce a comparable moral legitimizing discourse, the newly emerging opportunities were simply imported by many into their existing worldviews without experiencing any need to amend them.

Much of what has been said above applies equally well to the more prominent beneficiaries of globalization featured in this article, Zhenya and Anton. While they seem to be the ones most susceptible to transnational rhetoric and, indeed, most affected by it, particularly in the sphere of consumer behavior and work ethics, they combine their competence with strong loyalty to the old lifestyles: traditional hiking reunions with friends and a complete disregard for politics in case of Zhenya, and cultivation of informal patron–client ties and networks in case of Anton. There is, however, one important difference between Anton and Zhenya, on the one hand, and the other characters in this chapter on the other – the former's reluctance to wholeheartedly embrace all global practices is more self-conscious and mercenary. In contrast to the other cases, both Anton and Zhenya are aware of the central role globalization plays in structuring their opportunities, and orient their careers accordingly. They do so, however, by defining themselves *against* global patterns: Zhenya in her leisure and everyday life, and Anton in his career, by cultivating, in the face of globalization, a particular "niche," or competence, that will make him attractive to international employers. National specificity (conceptualized by Anton as the non-transparent business structure) is seen as precisely one such niche.

Individuals described in this chapter demonstrate little evidence to support the "strong" thesis of cultural globalization as cultural convergence on the "global values" of rationality, individualism, human rights and political participation. Even in a "weaker" sense of globalization as a transformation of mental horizons and the free circulation of ideas and technologies, it has but a limited presence on the lower stages of involvement with the new economy. Furthermore, even where it does play a role, such a role may be the opposite of the "global culture" ideal outlined above. At the same time, this does not mean that post-Soviet actors are unable to cope with the transforming economic realities. Their rhetoric demonstrates that an ability to navigate the new open economy to their advantage does not entail commitment to the values that originally underlay its development and expansion. In fact, at least in the postsocialist context, the elements of the "globalization culture" are fragmentary, disconnected and variably present at different levels of one's involvement with the new economy.

Conclusion

The argument of this chapter has been that the seeming coherence of the concept of globalization is misleading, since it smuggles assumptions of synchronicity and causal mechanics that are just not there: one dimension of globalization does not presume another one, even in cases when individuals occupy a prominent and durable position in the new economy (Hay and Marsh 2000; Held *et al.* 2000). On lower levels of involvement, when contact with global actors is less direct, the very imagery of globalization is experienced as something alien and unrelated to whatever economic gains involvement the open economy can provide. It is not that, as some scholars argue, there is a split between what Kellner (2002) calls the global "haves" and "have-nots," but rather that the economic dimension does not translate neatly into the ideational one among either haves or have-nots, or, importantly, any of the many social groups that fall between these two extremes.

Individuals' mental horizons are transformed, but not in one direction and not at the same pace. The influence of information and images supplied from around the globe is not self-evident and their effect is often to the contrary, not in the least because there is great freedom to interpret them either way, and because, all across the forms of exposure to global forces, local sentiments co-exist, and, as we have shown, are reinforced by the global influences. We cannot assume, thus, that just by virtue of workers' exposure to global discourses or transnational actors, new ideologies will naturally be picked up, because people are free to extract very opposite lessons from the transnational life stories they observe. It takes not merely involvement with the new economy, but a prominent role in it for at least some of the global influences and rhetoric to become an important part of one's discourse. Considering that the ideals of participatory democracy are considered to be among the most important ideological "export products" of the Western tradition, such development is ironic, since prominent global actors belong to a group that is least in need of ideals of Western democracy in order to defend its interests.

It remains an important task to further disentangle the different dimensions of globalization and to understand relations that exist between them. From a political-sociological standpoint, the gamut of embedded experiences of globalization underlies a range of political expressions and of interest configurations. The questions to ask now are: what are the different political consequences of such diversity, and to what extent can we interpret political parties as ways of catering to different "globalizations" on this continuum, and exploiting the inconsistencies of postsocialist experience? What are the forces capable of bringing the ideological complexity of globalization up to par with its economic complexity, which is experienced by everyone? But this is for the future. For now, the landscapes of globalization have not caught up with the speed of economic restructuring, and although individuals don't live in the socialist camp anymore, they don't live in a global village either.

Notes

1 This is particularly true for the time of Khrushchev's thaw, although some amount of transnational activity and contacts persisted through the years of late socialism. For an in-depth study of such contacts see English (2000).
2 The fieldwork for the project was supported by the National Science Foundation under Grant no. 9901924.
3 An important and necessary test of Meyer's theory would be to examine it in its native, i.e. Anglo-American, context, where one is bound to find important evidence against the assumptions of individualism and rationality (see, for example, Herzfeld (1992)). More importantly in our case, however, is not that Vera and Nina exhibit attitudes contrary to the Western values of individualism and human rights, but that they are unaware of the need to censor themselves in accordance with the demands of political correctness, whatever their actual convictions may be.
4 The Russian Prime Minister at the time of the currency crisis.
5 In case of Zhenya, such a curtailment did not take place, since she can still afford to travel to Latvia. At the same time, contrary to what one could expect, she did not immediately use the opportunity to explore the world behind the "iron curtain" as Anton did.

6 The development of the oil and gas industries in Russia

Ella Akerman

Introduction

Oil and gas will remain crucial traded commodities in the global economy as world energy consumption is projected to increase by 60 per cent from 1999 to 2020, in particular in the developing countries.[1] Throughout the past decades oil has been the world's dominant source of primary energy consumption, and is expected to remain in that position in the twenty-first century. In addition, natural gas appears to be the fastest growing source of energy consumption and is expected to account for the largest increment in electricity generation because of its environmental and economic advantages. The former Soviet Union was the world's largest producer of oil and gas, exceeding the production of Saudi Arabia and the United States. Following the break-up of the Union the Russian Federation remained one of the leading oil and gas countries in the world. However, the development of Russian oil and gas industries in the last decade has been troublesome due not only to the political and economic crisis in the country, but also to the difficulties of the transition to the market economy.

This chapter examines the development of Russian oil and gas sectors throughout the 1990s and into the twenty-first century as a four-step evolutionary process, which involves survival, domestic consolidation, modernization and internationalization. Furthermore, it attempts to relate the development of oil and gas to the general debate on globalization, and explores how far the Russian hydrocarbon industry can be viewed as a part of this process. First of all, however, a brief overview of the oil and gas sectors in the former Soviet Union is provided.

Oil and gas sectors in the Soviet era

The history of the Russian oil industry begins in the 1880s. Up to the beginning of the Civil War in 1918, Russia remained the world leader in oil production. Over that period Russian oil production accounted for up to half of the total world oil production, originating mainly from the Apsheron Peninsula (Azerbaijan) and the Grozny District (northern Caucasus) oil fields. After a decline in production during the Second World War, oil production in the Soviet Union continued to grow when large oil fields in Volga-Ural region were developed, and increased in volume by 30 times by 1984 (Krylov *et al.* 1998: 3). Under Soviet rule attempts were made to discover oil fields in all regions of the Soviet Union, and only four of the fifteen republics – Armenia, Moldova, Latvia and Estonia – yielded no oil. Among all of the Soviet republics Russia appeared to be the richest in terms of oil resources, accounting for almost 90 per cent of oil production and about 85 per cent of the remaining proven reserves of the Soviet Union (Krylov *et al.* 1998: 59). In fact, before the mid-1950s, Soviet policy viewed coal and hydroelectric power as the major primary energy sources, neglecting oil and gas. However, by the end of the 1950s, Soviet planners became aware of their large oil and gas potential and began the accelerated development of oil and gas resources to meet the growth in domestic demands and to earn hard currency through export.[2] In the 1960s large oil reserves were discovered in the Tyumen region of Western Siberia, providing the bulk of oil production increases throughout the 1970s. By the end of that decade, Tyumen had overtaken the Volga–Ural fields as the greatest Soviet oil region, by the mid-1980s producing 60 per cent of Soviet oil. At the same time, new policies in the early 1980s accelerated drilling rates throughout the country. However, low yields made this drilling expensive as the older oil reserves were already being exhausted. Soviet planners relied on the discovery of major new oil fields comparable to those in Western Siberia, but by 1987 no important discoveries had been made for 22 years.

To make matters worse, in the beginning of the 1980s the first signs of economic crisis in the Soviet Union emerged. This period saw a considerable reduction in the annual increment in oil production. By the mid-1980s the absolute level of oil production had decreased, and after 1988 continued to decline steadily. During 1991 oil production in the Soviet Union fell by 9.6 per cent and in Russia by 10.4 per cent (Borseman *et al.* 1998: 82). The decline was caused by the deterioration of the quality of reserves and by the growing paralysis of the political and economic systems within the Soviet Union. The difficult political and economic situation led to a transition to self-financing of oil producing enterprises, as well as the introduction of free-market prices for equipment and materials. The lack of capital investment in the oil industry and the traditionally low level of oil prices contributed to the decline of the oil sector. In addition, low productivity of the new oil fields, as well as the difficult access to newly discovered oil fields in the northern taiga and the continental shelf, together with the increased demands of the environmental control bodies, contributed to the substantial decrease in Russian oil production. At the same time some local oil producing enterprises took advantage of their emerging independence from Moscow to make supply deals directly with foreign customers. To prevent this practice former President Gorbachev in December 1990 announced a ban on the unlicensed export of raw materials, stating that in the 'current economic crisis, an enterprise's first duty is to supply the state' (*Petroleum Economist* 1991(1): 17).

During the Soviet era, the gas industry was one of the most successful branches of the Soviet economy due to the extensive development of the Western Siberian gas reserves.

In the early 1980s, natural gas replaced oil as the 'growth fuel' of the Soviet Union, amounting to 536 billion cubic metres. Similarly to oil, the majority of the gas production until the 1970s originated from the Volga Urals and Central Asia, but by 1983 Western Siberia provided almost 50 per cent of Soviet gas. Soviet planners were successfully replacing oil with gas, drastically increasing the investment into the gas sector in the late 1970s and 1980s. Gas also represented a vital export product. Exports to Western Europe reached 88 billion cubic metres in 1988. Even during the economic disasters of 1990–2, gas production remained stable at 806–15 billion cubic metres a year, supplying the Russian government with much-needed hard currency for its economic reforms (*Petroleum Economist* 1992(6): 5).

The impact of the break-up of the Soviet Union on oil and gas industries: survival stage

The disintegration of the Soviet Union led to dramatic changes in the political and economic situation in Russia, introducing new actors and decision-making processes, as well as new issues in the regional economic development of the country. During the 1990s the regionalization of Russia's political and economic areas resulted in a change of the balance of power between Moscow and the regions. Throughout the early 1990s the Russian energy sector, and in particular the oil industry, suffered hard times. Following the disintegration of the Soviet Union, oil production in Russia decreased in 1992 by a further 14.6 per cent and in 1993 by another 10.1 per cent (Borseman *et al.* 1998: 82). Since the collapse of the Soviet Union, oil field equipment manufacturers in the Ukraine, Georgia and Azerbaijan have faced the kinds of crisis familiar to industrial enterprises across Russia (see Schwartz, Chapter 4, this volume), increasing prices for their deliveries, or in some cases stopping deliveries of equipment to Russian oil producers. At the same time, energy and transport prices were held artificially low despite the dramatic rise in inflation since the government effected a far-reaching price decontrol in January 1992, making it impossible for oil producers to afford their basic requirements. Despite the decrease in oil production, more crude oil has been exported as traders, not always legally, sought to profit from the major differentiation between the state-subsidized domestic prices and the hard currency prices overseas.

On 17 November 1991 the Duma accepted a presidential decree defining the framework for corporatization and privatization of the oil industry. Specifically, this document ordered all oil producers and refiners to transform themselves into joint stock companies before the end of 1992. The decree also defined the ownership structure of the three largest new integrated oil companies, Lukoil, Yukos and Surgutneftegaz, which together were to produce one third of the total Russian oil.

However, the decree is somewhat muddled, disregarding the conflict between the reformists and those who supported centralized control (*Petroleum Economist* 1992(12): 10). Moreover, some associations were preserved intact as entirely self-sufficient regional monopolies, preventing the development of market structures, as well as any competition among them, such as the autonomous republics' oil companies, Tatneft and Bashneft.

Faced with the energy crisis, the government was divided over how best to proceed with the reform of the industry. One school of thought supported by the ex-Prime Minister Yegor Gaidar favoured a rapid transition towards marketization, calling for the immediate decontrol of oil prices together with tight control over export tariffs to prevent traders from flooding foreign markets with oil. However, the opposing school of thought led by Victor Chernomyrdin, who since May 1992 was holding the dual portfolio of Deputy Prime Minister and acting Minister of Fuel and Energy, argued for a centralized control over the oil industry, because it provided the basis of the country's foreign revenues. Chernomyrdin repeatedly stated that oil prices could not be liberalized until late 1993 at the earliest, arguing that virtually all the oil companies would go bankrupt, forcing the government to provide major financial rescue programmes. At the same time, both opponents agreed that it was too early to launch wholesale privatization of the oil industry. Despite controversial debates, the impatient producers began to move towards corporatization themselves. Thus, the large production association Krasnoleninsneftegaz obtained permission from the State Property Committee (*Goskomimuchestvo*) to transform itself into a joint stock company. The state was to retain 51 per cent of the shares, foreign organizations were allowed to purchase up to 15 per cent of the shares, and the remainder was to be distributed among the company's employees. An interesting experiment was launched by several production associations in Western Siberia and in the Volga Urals, where foreign advisers helped to commence pilot restructuring projects. This could be seen as the beginnings of new 'globalist' thinking in the oil sector.[3]

Although there was a lack of consensus in Moscow as to the best way of rebuilding the oil industry, most experts agreed that the shortage of investment is the single most important factor behind the collapse of oil production. Considerable amounts of foreign investment were required for the development of the oil sector, and even those politicians and oilmen who regarded foreign companies with suspicion recognized that international investment was essential. In fact, foreign companies have been actively seeking opportunities for participation in the Russian oil sector; however, their contribution has been small in relation to the enormous financial requirements. In 1992 it was estimated that about 30 international companies were working in the Russian oil industry, and another 150 were in the process of negotiation (*Petroleum Economist* 1992(10): 13).

In the early 1990s, the government under Prime Minister Gaidar encouraged foreign investment and significant steps were taken to enact new investment legislation. However, this idea did not find strong support from much of the Russian oil industry itself as the Russian 'oil generals' did not see much sense in selling out the industry's most valuable assets to foreigners in a period of national and economic weakness. This was particularly true in many of the regions, where local governments wanted to maintain considerable control of oil enterprises located on their territories, in part because of the need to present a strong bargaining hand to Moscow. Furthermore, there was a major misunderstanding of what foreign investment actually meant. Russian oilmen regarded it as easy access to foreign equipment and technology without the commercial quid pro quo. Western companies often wanted to take over ownership and control of operations. Russian managers were cautious of allowing this to happen and did not appreciate foreign investors' demands for ownership and appropriate legislation.

The low level of foreign investments therefore resulted from the political and economic uncertainties within Russia, the lack of a legal framework for the development of the petroleum sector, and clashes between companies based on ownership and control disagreements. In 1993 a critical problem on the macro level was the resolving of jurisdictional disputes between the federal and local authorities over the resource base. Many uncertainties were associated with export tariffs, access to pipelines and custom duties. Former President Yeltsin's initiative to create a new Russian constitution was regarded as a means to resolve those conflicts. However, it also appeared to offer the regions the opportunity to assert their independence further. Moscow had recognized this problem and was attempting to increase its control. The Ministry for Fuel and Energy has been restructured to extend its influence in the day-to-day operations of oil production, and to allocate export and import quotas, which constituted critical components for the potential profitability of oil joint ventures.[4]

While the oil sector confronted major survival issues, the Russian gas industry developed as a unified entity under Gazprom within the former Soviet Union in terms of management, technology application and financing. This system enabled Gazprom to provide for uninterrupted domestic gas supply, as well as stable gas export. Gazprom responded to the break-up of the Soviet Union by recreating itself as a joint stock company with ownership shared between the Russian federal government, which holds most of the shares, and the governments of Ukraine and Belarus. It produces 93 per cent of Russian annual gas output.[5] Among other gas producers, Surgutneftegaz was by far the largest, accounting for over one-third of the associated gas produced by oil companies. However, gas-producing enterprises faced major strategic difficulties because of unsatisfactory laws regulating access to gas pipelines. By law, Gazprom is required to allow outsiders to use its pipelines as long as there is spare room in the system. In reality, information on availability was poor and the gas transmission tariffs very high. Gazprom seemed less than eager to share the export markets with its competitors.

Domestic consolidation: privatization and reforms of the oil and gas sectors

Under President Yeltsin the economic base of the Russian regime contained elements of the free liberal market and some mechanisms of 'non-economic' coercion. In fact, the privatization process 'was not about purchasing an enterprise's shares; it was about gaining access to an enterprise's management' (Shevtsova 1997: 15). In the oil industry, in common with other industries, the enterprise directors themselves obtained ownership of the companies via 'insider privatization'.[6] As many of the former directors were opposed to reform, following the first stage of privatization the enterprises languished economically, and few new owners were willing or able to adopt approaches more in line with the requirements of a Western market economy. Arguably this was because the income of the new businessmen 'depended on their links to power and their membership in a financial-industrial group and not on the quality or quantity of goods and services they produce' (Vasilchuk 1996). With time, however, more and more enterprise owners realized that the economic development of Russia was dependent on creating conditions favourable to economic growth. This new thinking resulted in the emergence of 'state capitalism', characterized by the creation of powerful monopolies closely connected with the state. On the political scene, the introduction of regional elections in Russia in 1996 led to the legitimizing of local governors, independent to a degree from Moscow, providing them with opportunities to influence economic developments of the regions.

The Russian government began restructuring the oil sector in 1993 with the initiation of the two-phase privatization process. The first phase, completed by the end of 1994, involved the reorganization of state-owned enterprises as joint stock companies, and resulted in the creation of a group of large oil companies operating in a competitive market. The largest of these vertically integrated oil companies were Lukoil, Yukos, Surgutneftegaz, Tyumen Oil (TNK), Tatneft and Sibneft.[7] The government retained a 50 per cent share in these companies, but they were free to make their own deals and export arrangements without interference from central authorities.

The second phase, which began in 1995, involved auctioning large amounts of government-retained shares in these companies to private hands. During this process the remaining shares were distributed in one of two ways: the disbursement of blocks of shares to investors in exchange for their commitment to maintaining employment levels and to making future contributions to the enterprise, or the sale of shares for cash.[8]

The final consolidation of the oil sector's assets occurred in 1995 under a presidential decree that gave rise to the current structure of 11 vertically integrated oil companies.[9] The same year, the Russian government implemented a shares-for-loans scheme under the shares-for-cash proposal, whereby a large amount of governmental shares in certain joint stock companies were auctioned to a group of Russian commercial banks for cash. The successful bidders were required to hold the shares in trust for a maximum of three years in return for providing loans to the government to reduce its budget deficit. However, controversy over the possibilities of corruption in the bidding process resulted in the termination of all future auctions and legal challenges to previous auctions.

In December 1995, the Duma adopted the Law on Production Sharing Agreements (PSA). The PSA formula appeared relatively simple, calling for a royalty or revenue tax, a corporate profits tax and an additional profits-based tax (or production share) that would escalate with the actual profitability of a project. However, this law was widely criticized for having failed to remove the restrictions that previously prevented foreign oil companies, as well as international banks, from funding energy projects in Russia. One of the major legal obstacles for foreign investment appeared to be the confusion as to whether civil or administrative law provisions apply under the PSA law, as this distinction greatly affects the right of foreign companies under the Russian legal system.

In 1997 the Russian government approved a plan to privatize Rosneft, the fifth-largest Russian oil company, which represented its last major holding in the oil industry. However, the Yeltsin government was under pressure to halt further privatization sales because it was argued that previous auctions had been marked by unfair deals, and a special commission was established to investigate the previous sales.

The following year marked a major increase in Russian crude oil export, as it totalled a record 3.5 million barrels per day (bbl/d), of which 3.1 million bbl/d were destined for customers outside the former Soviet Union.[10] Thus, the share of net exports to countries outside the former Soviet Union rose from 53 per cent in 1992 to 89 per cent in 1998 (*Drillbits & Tailings* 2000(9)). Even the Russian financial meltdown in August 1998 did not have a negative impact on the country's oil and gas exports, and the companies profited from higher oil and gas prices, building hard currency reserves through increased export to some $35 billion (Knox 2001: 1). In the following three years, Russia greatly benefited from the sharp rebound in oil prices, which helped the country's largest oil producers to make huge profits, resulting in billions of dollars worth of additional tax revenues to the Russian government.[11] Many oil companies also started to upgrade decaying infrastructure and to undertake new exploratory drilling. At the same time, the Russian government continued the process of privatization. In February 2002 Russian officials announced plans to privatize another 6 per cent share of Lukoil later that year.[12] In addition, 19.68 per cent of shares in Slavneft, a joint Russian–Belarussian oil company, were to be offered by the government for sale.

While the oil industry was undergoing substantial reorganization, the gas sector, however, remained intact under the monopoly of Gazprom. In 1993 Gazprom was converted into a state-owned joint stock company, and began to be privatized in April 1994.[13] Similarly to the oil sector, shares were divided among Gazprom employees and other domestic investors, while 40 per cent of its shares remained in the hands of the government for about three years. Nine per cent of Gazprom's stock was set aside for foreign ownership, but the sale of shares required Gazprom's approval. In general, the privatization process of the gas industry has had a number of considerable consequences for Gazprom's structure. First of all, many new businesses have been created in the gas sector outside the control of Gazprom, in particular in order to produce small fields and distribute gas within adjacent regions, such as Russia-Petroleum in the Irkutsk area. Second, the regional subsidiaries of the original Gazprom were declared independent companies by local authorities, for example in newly autonomous regions, such as Bashkiria and the Republic of Sakha. Finally, major parts of Gazprom's assets on Russian territory were gradually transformed into joint stock companies, establishing a unified Gazprom. This process has created the largest single natural gas company in the world, whose $80 billion in assets include 68 gas and gas condensate fields, and all pipelines in the Russian Federation.

In contrast to the oil industry, Gazprom succeeded in maintaining gas production, mainly located in Western Siberia, where 90 per cent of Russia's natural gas is produced. However, major investments were needed for field development, as well as for the rehabilitation of Gazprom's extensive network of pipelines. At the same time, the domestic customers, such as Russia's electric utilities, as well as some CIS republics, have accumulated large debts towards Gazprom and prompted a major crisis. The revenues that could have been used for projects had to be diverted to subsidized electric utilities of the country since cutting supplies to the utility companies is forbidden by law. Therefore, exports to Europe remain Gazprom's most secure source of revenue.

Current trends in Russian oil and gas industries: modernization and internationalization

Most of Russia's oil companies operate as regional monopolies. Others, like Rosneft and Lukoil, use their size and influence to expand beyond their borders to other countries and compete with the world's major oil firms.[14] The Russian oil production monopoly was separated along geographical lines, combining regional oil production associations with refineries and product distributors, which were transformed into integrated public and private stock companies. In the mid-1990s, Russia's newly created oil companies started to delineate their respective areas of interests and expand further, gradually absorbing a 'no man's land' in terms of reserves and refining capacities. In a parallel move towards diversification, Russian oil companies have shown a strong interest in the gas market, and are already attempting to ensure access to the still monopolized gas pipeline network owned by Gazprom. Thus, Lukoil signed a strategic alliance with Gazprom in 1998, and another alliance was formed in 2000 between Gazprom, Lukoil and Yukos for the joint development of the gas fields in the Russian sector of the Caspian Sea.

Foreign investment in the Russian petroleum industry was first regulated through joint ventures. Nevertheless, foreign participation was not allowed in the first phase of the privatization of assets. In the second phase, foreign investors were welcome to take equity stakes in Russia's petroleum industry.[15] However, there is a widespread opposition in Russia to the sharing of strategic resources with foreign companies. In fact, the progress in foreign negotiations has been slowed not only by 'emotional and even nationalistic factors', but also by economic considerations (*Petroleum Economist* 1996 (12)). Foreign investors often do not want to commit themselves to risky long-term projects because they do not trust the existing legislation, consider the taxes and the transport costs too high, and finally regard the oil supply to frequently insolvent domestic customers as highly unprofitable, whereas the access to more profitable export markets appears physically constrained by the bottlenecked, monopolistic pipeline system. Instead, political uncertainty, rapid change and the wide spectrum of opportunities for those who are willing to take risks have encouraged the Russian oilmen to prefer short-term projects. This mentality appears to be opposite to the attitude of foreign investors, who prefer long-term projects with minimal risks and do not want to launch a project until there are satisfactory laws to protect their investments. Another legal obstacle in the rapid conclusion of contracts with foreign companies is the Law of Lists adopted in 1996, which details projects to be made eligible for production-sharing contracts. Originally, the Lists included 250 projects, or almost 40 per cent of the undeveloped Russian oil reserves. However, new Lists, which had been proposed after the delay in the first reading of the Duma, appeared much shorter as the local authorities in the oil provinces responsible for nominating projects for production-sharing agreements (PSAs) became impatient with the slow pace of negotiations and deleted some fields from the Lists. In addition, oil transport appears to be a major obstacle in the operation of foreign oil companies, because oil trunklines are managed as a monopoly by the state-owned Transneft.[16] Tariffs for oil transport rise frequently, absorbing over 30 per cent of the cost of a barrel of export crude. At the same time, given its enormously strong strategic position, Transneft is unwilling to conclude long-term contracts with foreign companies to guarantee them access to international markets.

So far, joint ventures remain the main means for foreign investment, allowing Russian firms to gain access to capital and new technology, and foreign companies to gain a foothold in Russia. However, joint ventures in Russian oil and gas sectors contribute little to overall production, contributing only to 7 per cent of total Russian output in 1995 (*Nefte Compass* 1996(4): 7).

Foreign joint exploration and development projects are mainly located in Russia's three largest production regions – Western Siberia, the Arctic Region and the Russian Far East. In Western Siberia, Occidental is operating the Vanyoganneft joint venture, and Amoco has a 50 per cent interest in the Priobskoye field. In the Arctic Region, the largest PSA is the Timan Pechora Company (TPC) led by Texaco, and including Exxon, Amoco and Norsk Hydro. In the Russian Far East, three agreements have been negotiated on Sakhalin Island. Sakhalin I is being developed by Exxon Mobil (United States), Sodeco (Japan), Rosneft & SMNG (Russia) and ONGC (India); Sakhalin II by Shell (United Kingdom, The Netherlands), Mitsui (Japan) and Mitsubishi (Japan); and Sakhalin III by Exxon Mobil, Chevron Texaco (United States) and Rosneft & SMNG.

Even before privatization, Gazprom had relationships with foreign companies within and outside Russia. At present, Gazprom is working on various projects with European and Asian countries that could lead to the establishment of a connected gas network system throughout these regions. In addition, Gazprom holds an interest in a German natural gas transmission operation with Wintershall, its German joint venture partner. A major step towards the restructuring of Gazprom was taken by the Putin government in May 2001, when the company's board of directors replaced its chief executive, Rem Vyakhirev, with Alexei Miller, an ally of President Putin. Mr Vyakhirev, together with other senior managers of Gazprom, was accused of stripping assets from the company and placing them into entities controlled by family members. This move clearly demonstrated the willingness of the Putin government to reform the natural gas sector, aimed at opening up Gazprom's control over Russia's pipeline network through transparent pricing for third-party providers. Russia's Ministry of Economic Development and Trade has drawn up restructuring plans to split Gazprom's upstream operations into separate producing companies in order to foster competition in the domestic market. According to this plan, the state would take control of the company's transmission pipelines, allowing equal access of all gas producers to domestic and export markets, as well as retaining a role in coordinating export shipments. However, once approved, the implementation of this plan is expected to take several years, dividing the country's largest company along territorial lines, and turning the company's immense Siberian gas-producing subsidiaries in Yamburg, Urengoy, Nadym and Noyabrsk into independent regionally based enterprises. According to the latest restructuring plan, all Gazprom shareholders will receive shares in each newly created company and in the transportation unit. After the completion of this step, the government would make an offer to shareholders in the transportation unit to swap their equity for shares in the producing companies, in order for the government to become a controlling shareholder in the transport company, which would run as a state-regulated monopoly similar to Transneft. These measures would increase competition among producers on the domestic market and help raise the domestic natural gas price to converge with world levels. In June 2001, the Russian Federal Energy Commission announced that it is planning to allow gas prices to rise 'substantially' over the next decade, reaching $45 per thousand cubic metres by 2010. However, the Commission has ruled out fully decontrolling gas prices as in the oil and coal industry. According to this announcement, Russia instituted a 20 per cent increase in the price of natural gas on the domestic market in February 2002.

As a part of the reform process, Gazprom's investors have demanded the removal of restrictions on foreigners holding the company shares.[17] Under present rules, foreigners are not allowed to buy Gazprom shares on the local market and are forced to buy dollar-denominated depository receipts at a large premium.

On 28 May 2002 the Russian government approved the country's 'Energy Strategy Through 2020', which aimed to ensure stable development of the energy sector, Russian energy security and an uninterrupted energy supply for the country's growing economy. On this occasion, Russia's Economic Development and Trade Minister German Gref stated that Russia's energy market could be fully privatized, at the earliest between 2012 and 2017, and the Russian Prime Minister Mikhail Kasyanov advocated the liberalization of the energy sector, but insisted on preserving state regulatory control. Moscow plans to keep subsidizing energy prices to military, education and healthcare institutions, which account for about 20 per cent of the domestic gas market, but other consumers would pay unregulated market prices (*Johnson's Russia List*, 29 May 2002: 1).

However, pressures on Moscow to develop energy markets in accordance with international trade laws may intensify following Russia's rapprochement with the West. At the EU–Russia Summit on 29 May 2002, European Commission President Romano Prodi promised that the European Union would recognize Russia as a market economy, raising the prospect of the country's competition in European markets under international rules (EU DG External Relations, 29 May 2002), despite the fact that the Duma has still not ratified the Energy Charter Treaty, signed by Russia and 40 other countries in 1994, which outlines the fundamental rules of transit, investment and market liberalization.

At the Moscow Summit a few days earlier, the US President George W. Bush and Russian President Vladimir Putin signed a joint declaration on co-operation in the energy sector, which launched the bilateral energy dialogue between Russia and the United States. The dialogue is aimed at facilitating commercial co-operation between the two countries in the energy sector, encouraging investment and modernization of Russian energy industry, as well as at promoting access to world markets for Russian energy. It establishes the Russian–American Working-level Group on Energy Co-operation that will serve as a forum for the discussion of energy issues at future bilateral meetings between the two countries.

These measures allow Russia to exploit the instability in the Middle East, and position itself as a force of stability in world energy markets. At the same time, political developments on a global scale have had a great impact on Russian oil and gas sectors. Thus, the fluctuation of oil prices following the terrorist attacks of 11 September 2001 significantly affected Russia, which depends on energy exports for governmental revenues and payments of the country's large foreign debt.

In an effort to boost world oil prices after 11 September, Russia agreed with OPEC in December 2001 to cut its oil exports by 150,000 barrels a day during the first quarter of 2002. Despite the demands by Russian oil companies to end the cuts and to increase exports, Moscow decided in March 2002 to continue its self-imposed cuts through to June 2002. These measures can be viewed not only as a response to the situation in international oil markets, but also as a political willingness on the part of Moscow to play a stabilizing economic role in the global arena.

The relevance of the Russian hydrocarbon industry to debates on globalization

As described in the Introduction to this book (Chapter 1), globalization refers to a wide array of phenomena, which attempt to explain different aspects of reality in the contemporary world. There are three arenas through which the globalization process takes effect: the economy, the polity and the culture. In general, three views can be identified within the debate on economic globalization. The first two oppose each other strongly, the third is more of a synthesis. First, some argue for a radical, unprecedented development of a single global economy (such as Hardt and Negri 2000; Sklair 2001). The globalists posit that globalization has transformed the nature of economic activity, and that in this light the global economy can be characterized as an informational, knowledge-based, post-industrial or service economy (Carnoy *et al.* 1993; Castells 1989, 2000a; Bryson and Daniels 1998). Second, opposed to this view is the idea of the centrality of nation states in the management of most economic activities (such as Hirst and Thompson 1999; Ruigrok and van Tulder 1995), denying the new global capitalist order, and regarding multinationals as 'essentially national companies with international operations'. These counterclaims assert the continuity of economic development, stressing in particular the regionally grounded, political nature of economics (Amin 1996; McChesney 1998). Third, the 'transformationalist' position (Held *et al.* 2000) or the 'third wave literature' (Hay and Marsh 2000) argues for a more subtle approach, involving profound, qualitative paradigm shifts in some parts of the world economy, but a large degree of stasis and continuity in other areas.

If globalization is characterized according to this transformationalist approach, as a complex interaction of globalizing and localizing tendencies

(Scott 1997: 7), or as the transformation in the spatial organization of social relations and transactions in terms of their extensity, intensity, velocity and impact (Held *et al.* 2000: 17; Jessop 2000), it can indeed explain some aspects of change in the development of Russian oil and gas industries. First of all, the analysis of the Russian oil and gas sectors over the last decade shows the co-existence of localizing and globalizing tendencies in the form of the development of the hydrocarbon industry on regional bases (regionalization), and the application of external standards of operation and management to the development of this industry. If local transformations are regarded as 'much a part of globalization as the lateral extension of social connections across time and space' (Giddens 1990: 64), the dramatic changes that occurred in the regional operation of oil and gas companies in the phases of domestic consolidation and ongoing modernization can be explained by the impact of globalization. Second, there is evidence of the stretching of political, economic and social activities across regions and political frontiers, as well as the growing magnitude of connectedness. New actors, such as international companies, environmental NGOs, etc., have appeared in the local, regional and national arenas, acting on a variety of levels and promoting their particular interests. Third, there is evidence of growing extensity, intensity and velocity of global interactions, resulting in the impact of distant events on local developments, and of local events on global developments. Thus, for example, the progress of oil and gas projects in the Russian regions can have a significant impact on shaping external perceptions of the investment climate in Russia, and unpredictable events, such as 11 September, can have a dramatic impact on Russian oil exports. In addition, the shockwaves on the international scale caused by the Russian financial crisis do appear to demonstrate the growing importance of the Russian economy to global political economy. Finally, if globalization is defined as 'a social process in which the constraints of geography on economic, political, social and cultural arrangements recede, in which people become increasingly aware that they are receding and in which people act accordingly' (Waters 2001: 5), the increasing expansion of the activities of Russian oil and gas companies nationwide and abroad can be regarded as the emergence of a new 'global thinking' that enlarges the scope of Russian economic life.

Despite the presence of these new globalizing factors that can be viewed as the underlying dynamic of several of the economic features of Russia, one could argue that there are other more important factors shaping this country's economy and influencing the development of the hydrocarbon industry. For instance, Mike Brown points out that Moscow's desire to end its isolation rather than the globalization process itself led to the opening up of the country and integration into the international system (Brown 1997: 251).

Indeed, the development of the Russian oil and gas industries throughout the 1990s shows the predominant role of the internal political environment and governmental decision-making, rather than the impact of the globalization process. Undoubtedly, the increased worldwide interconnectedness, accelerating interdependence and the embedding of local, national and regional relations within the more extensive sets of interregional networks affect Russian economic life, but it would be going too far to regard the Russian economy exclusively through the lens of globalization. At this point, it appears more appropriate to distinguish between the processes of internationalization and globalization, as the former represents an underlying factor shaping the development of Russian oil and gas sectors at the present stage. According to Peter Dicken, the process of internationalization involves 'the simple extension of economic activities across national boundaries', leading to a 'more extensive geographical pattern of global activity', whereas globalization refers not only to the geographical extension of economic activity, but, more importantly, to the 'functional integration of such internationally dispersed activities' (Dicken 2003: 253). As described above, Russian oil and gas companies today are extending their activities across originally designated geographical areas and sometimes across national boundaries, but no functional integration has yet been achieved.

At present, the governmental policies in the hydrocarbon industry, as well as the relationship between Moscow and the regions are the major factors shaping the future of the oil and gas industries in the country. At the same time, the increasing co-operation with foreign companies leaves Russian oil and gas enterprises vulnerable both to the conditions of the international resource markets and the strategies of global resource companies. If foreign companies abandon their projects in Russia, that would have a small impact on their fortunes, but it would seriously damage the short-term economic prospects for Russian companies. In that sense, the dynamic and complex interrelationship between the regional, the national and the global determines the future prospects for the successful development of the Russian oil and gas sectors.

On the other hand, there are specific spheres in which the pressures of globalization made the Russian government adjust its policies with regard to the hydrocarbon industry. One of the main pressures concerned the creation of an investment-friendly environment and the elaboration of a legal framework for the operation of foreign businesses within the country.[18] Another pressure was to reorganize and restructure the domestic oil and gas sectors in such a way as to make them compatible with the operation of foreign companies, and to increase their competitiveness on the international markets. In this sense, globalization appears to go only one way – into Russia. This trend can be characterized as variable or asymmetric globalization. This represents a new leitmotif of oil and gas development in Russia in the twenty-first century.

Conclusion

The examination of the main trends in the Russian oil and gas sectors shows a wide spectrum of factors that shape the development of these industries.

On the one hand, since the disintegration of the Soviet Union there has been a strong trend towards regionalization of the oil and gas enterprises that were separated along geographical lines and asserted their control over the resources situated within their 'zone of influence'.

On the other hand, increased needs for major capital investments in the oil and gas sectors made more and more Russian companies turn to foreign investors, thus initiating the process of internationalization of the hydrocarbon industry. As described above, this process was slowed down not only by the political and economic uncertainties within the country, but also by the lack of a legal framework for the operation of foreign investors. At the same time, the deep identity crisis within Russia resulted in suspicion vis-à-vis foreign involvement in the country's most important industries.

In the course of the 1990s, the improved political situation and the domestic consolidation of the oil and gas companies together with the beginnings of the modernization of the hydrocarbon industry led to an increase in co-operation between Russian and international companies. On the one hand, more foreign companies than before participate in major projects in the Russian oil regions. On the other hand, Russian oil companies are becoming more and more aware of the limitations of oil development within Russia, and are starting to move towards foreign acquisitions and diversification of their energy services. The rapid development of social, political and economic activities across political frontiers and growing interconnectedness among world economies certainly have an impact on Russia, and some aspects in the development of Russian oil and gas industry today can be explained within the wider context of the literature on globalization. However, it is as yet too early to speak of the full integration of the Russian hydrocarbon industry into the world economy, not least because of the asymmetry in economic relations between this country and the leading global economic powers.

In addition, the present role of Western oil companies in Russia under the operating conditions is still relatively small. The Russian government has not been able to establish a transparent PSA regime, nor to achieve a stable or predictable export tariff policy. Major investments are being undertaken by the Russian oil companies Lukoil, Surgutneftegas, Yukos, Sibneft, TNK, Rosneft and Tatneft for modernization projects and equipment upgrades. The most attractive areas for future development are situated in the northern and eastern regions of Russia. At the same time, Russia is focusing on redefining transportation flows and opening new export routes to Western Europe, Turkey and China, as well as to Japan and Korea.

The government's policy towards the hydrocarbon industry, together with Putin's willingness to reform the vitally important energy sector, may in the next few years lead to important changes in the organization and operation of the oil and gas industries. However, the extent and the effectiveness of these changes are hard to foresee. If the political and economic situation in

Russia remains stable, and the legal system develops in a way as to equally protect the interests of domestic and foreign businesses, the future of the oil and gas industries could be viewed with a great deal of optimism.

Notes

1 *International Energy Outlook 2002*, Energy Information Administration, US Department of Energy, March 2002.

2 Interestingly, during the Soviet era the energy industries were under the authority of a dozen ministries (Ministry of Gas Industry, Ministry of Petroleum Industry, Ministry of Petroleum Refining and Petrochemical Industry, Ministry of the Coal Industry, Ministry of Power and Electrification). Two ministries of machine building and one of construction were directly and specifically geared to supply and serve the energy ministries with equipment and facilities.

3 Japan's Daiwa and the Moscow Center for Foreign Investment and Privatization (CFIP) were working with Surgutneftegaz and Udmurtneftegaz, and The Bankers Trust of the United States and CFIP were involved in Uganskneftegaz and Kuibyshevneftegaz, setting out proposals for the revitalization of the oil industry and its successful integration into the global oil industry.

4 Following the disintegration of the Soviet Union, the state export agency Soyuzneftexport remained the country's unchallenged oil exporter. However, by the end of 1991, the Russian government gave up its total monopoly of foreign oil trade by awarding producers and refiners the right to market up to 10 per cent of their oil independently.

5 Turkmenistan, the only CIS republic outside Russia with a large-scale gas production, refused to join the Slavic trio in Gazprom.

6 One of the most prominent examples for insider privatization is Lukoil. The founder of Lukoil, Vagit Alekperov, was the first deputy minister of the Soviet oil industry in 1991. Ahead of anyone else, Alekperov sensed the coming break-up of the state-owned oil sector and assembled a producing company from three of the best oil properties in Western Siberia, together with two refineries, and took control of cash flows generated by the oil exports of these companies. Almost from the start he began moving his base from Western Siberia to Azerbaijan, Central Asia and the Middle East. Today Lukoil is a partner with the largest Western companies in some of the most prospective oil regions in the world.

7 Lukoil, until very recently, was the largest Russian oil producer with estimated reserves of more than 15 billion barrels. It was the best-integrated Russian oil company, and led the way in the consolidation of various companies from which it was assembled. In 2000 Surgutneftegaz accounted for over 13 per cent of the oil produced in Russia. Surgutneftegaz's marketing operations are focused on northwestern Russia, where it has product-trading enterprises, as well as around 300 retail stations. Yukos attempted to merge with Sibneft in 2003, to create Yukos-Sibneft. This would have been Russia's largest oil producer, pumping 2.2 million barrels a day, with 20.7 billion barrels of reserves. It would have been the fourth largest oil producer in the world. (http://www.petroleumworld.com/story1005.htm).

8 In 1999, the government auctioned 9 per cent of Lukoil for 200 million US dollars and 48.7 per cent of TNK for 90 million US dollars.

9 Eight of the 11 integrated Russian oil companies were ranked in *Petroleum Intelligence Weekly* among the 'World's Top 50 Oil and Gas Companies for 1994' (*Petroleum Intelligence Weekly: Special Supplement Issue*, 18 December 1995).

10 Since 1991, Russia has exported outside the former Soviet Union, mostly to European customers such as the United Kingdom, France, Italy, Germany and Spain.

11 In 2000 the Russian oil industry continued benefiting from the cost deflation stemming from the 1998 crash and high oil prices. The oil and gas condensate production of 6.46 million barrels per day (bbl/d) was 360 thousand bbl/d higher than in 1999. Forty-four per cent of the production has been exported, and capital investment reached $4.66 billion, representing a 150 per cent increase compared to 1999 (Mikhailov 2001: 2).

12 The Russian government is expected to raise around $600 million to $800 million from this sale.

13 In 1993, the government issued a decree: 'Transformation of the State Gas Concern Gazprom to the Russian Joint-Stock Company' to enable Gazprom to operate in much the same way as large foreign companies. On 7 December 1993, a follow-up decree was promulgated, 'Ensuring Reliable Gas Supplies by Gazprom', which designated Gazprom as a state buyer for both domestic and export sales.

14 In 1994, Rosneft and two of its subsidiaries purchased a 24 per cent interest in the planned Leuna refinery in eastern Germany.

15 ARCO became the first foreign company to buy an equity stake of up to 6 per cent in Russian Lukoil.

16 The company is charged with ensuring the transportation of crude oil by appropriate volumes and routes specified in the transportation schedule produced by the governmental Interministerial Commission. The schedule is based on annual transport contracts that producing companies draw up with Transneft, specifying the amount and quality of crude to be carried, starting and final points of shipment, route and terms and schedule for payment.

17 The Russian government owns 38 per cent of Gazprom, Russian companies 31.5 per cent, individual investors almost 20 per cent and foreign investors around 11 per cent.

18 These pressures, however, are also used to consolidate domestic power. For example, since Vladimir Putin became Prime Minister of Russia in August 1999, and especially since his election as a President in March 2000, he has placed a high priority on reasserting federal control over regional policy and politics. Putin declared that Russia would only succeed in attracting outside investment if it offered a 'unified legal, constitutional and economic space', and collected the country's 89 regions into seven 'super regions' to restrict the freedom of regional governors.

7 Novosibirsk

The globalization of Siberia[1]

Sarah Busse Spencer

Anatolii, a former civil servant, condemns democracy and "globalization of the world economy" for the closure of Soviet-era factories and widespread job losses. Evgenii, a disgruntled older man, blames the explosion of pornography in print media and television on American interference. Yuri, a recent college graduate, is proud of his marketing job with British American Tobacco. Katya, recent college grad, uses every opportunity she can to meet Americans and tries to get a visa to visit the United States. Dennis, a young factory worker, decries capitalism and mourns the collapse of the Soviet Union; his wife Natasha, also a skilled factory worker, joins a Western church and makes friends with foreign missionaries.

As these examples suggest, opinions about the increased contact with Western ideas, individuals and culture, since the collapse of the Soviet Union, vary within a city and even within families. Like Pandora's Box, once opened this contact with "the outside" has irrevocably changed the nature of daily life in Russia. To what extent is globalization actually affecting the lives of Russian citizens in the regions? What factors either intensify or minimize the effects of globalization in the regions?

To explore this question, this chapter looks at a city in western Siberia. The literature on globalization has emphasized the place of cities, both as instruments of the process and as sites reflecting its outcomes (Sassen 1991, 1994). This chapter examines the city of Novosibirsk for evidence of globalization. This examination "grounds" the search for globalization in ethnography (Burawoy 2000). The chapter is based on a larger research project comprising participant observation in two trips to this city in 1999–2000 and again in spring 2002. Data in this chapter derive from interviews and fieldnotes on visits to colleges, a church congregation and local NGOs.

The chapter first outlines Novosibirsk's place in the geography, history and social hierarchy of the former Soviet Union. Then it moves to a description of aspects of daily life – employment and social status, communication, transportation, media, consumption and politics – which mediate the effects of globalization on the local. This discussion draws on historical accounts as well as current conditions for understanding factors spurring or slowing globalization. While some aspects of the current situation in Novosibirsk are unique to its history and location, other elements are suggestive of ways in which globalization may be affecting ordinary Russian citizens in other cities in Siberia and other regions outside of Moscow.

Globalization and postsocialism

For ordinary Russians, the experience of globalization has come by means of, and as a consequence of, *glasnost* and the subsequent collapse of the authoritarian Soviet state, which had previously strictly controlled its citizens' access to the rest of the world. Ordinary Russians' experience of the collapse of the Soviet Union has been inextricably intertwined with a growing interconnectedness and awareness of other parts of the world; in other words, with globalization. The processes of globalization and the transformations of the *glasnost* era coincide to such a degree in the Russian Federation that most citizens do not – or cannot – distinguish between the two.

Much has been written on the postsocialist period in Russia, about economic transition (Spagat 1994; Lazear 1995; Leitzel 1995; Blasi *et al.* 1997; Gustafson 1999), political transformation (Fish 1995; Hahn 1996; Stoner-Weiss 1997; Bunce 1999), and the social costs of this dual transition (Lempert 1995; Klugman 1997; Silverman and Yanowitch 1997; Ashwin 1998; Bridger and Pine 1998; Clarke 1998a). But less has been written about the integration of this formerly isolated nation that has arisen because of marketization and democratization.

On the other hand, studies of globalization often discuss changes in local culture that are shared "globally" or a "global" standard of living (Waters 1995). Robertson defines globalization as a process of the world becoming "one place" (Roberston 1992), one system in the Parsonian sense, hindered only by religious, legal or industrial differences. Giddens sees globalization as a continuation of the process of modernity, of time and space "distanciation" and embeddedness beginning as early as the sixteenth century (Giddens 1990). Harvey also connects globalization with modernity, or rather postmodernity, and the "compression" of time and space, i.e. taking less time to transcend space (Harvey 1989).

One difficulty in applying theories of globalization as extended modernity to the case of Russia is the fact that in some ways Russia is not, and nor was the Soviet Union, a fully modern society. Rose refers to Russia as an "antimodern" society (Rose 1999, 2000, 2001). Instead of universalism, which was expected to characterize modern society (Parsons 1960), the Soviet Union was characterized by particularism (Clark 1989) and personalism, the traits of which have carried over into the post-Soviet era. The personalism of patron–client relations (Eisenstadt and Roniger 1984) and of barter transactions (Ledeneva 2000; Seabright 2000) continue in the Russian Federation. The use of special or multiple monies (Woodruff 1999) undermines attempts at universalism, and the rise of barter contributes to Russia being a "nonmonetary" society (Ashwin 1996). If Russia never experienced complete "modernity," then its experience of globalization would be different from that found in fully modern and "postmodern" societies.

Novosibirsk: capital of Siberia

Founded in 1893, Novosibirsk straddles the Ob' river where the Trans-Siberian railroad crosses this major Siberian waterway 1,750 miles east of Moscow. The intersection of major transportation lines may account for its existence (in accordance with the traditional ecology approach to urban studies (Park and Burgess 1925)), but the city owes its growth and present size of 1.7 million inhabitants to the Great Patriotic War (WWII). Halfway across this vast country, Novosibirsk experienced extensive concentration of wartime production, including tanks, airplanes and chemical weapons, far from enemy lines. With the largest concentration of military, industrial, cultural, transportation and trade resources east of the Ural Mountains, Novosibirsk is often considered the unofficial "capital of Siberia."

Urban Siberia: industry and academics

Novosibirsk was built almost exclusively during the Soviet period, and, like other urban areas in Russia, follows Soviet urban planning schemes in its architecture and infrastructure (Andrusz *et al.* 1996), displaying many features of the classic socialist city (French and Hamilton 1979). The city is divided into nine administrative areas, or *raiony* – seven on the right bank of the Ob' and two on the left bank. The careful hierarchic circles so favored by Soviet planners are disrupted by the scattered factories, each with its own housing tracts, hastily erected during WWII. Urban legend tells that, in the frantic pace of wartime production, supplies were simply thrown from moving freight cars, and people worked where the supplies landed. Workers labored year-round under open skies as factories were built up around these emergency workstations, while themselves remaining in temporary barracks for years. After the war, factories began construction on workers' housing clustered around each factory, and this patchwork continues to characterize the city – and makes urban transportation difficult.

Patchwork aside, in most respects Novosibirsk presents an urban milieu identical to any other mid-sized Soviet city, with its Soviet-era transport and the housing and public buildings built from the 1950s through to the 1980s. From the statue of Lenin dominating the central city square, to Soviet-era neighborhood and street names, the Soviet era remains everywhere inscribed on the urban landscape. The Soviet legacy is particularly important for Novosibirsk, which has little pre-Revolutionary history. This legacy is visible not only in the urban landscape, but carries over into local politics as well, in a city still run by the same Soviet-era leaders who, according to locals, continue many habits of patron–client leadership that characterized Soviet-era politics (Eisenstadt and Roniger 1984; Clark 1989).

Novosibirsk derives its national and international reputation in great measure from its prestigious university (Novosibirsk State University, NSU), numerous research institutes and the Siberian branch of the Russian Academy of Sciences, as well as several well-known technical schools. NSU and many of the research institutes are located in an outlying district of the city known as Akademgorodok (or "academic village"). Akademgorodok was intended as a cutting edge scientific center, where researchers could work with some degree of freedom away from the bureaucracy of Moscow. However, the technical innovations emerging from the academic village could never be put to use by Soviet industry, as that would have required shaking up the rigid production process (Castells 2000c: 33–4). Nevertheless it was here that several of the leading academics behind *perestroika* emerged. Though academics living here have often represented this area as an entity distinct from the city, Akademgorodok is nonetheless officially part of the Sovietskaia *raion* of Novosibirsk.

For local residents, Novosibirsk's primary identity is as a major center of military-industrial production, and they are justifiably proud of their city's crucial role in victory in WWII. Military production continued as the mainstay of Novosibirsk's economy until the collapse of the Soviet Union. Having survived and flourished due to the high position of the military-industrial complex and of research in the hierarchy of the Soviet command economy, Novosibirsk benefited greatly from a strong Soviet Union and its economy suffers from the Soviet demise, including demilitarization, unemployment, poverty, inflation of prices, devaluation of the rouble and the emigration of highly educated residents.

As a provincial city, Novosibirsk was dependent upon payments from Moscow for improvements and maintenance in urban infrastructure, transportation and housing. When those subsidy payments ceased, so did construction and maintenance of public works, including a partially completed subway system, half-finished housing blocks and planned schools and stores.

In the past five years the economy in Novosibirsk shows signs of improvement. Active efforts by government and business leaders have resulted in the payment of most back wages, modest increases in salaries or pensions, and ongoing business growth and investment. The economy has been relatively stable: inflation and prices continue to rise but at a slow and steady rate, particularly since Putin's election in spring 2000. Employment in Western-owned firms or joint ventures had been on the rise until the crash of August 1998, after which it dropped dramatically and now comprises only a small fraction of total employment in the city.

Against the backdrop of a monolithic Soviet-era high modern urban landscape, dominated by 9- and 12-story housing blocks, Novosibirsk serves as the vibrant trading center for Siberia connecting East and West, where cheap Chinese goods and expensive European foods are sold in shops, markets and to wholesale traders who take their wares to other cities and regions. Novosibirsk has become a city of contrasts: of huge colorless concrete apartment blocks and tiny brightly lit kiosks and stores with goods of all descriptions; of wealthy new Russians and impoverished teachers; of young people buying European pop music and older people marching in Soviet-style May Day parades. Although the city is experiencing dramatic social change, Novosibirsk retains many features of its Soviet existence, from street names and high-rises to long-lasting social networks, in the post-Soviet present.

Social composition and employment

The industrial core of Novosibirsk explains the working-class background of most residents of this city, a background that meant good wages and excellent benefits under the Soviet regime's priority for military production. However, in present conditions, more than a quarter of the city's population have wages below the official poverty level. A few lucky individuals have been able to benefit under gradually improving business conditions by running local businesses and turning a profit by staying one step ahead of the tax inspection police and the mafia.

The residents of Novosibirsk are rapidly being divided into "new rich" and "new poor," like countless others across Russia (Silverman and Yanowitch 1997). Soviet-era inequalities of access based on education, occupation and sector of employment persist in this Soviet-era city. These inequalities affect the access of individuals to the many changes which increased globalization has had on Novosibirsk.

In the new pattern of inequality, the "new poor" earn near or below subsistence wages and call their lifestyle "not living, just existing," "just survival," or "not getting by." This group includes many state-sector positions, including doctors in government hospitals or clinics, school teachers, as well as unskilled factory labor, doorkeepers or cleaning women and pensioners. In 2000, the minimum subsistence was officially considered $35 per person per month (1,000 roubles), including a (very) basic food basket and utilities, but not rent (assuming privatized or state-owned apartments). Despite this official "minimum," countless state-sector jobs had a base salary of only 600 roubles ($20) per month in 2000.

Though Putin has ensured his popularity by raising the minimum payments to pensioners and state employees by as much as 20 percent in the first two years of his administration, inflation-driven prices have risen higher than this, so that the increased salary buys even less. Most people I talked to in 2002 suggested a bare minimum of 1,500 roubles, or $48 per month, was necessary to live on. Those who did not have an apartment to privatize, such as those now reaching adulthood, have the greatest difficulty, since market prices for renting an apartment start at $100 per month. Those who own, however, were also starting to see some hope for the future by 2002, at least in the greater stability since Putin assumed office.

The "new rich" in Novosibirsk are the small but growing number of residents who consider that they are "doing alright," or "earn well." In advanced market economies they would be considered middle-class, and are only "rich" by comparison to the poor. These are people who feel that they can look beyond survival, who say they "don't have to deny themselves anything" and can plan for the future and consider saving for an apartment, car, computer or vacation.[2] By 2002 standards, disposable income (after paying for housing) of the equivalent of $120 per person per month in Novosibirsk seems to be the minimum threshold for "earning well."

While small in 1999, this group was becoming more visible by 2002. These are managers or owners of local businesses, private doctors, private English teachers and employees of foreign companies, joint-ventures or successful local businesses. The growth of this group has been stimulated in part by Western multinationals with established presence across Russia, such as Coca-Cola, Proctor and Gamble, and Phillip Morris (BAT). They offer well-paid jobs to young people (typically under 35) with degrees in English, accounting or computing, employing them in distribution and marketing. Western foundation money (from groups like USAID, the Soros Foundation and TACIS), which funds local non-governmental organizations (NGOs), allows these groups to hire local employees at anywhere from $200 to $500 per month.

A few "new rich" earn good salaries through telecommuting (working over the Internet) for computer companies in the United States and Canada. Local Novosibirsk companies regularly solicit programming jobs from Western firms through mass emails advertising "Siberian Programmers $20 per hour!" Since this is far less than programmer salaries in the United States, but far more than local salaries, both sides benefit. For local programmers, typically recent NSU graduates, who at least read English well, but do not speak it, this can be an attractive alternative to emigration.

According to the vice president of one local company (as yet quite small), their biggest competition comes from programmers in India, which is a much better known source of labor in the Anglophone countries. He seeks market share by undercutting Indian prices and extolling the higher educational credentials of the Siberian programmers. Some employees of this small firm staff a toll-free help desk to answer their international clients' questions, which means they work from 8 p.m. to 4 a.m., roughly corresponding to working hours in the United States. For these staff and others like them, New York time has become as important as local time (which is six hours ahead of GMT). We can assume more will come, but for the time being telecommuters remain rare in Novosibirsk.

Rarer still are the "*Novorusskie*" (New Russians), the super-wealthy who turned position into financial advantage during the early years of privatization (1992–3). Still imbibing the Soviet notion that Moscow is "the" city, most super-wealthy regardless of origin have moved there. The oil giant Lukoil has offices in Novosibirsk, so that some of its top managers at least occasionally eat and shop in the city. A few high-end shops and restaurants are located directly across a central square from Lukoil headquarters in downtown Novosibirsk, but the super-wealthy, whether businessmen or mafia bosses generally live quite separate lives from other Russians.

Globalization: forces for and against

Media

The first agent of the globalization of culture (Robertson 1992) is television. Recent research suggests the importance of the plurality of choice and the internationalization of Russian television (Mickiewicz 1999), with Russians "changing channels" for the first time. But the increasing diversity of programming, with news and entertainment from many countries, covers not only television, but also newspapers, books and movies, an increasing number of which are well-dubbed imports from the United States. Though nearly all urban Russians own television sets, not all can afford the movie ticket prices of 100 or 150 roubles (approx $3 to $4). In October 1999, *Star Wars Episode I* opened in Novosibirsk, six months after the US opening. The first Harry Potter movie, marketed under its UK name (*Harry Potter and the Philosopher's Stone*) opened in Novosibirsk a few months after its release in the West. Upon my revisit in 2002, a five-year-old boy neighbor, wearing his Harry Potter shirt, had to tell me how excited he was about the Harry Potter video game. In May 2002, *Star Wars Episode II* opened in this city on the same day as in the United States, attended by some of the paraphernalia as well.

In a more dramatic example of time–space compression (Harvey 1989), people in Novosibirsk watched live on the evening news as two commercial planes crashed into the Twin Towers in New York. Many residents of Novosibirsk, meeting me in June 2002, had to tell me how shocked they were to see this; I was the first American they had met since that time, and they had to share with me their outrage and sympathy at this tragedy. Their expressions of condolence were the single greatest example of the compression of space and time, of the globalization of tragedy.

Consumption

The most visible signs of the "internationalization" of this formerly closed society are the foreign consumer goods available in shops, street corner kiosks and wholesale markets. Expensive Italian jackets and shoes vie for attention with French lingerie, German knives and Korean electronics, along with countless inexpensive items made in China (slippers, housedresses, etc). Consumers in Novosibirsk have a new and bewildering array of clothing to choose from, in addition to the electronics (stereos, recorders) and household appliances (washing machines, irons) gradually making their appearance in the past decade.

The super-wealthy can buy anything wealthy Europeans have, such as perfume from France or furniture from Sweden. Even the more modest "new rich" can afford imported clothing or German washing machines,[3] microwaves or stereos. By 2002, a new building craze had begun, with developers putting in new high rises in every available corner of the city center, offering "luxury" apartments. For those remaining in their 1970s-era Soviet cinderblock buildings, renovating apartment interiors, in a European style ("*Evroremont*") has become popular (as we have seen in Moscow, (Shevchenko and Schukin, Chapter 5, this volume)) and home supply stores in many neighborhoods sell everything from new ceiling lamp fixtures to Italian faucets.

The "new poor," already coping with unfamiliar financial constraints, are faced with an increasing sense of relative deprivation, as Japanese technology and European clothes (or even Chinese imitations), which they cannot afford, are translated from television shows to their corner store. This new inequality is especially difficult for schoolchildren, since, unlike in capitalist cities, housing and districts are not yet segregated by income, and children of newly prosperous families show off in front of poorer schoolmates and teachers who have no chance to imitate them.

The globalization of consumption includes foodstuffs, and consumers in this city are faced with an unprecedented array of food and drink alternatives. French and German yogurt and pastries vie for attention with domestic Soviet-style milk and bread products, while Indian tea and Brazilian coffee edge out Soviet ersatz products, and Coke and Pepsi carry their global duel to new sites as they contend with local beverage producers Vinap (sodas and alcohol) and Champion Juice. The rising inequality of incomes has created a new inequality of consumption, as wealthy residents buy imported foods and poor residents eat food grown in their gardens. The 1998 financial crash provided a boost to domestic food production by making domestic brands cheaper than imports, but this does little to reduce the disparity between the consumption of rich and poor. Some Russians reject Western foods with the suspicion, "how can it be healthy with all those preservatives?," but some of this reaction to "not our (*ne nasha*) food" (Humphrey 2002) might just be sour grapes.

No Starbucks calls Novosibirsk home, but next door to the "Irish Pub," a small elegant café serves all the latest in latte for at least as much as in New York. There are also (less pricey) outdoor cafés, impromptu eateries of brightly colored umbrellas and plastic lawn furniture on sidewalks outside stores or restaurants. Locals call them "summer cafés," since, in Siberia, eating outdoors can really only be enjoyed from June through August.

Fast food was not part of the Soviet experience, and has only begun to appear in Novosibirsk in the past six years. In 2002, Novosibirsk did not yet have any of the Western chain restaurants which operate in Moscow, such as McDonalds[4] or Pizza Hut, though in their absence a number of local alternatives flourished. A chain of eateries under the name "New York Pizza" was opened by an American, Eric Shogrun, who now makes Novosibirsk his permanent home (Montaigne 2001). Especially popular among young people, many assume it is a well-known chain in the United States, but do not realize it costs more than (the equivalent) 50 cents for pizza in New York. "GrillMaster," started by a local businessman, offers hamburgers (for just over a dollar), fried chicken and other American foods on Lenin Street across from the still-intact statue of Lenin in Lenin Square. Fancier restaurants, where a full meal might cost from 300 to 500 roubles ($10 to $16), or half a teacher's base monthly salary, are frequented mostly by foreigners and a few of the new rich. Some, like the Levis 501 restaurant, the authentic Mexican restaurant and a Chinese restaurant, appeal to locals who like the feel of the West. Others, like the elegant "*Zhili Byli*" ("Once Upon a Time") suggest Russian tradition in food as well as decor and are popular with local elites.

Globalization has also a tangible expression in the layout of new stores. Most Soviet stores held commodities, all precious because all scarce, on display behind the counter, with shop clerks to hand down items for inspection, and the cashier at a separate island in the back of the store. Shoppers paid the cashier and took a receipt to the clerk in exchange for the item. Many grocery stores still operating from Soviet times have not altered their layout, thus conforming to the expectations of most Soviet-raised adults. In contrast, some grocery stores in Novosibirsk now sell goods in the "supermarket" style (Charvat 1961), with goods accessible on shelves for shoppers to put in baskets and bring to the checkout counter, teaching adult Russians new habits of shopping long familiar in the West. Some new stores modify the traditional style by keeping goods behind a counter, but a cash register at each counter instead of across the store. Though everyone who has been in the supermarket-style stores prefers the ease and convenience, the new poor rarely shop there, because prices are slightly higher.

Communication

The hierarchy imposed by the Soviet command economy in the face of shortages and ideological need for control affected the life chances of Soviet citizens (Zaslavsky 1995). One's position in the geographical and occupational hierarchy determined one's access to power (*dostup k vlast'u*), access to critical resources and access to luxury or non-necessary items. The consequences of this hierarchy continue to affect ordinary citizens in countless ways, including the experience of globalization for the city and the "global" life chances (or opportunities for increased globalization) of its various residents. This has already been suggested in the eating habits of the new rich and new poor, but is true also in communication and travel.

Residents of Novosibirsk describe with nostalgia the affordable travel, phone and post in the Soviet period in contrast to the present day. The truth is that the Soviet postal system was never fully reliable nor the telephone system fully complete. There was overall a low level of investment in residential infrastructure (communications, transportation, plumbing and electricity), reflecting Soviet economic priorities in heavy industry rather than consumer needs, and housing with these amenities was distributed unevenly in respect to the social hierarchy.

Only Muscovites can assume a telephone in each apartment; telephonization declines sharply outside the capital, being implemented in Soviet times based strictly on city size and significance to the military-industrial complex. On both those scales, Novosibirsk rated highly, but at least half the apartments still had no phones by the end of the Soviet era. Within the city, coverage is also uneven. In the Central *raion*, where most of the Soviet elite and party members lived (and in Akademgorodok) phone coverage is very high, while in the outlying districts, telephonization is good in some neighborhoods, incomplete in others. Though intelligentsia and managers assume that everyone they meet has a phone, most ordinary blue-collar residents first ask whether a person has a phone before asking for the number.

Having a phone installed, even with the money to pay for it, is a long and complicated affair, accomplished only through connections. A simpler solution in Novosibirsk is to leapfrog the landline and move directly to mobile phones. Though ads for Beeline (one of Moscow's largest cell phone providers; see Freeland (2000: 239–44)) and other GSM-based phone companies were visible in 1999, few I met had mobile phones. By 2002, all my sociology colleagues had (at least one) "*mobilnik*" and wondered why I did not yet. Among businessmen and many other of the "new rich," mobile phones were *de rigueur*. The price for phones (between $60 and $100) and air-time (10 cents per minute) makes this a viable option for many of those well employed.

A recent innovation for mobile phone users is the use of "federal numbers," which offer national coverage instead of only the city of Novosibirsk. Though similar in appearance to Moscow numbers (a three-digit city code with seven-digit numbers as opposed to the four-digit city code and six-digit numbers in Novosibirsk), callers from home lines or other mobile lines pay no long-distance charge. However, public pay phones (operated by prepaid phone cards) cannot dial long distance numbers, reifying a literal divide between those with no phones and those with federal mobile phones.

Internet access time can also be bought, like pay-phone cards, as prepaid cards from kiosks at any bus or subway stop, but a computer, modem and phone line are more difficult to access. Personal computers are increasing in usage and popularity in Novosibirsk, though owning one, which may cost from $200 and up, is nearly impossible for the new poor. Enough computers existed by 2002 for an entire shop in Novosibirsk to sell nothing but computer games, and a network gaming facility was advertised via stickers on buses and lamp-posts. The Internet is considered an essential medium of globalization, creator in part of the "network" society (Castells 2000a), so those without access are left on the other side of the "digital divide." Those who might know a friend or co-worker with a computer can count on access to it, but with so many with no hope of buying one, the new rich and new poor are again segregated into those with access to the world and those without.

Thus the same force which serves to globalize some residents of this Siberian capital serves also to permanently exclude their neighbors from direct contact with the rest of the world. This supports the theoretical approach to effects of globalization as suggested by Bauman (1998), Sassen (1998) and Castells (2000a). Built on the legacy of Soviet hierarchical inequality, globalization has had, and will continue to have, an asymmetrical impact on the people of Novosibirsk.

Travel and transportation

Transportation, like other consumer services, is also unevenly supplied across and within Soviet cities, particularly in the vast spaces of Siberia. Because of its military-industrial significance, Novosibirsk was supplied with excellent transportation by rail and air to and from Moscow and is a major transfer point on the Trans-Siberian Railway.

Thanks to the railroad, Novosibirsk is a hub for the formal and informal trade which connects cities across Siberia with Kazakhstan, Tatarstan, Mongolia and China. Products from Europe, the United States and the Far East are imported to Novosibirsk both through formal means (importing goods through customs) and informal channels, including the "shuttle" traders (*chelnoki*) who carry goods by train across the border from China or Kazakhstan. Traders buy inexpensive goods in China, pack them in bags and carry the bags as private luggage on trains, because, in contrast to airports, customs inspections on trains are extremely lax.

Other cities in western Siberia were less privileged than Novosibirsk during the Soviet era and are thus less well connected today. While Omsk, 12 hours to the west, is on the Trans-Siberian Railway, getting to and from anywhere but Moscow or Novosibirsk is nearly impossible. Tomsk, of similar size to Omsk, is not connected by rail, and getting there involves a five-hour bus trip over village roads from Novosibirsk or a flight from Moscow. Paved roads are on the whole less reliable than rail throughout Siberia. For many smaller towns and villages, travel to anywhere else involves first traveling to Novosibirsk, by bus or *elektrichka* (suburban train) and then further by rail or air. Residents of Novosibirsk have better access to travel (if they can afford it) and see more foreigners come through their city than those living either in Omsk or Tomsk.

Usually thought of as more flexible than rail or ground transport, air transportation is also constrained by historical patterns. Novosibirsk has an airport with runways large enough to handle large modern commercial jets, but other cities are not as fortunate. Russian cities continue to have air travel in one primary direction – Moscow. Even Novosibirsk air traffic flies primarily to and from Moscow. During the Soviet era, this arrangement served the interests of the command economy, where everything centered in Moscow. Aeroflot, the primary carrier in Russia, still routes all international flights from Novosibirsk through Moscow. A competitor airline, Sibair based in Novosibirsk, offers flights to Frankfurt, connecting to services with their partner Lufthansa. These flights, while avoiding Moscow, are significantly more expensive and less well known.

The "hub and spoke" pattern of Soviet transportation is repeated within the city of Novosibirsk, too. In the center transport is easy and quick. But the patchwork nature of the city's neighborhoods makes some outlying areas difficult to reach by public transportation. Each trip to such an out-of-the-way location once required going into the center and back out, making long trips and several transfers. This pattern, long inscribed on the city's transportation scheme, is gradually changing with marketization; in 2002, the private bus lines that compete with city buses began offering new routes that connected distant *raiony* without transfers. Gradually the geographical inequality inscribed on the city by Soviet decree may begin to be eroded by this commercialization of transportation. Commercial buses, though cheaper than taxis, are accessible only to those with the extra cash to pay more than the municipal fares. From a Soviet legacy of inequality of access, in the post-Soviet period Novosibirsk is becoming a city of inequality of outcome, transforming stratification patterns as the market, rather than the government, decides who has access to globalization through communication and transportation.

Migration and the state

An important component of globalization is the "intensification of worldwide social relations" (Giddens 1990), which in part comes about by increased face-to-face contact, through migration, travel and tourism of people of different cultures and national identities. This is occasioned, according to popular notions of globalization, by the decline in importance of nation states.

The Russian state, though significantly weakened from the Soviet era, has with Putin's administration begun tightening its grip on this vast country and its resources and citizens, rather than relinquishing control as many might assume under pressures of globalization. Control over citizens' internal passports,[5] residential registration (*propiska*) and visas for foreigners was temporarily loosened in the immediate post-collapse period (1992–4), making it easy for citizens to relocate and emigrate and simple for foreigners to enter. Since then, restrictions on relocation and exit/entry have again stiffened, making it difficult for Russian citizens to leave and administratively very complicated for foreigners to enter.

Travel to Russia for non-nationals still requires a visa, which needs a letter of support from an organization or individual inside the Russian Federation. While in the early 1990s this requirement was only loosely enforced, by 2000 applications for both exit and entry were being much more closely examined. This effectively limits foreigners to three groups – business travelers, academic exchanges and tourists – and all three groups are effectively confined to visiting those cities in which they already have some contact, thus limiting the possibility for foreigners to see other parts of Russia. Tourists primarily visit Moscow, St Petersburg and the Volga, while business and academic visitors also overwhelmingly choose the two largest cities, Nizhni Novgorod (near Moscow) and Vladivostok, and few ever see the beauties of Siberia.

Internal political history and international relations affect contact with foreigners in separate regions. During the Great Patriotic War, a suspicious Stalin resettled Volga Germans in Novosibirsk *oblast'*. In the early post-Soviet years, these "Russian Germans," primarily rural villagers, emigrated to Germany in the thousands, taking advantage of German laws favoring "heritage" immigration. To help stem this tide of (mostly poorly educated, non-German speaking) immigrants from Russia, Germany has invested in Novosibirsk, both in commercial and educational sectors, trying to discourage further migration by making this city more attractive. Yet, around the German consulate on the main thoroughfare, several travel agencies still offer discount prices for visiting Germany, by air, rail or bus – both round trip visits or one-way "resettlement" trips. Every week more people line up outside the consulate, applying for either visitor (non-permanent) or resettlement visas. Because the consulate also facilitates German business and visits to Novosibirsk, if a local resident has met a foreigner, he or she is most likely to have been German.

But the largest and most dramatic departures from Novosibirsk have been by Jews. Many thousands left Novosibirsk for Israel in the early 1990s, many of them well known in the city, including the rector and many faculty from the State Technical University (NSTU). Israel, unlike Germany, has encouraged this emigration, since the roughly 1.5 million Russian Jews in Israel have strengthened their West Bank settlements and improved population figures. In Novosibirsk, the Israeli consulate serves as an "Israeli cultural center," supporting both cultural and religious activities within the Jewish community and the city as a whole. The consulate director, well connected with the mayor and other important local political and cultural leaders, is always asked to trot out the standard "Jewish ethnic" songs or dances for the usual city-wide ethnic festivals, but the consulate also serves as a synagogue and offers free classes in Jewish history and Hebrew, especially for those considering emigration.

The third category of migrants, somewhat overlapping with the second, concerns the much lamented "brain drain" of highly educated or skilled professionals. Scientists or academics from NSU or the research institutes seeking emigration have primarily chosen Canada or the United States as their destination. Again, in the first few years many thousands left for the United States, taking advantage of liberal US policies which tightened only after 1994. Since then, not only has getting a visa to the United States become increasingly difficult for Russian citizens, but the Russian government has itself restricted the number of exit visas it grants. Canada, in contrast, still pursues a liberal immigration policy for Russian citizens, in particular those with high financial or human capital resources. Canadian firms in sciences or computers frequently offer one- or two-year contracts to educated Russian scientists or talented Siberian programmers to work in the West. Though the contracts are often of short duration, most who intend to permanently relocate are able to do so. So many have taken advantage of these opportunities that, as one faculty member at NSTU put it, "only the less talented are left behind."

As Sassen (1988) and others (Menjivar 2000) have suggested, migration serves to spread social networks over space between sending and host countries, which often spurs further migration. In the case of Novosibirsk, the increasing difficulty of exit has dramatically slowed this process, but many people know someone who has emigrated. For less educated, lower-status individuals, this knowledge is often third-hand or by hearsay, such as the street vendor who boasts, "my neighbor's daughter married an American!" For higher-status individuals, most know someone who emigrated somewhere. Some groups, such as recent college graduates of NSU, are devastated by this brain drain, with every third or fourth member of a cohort finding work in the West – and not returning. Those left behind are split into two basic opinions: those that think of emigrating themselves see this as a resource for their own move, while the majority who want to remain in Novosibirsk see the permanent diminution of their social circle. Many keep in touch via email or phone, but will probably never see one another again. One woman who had graduated in 1998 and saw half of her cohort leave, insisted "for Russians, email is just not the same!"

Migration, when permitted, serves to foster social relations among peoples of different cultures and nations. Foreigners are allowed to enter, however cautiously, and many "new rich" in Novosibirsk have been or plan to go abroad, if not to the United States, then to Turkey, Greece or Germany. Face-to-face contact aids in transforming impressions of "outsiders," as I saw the people I met become more comfortable over time with me as an American. But chances for exit are few, and my visa to Russia expired long before my social welcome. Thus a state such as Russia (despite so often labeled a weak, or even a 'failed' state in the transition literature) still influences all potential contact between locals and foreigners, limiting opportunities for globalization and attempting to preserve the age-old gap between Russia and the "outside." Visas and immigration policy are left out of the transition literature and much of the first-wave globalization literature. Although something as small as a visa appears irrelevant to the abstract debates of those literatures, local research reveals just how important they are to the lived experience of people.

Foreign organizations

During my stay in Novosibirsk, I had extensive contact with three types of organizations that facilitated the arrival of foreigners to the city: the educational system, NGOs and Western Christian churches. The educational system, particularly in higher education, including NSU and NSTU and other smaller colleges, institutes and academies, allows both teachers and students from abroad to come and spend time teaching or studying in local universities. With Novosibirsk's academic reputation, scholarly international exchange has existed in this city for decades, even during the Cold War. For those residents who could not understand, even in today's global possibilities, how an American could have gotten to their city, all I had to do was mention that I was on an academic exchange – a form of travel even the least educated had heard something about. The other two types of organizations – NGOs and churches – arrived in Novosibirsk only as a result of the collapse of the Soviet Union and the project of building democracy.

Global grassroots associations

In 1993, two Americans came to Novosibirsk to encourage democratic change through supporting grassroots efforts of collective action. Beginning from an apartment, this group which snowballed to a network of collaborators eventually gained enough funding, from a variety of US and European agencies, to establish themselves as "the Siberian Center" and rent permanent office space from 1994 (SCISC 1999). Gradually their actions grew into a network of centers across Siberia supporting local NGOs through opportunities to share experiences and learn from activities in other Siberian cities. At the beginning of 2000, the Center employed an all-local 16-person full-time staff, with numerous part-time consultants, trainers and speakers, and a variety of unpaid contributors. Except for one of the original Americans who decided to settle in Novosibirsk, everyone who works for the Center is Russian. The Center hosts occasional visits from British and American representatives from various donor foundations (for example, the Charities Aid Foundation and the Charles S. Mott Foundation), but most of their activity focuses on educating and "incubating" local grassroots associations.

Ordinary Russian citizens who come to the Siberian Center for the first time are surprised to see knowledge and information being dispensed for free as part of the Center's support activities. In theory, in a democracy knowledge is taken for granted as a right by citizens, but in a closed society such as the Soviet Union, knowledge was a privilege, granted only on a need-to-know basis. In Russia today, knowledge is often still guarded as a valuable and scarce resource; people are used to having information withheld from them, or rationed out on a need-to-know basis. At the Siberian Center, the novelty of free training seminars, free informational flyers and free booklets available to anyone (and not a privileged few) is surprising to newcomers.[6]

Publishing booklets and holding training seminars is an integral part of the Siberian Center's mission as a resource and incubator for local grassroots initiatives. The Center offers to any registered organization or group-information free use of computers with Internet access and printing and photocopying for a moderate fee (thus offering something like the services in US public libraries). The goal of seminars and computers is to increase the "effectiveness" of local NGOs. For the Siberian Center efficiency is equated with Western professionalism, such as that put forward by US corporate management gurus (Drucker 1990). Local groups vary in their ability or desire to imitate these "American" ideas of what constitutes professional behavior for an NGO, but the introduction of these ideas and practices at the grassroots level is a dramatic example of the globalization of ideas at the micro level.

Local NGO support was also offered by the Sib-Novo-Center, founded in December 1995 by a well-known sociologist affiliated with NSU, Frederik Borodkin. All of his eight staff members are locals. In 2000, projects at the Sib-Novo-Center included an NGO information center and a "leaders' club" for networking among third-sector leaders, plus seminars, conferences and round tables. Their seminars focused on "scientific" (academic) knowledge and on relations with local government officials and thus little in the way of globalization, in contrast to the Siberian Center's emphasis on Western professionalism. On my return visit in 2002, I found that the Sib-Novo-Center, while still officially open, had ceased any meaningful operations because its founder and director had moved to Moscow.

However, the Sib-Novo-Center had, while operating, received major funding from TACIS and *Deutsche–Russische Austauch* (German–Russian Exchange; DRA); the latter organization sent resources as well as youth volunteers and one full-time staff member. The full-time representative from Germany arranges exchange programs of German youth to volunteer in Novosibirsk's third sector. In addition, DRA funded several of the Sib-Novo-Center's publications and conferences while it operated. DRA continues to underwrite other German cultural programs in Novosibirsk in connection with the German consulate. With these influences, German culture and German language are receiving more recognition in this city than they had under socialism, contributing to increased globalization in Novosibirsk.

Globalizing church

The third category of globalizing organizations I encountered in Novosibirsk comprises Western Christian churches. Novosibirsk has fewer foreign religious groups than Moscow or St Petersburg, yet at least three Western churches have a visible presence in the city: the (Roman) Catholic Church, a Lutheran mission (Missouri Synod) and the Church of Jesus Christ of Latter-day Saints. New national laws, the result of democratization, formally permit associational life, including religious groups (Protopopov 1996), but at the same time stipulate rather cumbersome registration requirements, which are implemented ad hoc by local authorities. Despite the verbal tolerance for religious freedom at the national level, in practice at the municipal level, suspicion of foreigners and "cults" leads local bureaucrats to drag their feet over processing applications from religious organizations. This in turn leads to delays of many months for simple requests such as formally renting a meeting space or opening a bank account.

Once these difficulties are surmounted, however, a group with evangelical plans like the Church of Jesus Christ, must convince locals to be interested in new religious ideas espoused by this church (Shipps 1985) and act upon those ideas by joining this new faith. Seen by many Russians as being an "American" church, the Church of Jesus Christ is in fact a worldwide church with over 11 million members, fewer than half of whom live in the United States. This Church has had a presence in Russia since 1992 (Browning 1997) and in Novosibirsk since 1994. Initially founded by a corps of volunteer missionaries, the three mid-sized congregations in this city are now staffed entirely by local volunteers, with a total membership of over 500. As the Church has attracted more members it has sought additional meeting space, but has difficulties with permits, which it refuses to solve by giving bribes or "gifts" to local officials, a common local practice which would expedite matters.

The volunteer missionaries, mostly 19–22-year-old single men and women who come from many countries but primarily from the United States and Canada, devote most of their time to attracting new people into the Church. While most missionaries come assuming that Russians are all firmly Russian Orthodox, in reality the vast majority in Novosibirsk are communist-sponsored atheists. For most residents of Novosibirsk, the Bible and Jesus are as unfamiliar to them as is Islam; few can explain Easter or Christmas, even though attendance at the holiday services at the large Orthodox cathedral in Novosibirsk has become quite popular.

Russians who join the Church of Jesus Christ of Latter-day Saints have regular contact with missionaries and other foreign Church visitors at Sunday meetings. Many Russians, besides picking up some English slang, also become familiar with the names of missionaries' home towns in Utah or California, putting them on their mental maps. In this Church Russians learn a new religious doctrine, and feel connected to fellow members around the world through the Church's international periodical (the *Liahona*); they learn about and feel connected to America. Finally, they learn about insistence on rules and proper authority which this Church stresses in its hierarchical administration of congregations, in contrast to the typical Russian view of formal rules as something to evade rather than obey.

In addition to explaining their faith, missionaries also perform volunteer work in the city, including visiting invalids and conducting free English conversation classes. Hundreds of people have attended at least some sessions of these classes since they began more than four years ago. Though the locations have changed from the public library to the Church's rented facilities, most people in Novosibirsk who actively want to learn English have at least heard of the "Mormon ESL classes." Those who attend the classes typically are meeting Americans for the first time, and spend lots of the class time learning about life in America.

Globalization and place

As the above discussion illustrates, some factors lead to an increased interconnection of Novosibirsk with the world, including the media, consumption patterns, communication, travel, migration and foreign organizations. Other factors inhibit or hinder this process, including new poverty, historical legacies of Soviet inequalities in communication and transportation, and the control of the Russian state over migration and travel. In some ways (through television and foreign organizations), all residents of Novosibirsk have access to globalizing elements. In many other ways (communication and transportation infrastructure, inflation and migration), the "new rich" have a chance to become more global than the "new poor." Despite all these changes, Novosibirsk is not one of the world's "global cities" (Sassen 1991, 1994), so how can examining this city inform the study of globalization? The answer is in four aspects of place.

First, how much of the global reaches a given locality depends on the position of the locality and how well it is (or can be) connected to the rest of the globe. Europe, with its contiguous nation states and relatively smaller distances, is the first to feel the effects of "globalization" as far back as the Renaissance. Transportation and telecommunications infrastructures have the capacity to bind peripheral areas to the center and/or to one another, allowing for the reduction of time needed to transcend that space. Though geographical distances pose a challenge for establishing this infrastructure, as Siberia illustrates, Novosibirsk because of its size and importance is more connected to Moscow and hence to the rest of the world than its neighbor Omsk, which is 2,555 km from Moscow (42 hours by train). Novosibirsk residents have greater potential to be connected to the world than any other Siberian city.

A second principle is suggested by the first. Novosibirsk is more connected because of its position in the Soviet command economy, which established its infrastructure. Except for Sassen's work on the resilient importance of New York or London as global cities, few scholars recognize the path-dependence (Stark and Bruszt 1998) of globalization. The "place" which a locality once occupied in the social, economic or political hierarchy of its governing political body affects its present connection with the world. Compressing time by transcending space involves the investment of resources over many years, so that cities which were once hubs continue to serve that function. Runways and rail lines take years of investment, so that globalization can only reshape the world along (air)lines already laid down in the past, even when those lines no longer serve the purpose once intended.

Third, mirroring the social hierarchy of localities, individuals within a given locality share in the compression of space–time based on *their* place within that locality. Place is both geographical and social – those who live in the center and those with higher education or occupation have more global opportunities. As other research has suggested, those with high status (or the new rich) have greater access to the benefits of globalization, while those with low status (or the new poor) face more of the disadvantages (Bauman 1998).

Fourth, individuals' social place, and their attendant "global" life chances, are as path-dependent as that of their localities. Education, occupational history and political connections are not (re)created overnight, but are the result of years of investment. Wealth accrued over time (Keister 2000) confers present advantages in the way that previous poverty confers present disadvantages of social isolation (Wilson 1987). In the US context, the importance of history is often used to blame individuals who chose not to get an education or amass wealth; in the post-Soviet context, such blame is harder to assign, since some of the best Soviet-educated are now the poorest and worst off.

While these conclusions of the importance of place are not unique to Novosibirsk, studying Russia sheds new light on these and other aspects of globalization in two ways. First is the importance of including Russia in comparative studies of globalization. Because of the sudden transition from socialism and introduction of globalization almost overnight, contrasts are starker and more vivid in the Russian context than in the English-speaking world where change has occurred gradually. Because 50 years of social, technological, cultural and economic change have been compressed into little more than a decade in Russia, the old and the new coexist in surprising ways, helping researchers long familiar with modernization and globalization to see these processes in a new light. Second is the importance of including "provincial" areas in these comparative studies. Western observers of Russia are often deceived, either in thinking Moscow is like any other cosmopolitan, proto-global city, or in thinking that the rest of Russia must be like its capital, when neither assumption is correct. Only in the provinces, at the periphery, can Russia truly be seen for what it is. Studies of globalization in other societies might also look beyond global cities or capitals, to regional cities like Novosibirsk – places globalization has not fully transformed. Places where Starbucks has no presence – yet.

Notes

1 Research for this chapter was supported in part by a grant from the International Research and Exchanges Board (IREX) with funds provided by the National Endowment for the Humanities, the US Department of State, which administers the Title VIII Program, and the IREX Scholar Support Fund. None of these individuals or organizations is responsible for the views expressed.

2 According to the director of a local tourist firm, popular destinations for this middle category are the "exotic" (and warm) but relatively inexpensive locations of Turkey, Cyprus or Thailand.

3 Only those who have struggled with Soviet-era washing machines, some of which have no spin cycle (requiring clothes to be wrung by hand), or which neither fill nor empty manually, can appreciate the complete lifestyle change (less labor, increased ease) which being able to afford a new imported washing machine brings.

4 As of 2003 McDonald's had 103 outlets across Russia, in Moscow, Moscow *oblast*, St Petersburg, Kazan, Samara, Nizhnii Novgorod and Yaroslavl, serving over 200,000 customers per day. See http://www.mcdonalds.com/countries/russia/.

5 In 2002, citizens still holding Soviet internal passports (identity cards) or travel passports are required to convert them to Russian Federation documents, which involves proving where one has lived in the past 10 years. This process will shut out some of the former Soviet citizens who consider themselves Russian but who were left behind in former republics when the Union collapsed and who wish to return to the Federation but have been unable to do so.

6 The surprise at information liberally provided at no cost in this third-sector organization also speaks of the lack of other information sources such as public libraries. Libraries exist and are well utilized in this nation of well-educated individuals, but Soviet libraries existed to allow citizens to access (certain politically allowed) books, and did and do not play the role in civic life that many libraries do in the United States.

8 Why work "off the books"?

Community, household, and individual determinants of informal economic activity in post-Soviet Russia

Caleb Southworth and Leontina Hormel

Substantial numbers of people in post-Soviet societies exited formal employment and became self-employed in informal work arrangements (Clarke 2002b; Busse Spencer 2001; Burawoy *et al.* 2000; Crowley 2000; Tchernina 2000; Vorobyov and Zhukov 2000). Informal economic activity includes income-earning activities that are unregistered and off-the-books, that do not involve legal protections, contracts, or government regulation, and that are not reflected in official employment statistics. Examples include activities like petty reselling, repair work, small-scale manufacturing, gardening and selling produce, day labor, teaching and tutoring, and shuttle trading with goods imported into Russia from the near abroad.

Many analysts have argued that informal economic activity is related to the growth of market capitalism (Åslund 2002; Sassen 2000; Castells 2000a; Portes and Sassen-Koob 1987). However, two contradictory theories are put forward on the relationship between the expansion of trade and markets – globalization in the economic sense – and the choice of people and households to work outside the legal, regulated economy. The first explanation views the informal economy as transitory and non-market (Åslund 2002; Vorobyov and Zhukov 2000; Buhuslav and Stoffers 1996). Åslund (2002) argues that the sudden growth of commodity markets in Russia occurred as the state was in disarray and caught regulatory officials and tax inspectors off guard. While there was an incentive under the Soviet socialist system to register all forms of output in order to receive political credit with higher levels of government, with the rapid expansion of commodity markets in 1992 there was suddenly an incentive to hide all forms of output and profit that might be taxed (Åslund 2002: 285):

> With the start of transition, the underground economy expanded everywhere. Soon, however, it shrank both in successful reform countries and the most repressive state-controlled economies, while continuing to grow in partially reformed countries. Hence, the unofficial economy peaked in 1991 in the most successful transition economies (Poland, Hungary,

> and Estonia), while in less reformist countries (Russia, Ukraine, and Azerbaijan) it was still rising in 1995. Mostly, the unregistered economy peaked when the official GDP hit its nadir.
>
> (Åslund 2002: 124)

While Åslund's argument is comparative, the implication of his theory for Russia is clear: the informal economy is a way to hide real incomes and when trade and markets penetrate a country so that rational, market-based planning becomes possible, people will switch from the informal economy to the formal economy.

The second explanation for informal economic activity views it as a durable feature of both developing markets and industrialized capitalist economies (Tabak and Crichlow 2000; Lippert and Walker 1997; Portes and Sassen-Koob 1987). Researchers have examined the expansion of global markets through trade and found persistence of marginal employment (Standing 2002, 1999), demand for flexible (non-factory, unregulated) labor arrangements (Mies 1998), and expansion of informal work arrangements (Beneria 2001). These patterns, in fact, are prevalent in industrial economies as well as in the resources-extracting economies of the Third World (Sassen 2000: 106). In this perspective, the rise of employment insecurity and the growth of informal work are *symptoms* of globalization and the integration of economic regions into the world trade market.

In Russia, there is evidence that workers withdraw from the market into informal activity – gardening, manufacture, and reselling – because they are not fully separated from the means of subsistence and have more access to land, tools, and trade than was the case in Eastern Europe (Southworth 2001a, b; Woodruff 1999; Clarke 1998b; Szelényi 1998). In this case the expansion of trade results in greater participation in the informal sector. Where commodity markets expand, the labor market bifurcates into formal wage labor and informal survival (Vorobyov and Zhukov 2000: 29). Rather than eliminating informal activity, engagement with the imported goods of the global market bankrupts local manufacturing employment and workers in those firms turn to unregulated labor.

This chapter attempts to sketch the broad outlines of informal employment in Russia from 1992 to 2000, and then model the particular dynamics of informal work and its causes in the year 2000. We ask: What is the relationship between, on the one hand, the presence of global trade, finance, and state regulatory apparatus, and, on the other, the level of informal economic activity within Russia's regions? We examine the determinants of informal economic activity among individuals, households, and communities. Specifically, we want to know: What individual and household circumstances – income levels, pensions, and wage delays – lead people to participate in the informal economy? And: How do wage levels, bankruptcies, and capital flows explain variation in the size of the informal labor market between regions of Russia?

Mapping workers' responses to Russia's reforms

Our effort to map the informal labor market in Russia is linked to a broader debate on the creation of a capitalist market economy and the extent of global economic forces operating within the former Soviet Union. While the chapter is not explicitly comparative, many social scientists and policy analysts expected that the creation of private property and reduction of state planning would lead to the development of market capitalism. They expected that the institutional changes of the last decade – particularly liberalization and privatization – would result in markets allocating resources and prices transmitting information to firms about what to produce (Åslund 1995; Boycko *et al.* 1995; Sachs 1992). Boycko *et al.*, for instance, argued that political control over property was the clear reason for inefficiencies, which could only be solved through privatization (1995: 19–21). Indeed, Åslund hailed Russia's privatization program and gave credit to "a prevailing reverse Marxism, which implies that no market can exist before private property has achieved hegemony" (1995: 223). The expectation is that similar paths of reform lead to a developed market economy. The International Monetary Fund's advice and loans to the Russian government "has centered on supporting the transition to a market economy through the adoption of appropriate macroeconomic and structural policies, and the creation of necessary institutions" (Spatafora 2001: 8).

Despite divergence on the reasons, there is widespread agreement that the Russian economy has not converted to market capitalism in a decade, despite the creation of private property, deregulation of prices, and creation of a floating currency with an international market price (Hough 2001). Researchers point to the distinct qualities in the Russian economic system, which deviate from those of the model market economy.[1] To foreshadow our main conclusion, we argue that the economic transformation leads to high levels of participation in informal work arrangements which amount to a partial exit from the labor market.

There are various reasons that informal work arrangements would gain ground in post-Soviet Russia. One reason is to defend against precarious employment situations, such as administrative layoffs, shortened hours, and unpaid back wages. In 1997, OECD researchers reported:

> The fact that enterprises had to continue the practice of underemployment in 1996 largely determined the dynamics of the labour market. In 1996, an average of about 3.2 million (6.7 per cent) of the employees of large and medium-sized enterprises worked short hours or short weeks, which was 1.6 times more than in 1995. In all, 7.5 million (16.9 per cent) of the employees of large and medium-sized enterprises spent some time in forced administrative leaves in 1996. The use of short working hours or short working weeks as well as forced administrative leaves led to the loss of 464 million person-days of work in 1996, or the equivalent of roughly 2 million standard full-time workers.
>
> (OECD 1997: 91)

In this context, then, workers are motivated to seek other income-earning activities. Those employed in declining branches of the economy are more apt to face the above circumstances, such as those who work in the sectors of engineering, light industry, timber, woodworking, pulp and paper, geology, geodesy and hydrometeorological services, design services, science, and scientific services (OECD 1997: 91).

It may turn out, with the hindsight of several decades, that informal employment in Russia was indeed characteristic of a "temporary" period of transition from socialism to capitalism. However, transition has already lasted more than 12 years and constitutes a meaningful period of economic change. The aggregate evidence on the country as a whole is that informal economic activity is increasing as trade grows and integration into the world economy proceeds. First, massive immigration generally seems to augment informal employment because the formal economy does not absorb all the new arrivals and immigrants and their employers wish to avoid both formal work rules and registration (Visaria and Jacob 1996: 145–6). In Russia, "the combined share of re-settlers and illegally working temporary migrants can be conservatively estimated at 12–14% [in 1999]" (Vorobyov and Zhukov 2000: 4). Second, informal employment existed during the Soviet period and the motivations for such work have only increased since the collapse. Treml (1992: 40–2) estimates that 10–12 percent of the Soviet labor force in 1988 worked, either exclusively or as a sideline, in the informal economy. Analysts often called this work for cash outside of official plans "the second economy." Research has shown that participation in the second economy under socialism had both formal and informal dimensions (Böröcz and Southworth 1998; Böröcz 1993). As a consequence of nearly full employment in the Soviet Union, the informal economy before 1992 was "supplementary and not substitutive of regular working time. Therefore, labor supply is entirely made up of moonlighting of primary workers and of labor by marginal workers who do not accept a regular job" (Dallago 1987: 152). Without the legal requirement of a formal-sector job and the massive decline in Russian industry after the collapse, workers can more readily pursue informal employment.

Both individual- and community-level factors shape the decision to participate in informal work. The individual's choice to take up informal work is situated within the household. Burawoy *et al.* (2000) describe the effect of economic changes in the formal sector as generating a split in work tactics in the household sector. Households often adopt either a defensive "survival strategy" that is often called "the household economy," or they choose "entrepreneurial strategies" by participating in some sort of business, resale, or distribution work. Some household members retain their formal-sector jobs even if they are not being paid at present and/or are owed wage debts by their firms (see Schwartz and Southworth, Chapters 4 and 10, this volume), while others in the household take up informal work. Wage arrears have steadily grown in Russia over the past 10 years with rapid expansions in times of crisis, such as the currency crisis of 1998 when the rouble was devalued by a factor of four or more (Goskomstat 1999b). Our own fieldwork in firms in Russia and the Ukraine leads us to hypothesize that households often retain some formal work, especially when such work provides access to resources, tools, food, day care, and other benefits. Households turn to informal work to meet their need for cash in order to buy medicines, to pay for education, or to obtain other goods unobtainable through the workplace (such as high-quality meats and liquor). The choice of individuals or families to have some household members work in the informal sector is likely influenced by the ease with which legal permission to work can be obtained. Further, access to gardens, tools, trade routes, and other "entrepreneurial" possibilities may also play a role in the choice of informal activity. Some households may have pensioners receiving somewhat more regular, if paltry, cash payments from the state. Still others may have relatives in the nearby countryside who provide a ready opportunity to participate in animal husbandry, gardening, or construction, but possibly also provide enough food to lessen household needs for labor market participation, either formal or informal. Finally, the skill assets and health of the individual also come into play. It is not everyone who can be a street-level auto mechanic or carry the heavy bags of the shuttle trader in a Turkish bazaar.

Like the neoliberal economists, we suspect that informal activity is related to the economic health and opportunity present in a region. Informal activity, however, does not simply expand where trade and market are curtailed and disappear where imports, competition, and labor market growth take place. Where privatized state firms (mainly industry) remain relatively healthy – disposing of product, paying wages, able to purchase raw materials and necessary inputs – employees have less of an incentive to seek informal work. We expect such conditions in export-oriented, resource extraction industries such as oil, minerals, and metals. Such conditions are more common in the major urban areas, Moscow and St Petersburg, where more government money is spent on goods and services, the economy is larger, and a greater proportion of business is conducted in cash (instead of barter) than in other regions. In contrast, in regions where industry more often barters, delays wages, and puts a relatively greater proportion of the workforce on reduced hours or administrative leave – conditions favor informality.

If the market is reorganizing economic enterprises, then bankruptcy should be an important mechanism closing firms that do not produce products in demand, reallocating labor to profitable enterprises, and ending management priorities, such as excessive employment, not in line with those goals (Center for Strategic and International Studies 1998). As with trade, however, we hypothesize that the relationship between bankruptcy and informal labor market participation will be the opposite of that expected by neoliberal economists. Rather than indicating the presence of a competitive market and firms opting for reliance on the labor market, we expect bankruptcy to be related to the non-payment crisis, firms relying on off-the-books production, and informality generally. During the period under consideration, two different bankruptcy laws were instituted. The first bankruptcy law established in 1992 called for enterprises to be bankrupt when "the total amount of outstanding debt . . . exceed[s] the total balance sheet value of company assets" (Sonin and Zhuravskaya 2001: 6). This law made bankruptcy a rare event in Russian business as managers could easily manipulate their balance sheets in order to add debts owed to the firm (which appear as assets held). That alone is an incentive for use of the non-cash and barter economy. Where workers are not paid cash wages and continue to work for goods received in kind they more readily accrue debts to the firm in the form of loans or goods taken from the company store beyond their nominal pay (Southworth 2001a, b). Moreover, while back wages are not indexed for inflation, debts owed to the firm are accounted for in dollars and typically have an interest percentage as well. Such practices increase the "assets" of insolvent enterprises. A new bankruptcy law was enacted in 1998; one more in line with western standards and which lets any creditor with approximately $5,000 in holdings file for bankruptcy. Under this procedure a commercial court (*arbitrazhny sud*) investigates the claims against the firm and then appoints a manager to reorganize or liquidate the company. While this law in principle permits quick liquidation of insolvent enterprises and protection of creditors' rights, the courts in question lack independence both from regional governments and from the businesses themselves. Because the courts are not federally funded, and the bankrupt firms in question often owe substantial back taxes to federal authorities, local political officials and directors of larger economic organizations can influence the court to appoint insiders to handle the reorganization. "[R]egional governors are interested in keeping revenues inside their regions as well as keeping high employment at regional enterprises and they are opposed to liquidation of large and politically important enterprises" (Sonin and Zhuravskaya 2001: 8). While bankruptcies have increased slightly, they do not generally result in the closure and liquidation of enterprises, particularly if bankrupt firms are major employers. This facilitates the conditions of informal work: insolvent firms that owe wage arrears are not closed and employees are not reorganized through the labor market. Instead, they retain their formal-sector jobs, being paid in kind and through barter arrangements, and use informal activity to meet the cash needs of the household.

Where trade involves importing consumer goods and exporting mainly raw materials, competition and market reallocation occur. Firms producing for the local market face price and quality competition from the world market, while extracting and refining industries are subject to the efficiency requirements of their competitors. Because Russian labor is below world productivity standards and companies have no source of credit to upgrade their equipment, the encounter with global markets results in increased informality as firms either close or become moribund and cashless, often through bankruptcy. There are fewer formal sector jobs as a result.

What do informal activities look like in Russia?

Before discussing how we conceptualize informal activities in our analysis, it may help to look at what types of activities we wish to map and how they look through the lens of everyday life in Russia. Many occupations can engage in informal work. Teachers tutor; repair personnel take jobs in private homes or after hours at work; street markets provide the opportunity for reselling goods from local wholesalers or those of one's own manufacture; and the produce from local gardens is sold on the street. The following vignettes come from fieldwork in St Petersburg and Novosibirsk.

In St Petersburg, as in many Russian cities, it is common to see street selling. Typical scenes at metro stations and along the underground crosswalks are of clusters of individual sellers who hold second-hand goods (such as leather shoes, belts, and coats), homebred kittens and puppies, self-manufactured clothes and foodstuffs (such as knitted socks and preserves), and imported housewares and sundries. One street vendor, who regularly plied his trade, located near the Peter and Paul Fortress, sold Barbie doll costumes (Red Army uniforms, Soviet Navy, and Aviator uniforms) that his wife sewed at home.[2] They are both formally employed, but used the sale of souvenirs as a means to earn additional cash. For him, the advantage of selling on the street was that it can be easily relocated (though it is difficult to imagine a better location than the Peter and Paul Fortress for his merchandise) and he only stood on the street when his household desired the additional income.

The street selling does not disappear as you travel away from the country's centers – Moscow and St Petersburg – but the assortment of goods changes. The most visible difference is that the sale of garden produce and home preserves seems to increase in the smaller communities and more agricultural regions. In Akademgorodok – a small city 45 minutes away from Novosibirsk – street sellers line up along sidewalks and surround the tiny outdoor market with fresh produce from their gardens.[3]

Some of these sellers reside in villages that are only reached by train and bus. In summer 2001, in Lebedevka, a small town located 30 minutes from Akademgorodok by train, a retired couple discussed the popular scheme[4] of selling garden produce.[5] The woman discussed how her neighbors – two retired women – constantly tried to persuade her to pursue this opportunity for additional income. She and her husband opted not sell their produce since they felt their pensions combined and produce from their *ogorod* (kitchen garden) were sufficient to get by.

In neighboring towns where unemployment among working-age residents is prevalent, sale of home produce is sometimes the only means to obtain cash. For example, in Sosnovka (a village that is another 30 minutes by bus from Lebedevka) job opportunities are now only available to a small number of men who work at the machine tractor station – the only enterprise that remains on a local collective farm that once raised 500,000 geese. The village's residents rely mainly on subsistence farming, which enables households to eat and to trade with neighbors. But, some goods still need to be purchased with cash, such as soap and fabric. Since cash cannot be generated locally through Sosnovka's one small employer, residents must travel outside of the village to sell goods for cash.

Informal services depend partly on the local market. In St Petersburg and Novosibirsk, *chastniki* ("private" cabs, sometimes known as "pirate" cabs in English) are a taken-for-granted feature of urban life and a ready means for automobile owners to earn extra cash. In Russia today (and even more so during Soviet times) the majority of cars will stop to pick up a hitchhiker for a small fee, assuming it is not too far out of the driver's way. However, working as an unregistered taxi is less regular and profitable in smaller communities.

Construction and carpentry skills, on the other hand, are saleable in both large and small communities. In St Petersburg, for instance, the workers who renovated the dormitory rooms for *Sankt Peterburgskii Gosudarstvennyi Universitet (SPGU)* (Saint Petersburg State University (SPSU)) throughout 1999–2000 were moonlighters who performed this work in addition to their primary occupation. This was widely known among the dorm residents since *remont* (repair work) in the building was normally audible after five or six o'clock in the evening, when the majority of residents had returned home for the evening. In Akademgorodok, moonlighting employees of local industry typically undertake remodeling or repair. They are said to be popular since they are most affordable and come with references from satisfied relatives or neighbors.

Theoretical considerations and hypotheses

Informal economic activity is a notoriously slippery concept and, consequently, difficult to measure, especially in survey data (Portes 1994: 438–43). Again, we identify informal economic activities as off-the-books, unregistered employment that does not pay taxes and is not registered in official employment statistics. The OECD puts forward measurement standards and models for assessing aggregate statistics about the "non-observed economy." In this, it includes:

> *underground production*, defined as those activities that are productive and legal but deliberately concealed from public authorities to avoid payment of taxes or complying with regulations; *illegal production*, defined as those productive activities that generate goods and services forbidden by law . . .; *informal sector production*, defined as those productive activities conducted by unincorporated enterprises in the household sector that are unregistered and/or less than a specific size . . ., [and] *production of households for own final use*, defined as those productive activities that result in goods or services consumed.
>
> (OECD 2002: 13–14)

Here we focus on the first three, except that, unlike the OECD, we exclude legal, registered household or self-employment, and small businesses.

In Russia, every legally employed adult has a *trudovaya knizhka* (workbook) in which the employer must place a stamp. Within five days of being hired, the workbook must be presented to the employer along with a valid passport and registration, certification of education, and, for those discharged from the army, a military card. This booklet is usually kept in the *otdel' kadrov* (personnel department) of the employer. Thus, it is not peculiar to expect individuals to know whether or not their employer is formally registered, since only registered employers keep records of their employees in these books (Clarke 1999a: 142).[6] Many employers, particularly in privatized Soviet firms and in manufacturing, also require that an employee present a *propiska* (residency permit) before being hired, and information on place of employment would also be recorded at the time a residency permit was made out at the local passport desk. That is, Russia has a strong passport regime and this, to some extent, simplifies what constitutes unregistered work. When an employee does not have a stamp in his or her workbook, the job is unregistered.

The transformation of Soviet economic institutions over the past decade has been thoroughgoing. The vast majority of state enterprises were sold off at auction or converted into joint-stock companies with their employees as the initial shareholders by the mid-1990s (Shleifer and Treisman 2000; Blasi *et al.* 1997; Boycko *et al.* 1995; Åslund 1995). Price controls have been eliminated on all but a few foodstuffs in particular localities (Hough 2001). State financing through industrial ministries was dramatically curtailed in the 1990s and ended altogether in the currency crisis of 1998, in which the rouble was devalued by more than a factor of four. Many areas of institutional change are still in process – bankruptcy laws, the labor code, and land ownership to name a few – but in broad outline Russia quickly set up the formal institutional framework for market capitalism.[7]

The Russian economy went into a dramatic depression during the 1990s in which gross national product fell to less than half the level of the decade before (Hough 2001) and unemployment went as high as 20 percent. Though, interestingly enough, in 1999 fewer than 14 percent of the unemployed were registered with the Employment Service and eligible for unemployment benefits (Clarke 2002b: 3). Wages in Russian enterprises were commonly delayed by months and even years in some provincial republics, while firms operated largely in a barter economy (Clarke *et al.* 1996). While employees often kept their formal legal jobs, and their employers provided them with products procured through barter or even the produce of the enterprise itself, there was a strong incentive to find additional sidelines that might bring in some cash. The research questions at hand are: How did non-payment of wages and low wages themselves influence participation in the informal economy? Is informal work particularly the province of pensioners and others who have left the formal labor market? And for communities: Did the bankruptcy of state firms influence workers to seek informal employment? Does the presence of the world market, measured through import and export trade, create conditions favoring informal employment?

Of course, informal work also existed in the Soviet era. People resold goods obtained through the workplace or other connections (Grossman 1989; Stark 1989; Mattera 1985). Unofficial repair services, language lessons, and the sale of garden produce also occurred. The differences are both in quality and scale. Those activities were formerly the province of *spekulanty* (speculators) and their activities were illegal and sometimes punished (Grossman 1989: 154). Moreover, nearly everyone of working age had a formal job, an employer with their workbook, and there was very little unregistered employment within legal organizations. Now the state has neither the inclination nor the resources to monitor such employment and the petty sidelines are legal and unimpeded.[8]

The intersection of market forces and economic decline leads us to a set of hypotheses about the connection between changes in institutions and participation in the informal economy.

> H1: Workers who are currently owed wages will have a higher rate of participation in the informal economy.

> H2: Workers who were paid wages in the last month are less likely to participate in the informal economy.

These two hypotheses suggest that a central motive for participating in the informal economy is to get cash. Workers who are not owed back wages, who were paid the proceeding month, and who receive relatively high wages have less of an incentive. There is a regional pattern to the non-payment of wages, low wages, and wage debts. Provincial areas where market forces operate to a lesser degree, and where privatized but formally bankrupt firms remain open, have more non-payment problems.

> H3: People with regular government support, such as a pension, will be less likely to participate in the informal economy.

People with pensions receive their payments with more regularity – although delays do occur, they are typically paid in full within a few months. Pensioners have more time to engage in the informal work of gardening and selling, but this is offset by the household economic situation. Informal work is not simply for people who are poor, but rather for those without access to cash, or for whom access to cash is irregular due to unstable or irregular work arrangements.

Like many economic decisions, the proper unit of analysis may actually be the household and the key determinants may be factors acting on the household budget. This is the standard way that poverty is assessed in multinational studies (Deaton 1997). We expect that households that are owed back wages or have members who did not receive wages will be more likely to have at least one person in the informal economy. Likewise, households with pensioners, and the regular access to cash which this implies, will be less likely to have members in the informal sector.

If the individual-level hypotheses are not supported by those at the household level, this would suggest "family" decision-making. For example, if several households' members held formal jobs with wage delays, the household might decide that some members should keep those formal-sector jobs while others should quit. Retaining formal employment without wages might provide a hedge against the possibility of economic recovery or it might provide access to barter arrangements to pay the household electric bills, or access to credit in the form of a loan from the enterprise director. On average, if we did not account for such household-level decision-making, we might find that half of those with wage delays took up informal work while half did not. Represented as a two-by-two table, this would find "no effect" for wage delays. However, households with wage delays might well put some members to work in the informal economy more often than households without such delays.

H4: A greater proportion of households in which one or more members are owed back wages will participate in the informal sector.

H5: A greater proportion of households in which one or more members were not paid last month will participate in the informal sector.

H6: A greater proportion of households in which one or more members receive a pension will not participate in the informal sector.

We also want to look for the effects of the local labor market and the influence of economic context, particularly the influence of bankrupt state firms, levels of trade, and average wages.

Because many bankrupt firms remain open producing goods and "hiring" workers, our argument is the opposite of the neoliberal view: bankruptcy will be associated with informality. The point of the hypothesis is not that workers of closed enterprises themselves seek informal employment, but rather that those who are employed in bankrupt organizations operating in barter are more likely to seek informal work arrangements where they can obtain cash.

H7: Communities where state-owned firms have gone bankrupt will have higher rates of informal participation.

The main hypothesis of the neoliberal theorists put forward at the beginning of this chapter is that market development and trade, particularly in regions exposed to the world economy, should result in a decline in informal activity. Where competitive price pressure is applied to firms, there is a stronger incentive for a reorganization of labor. Firms close and new ones open as a result of the dynamism of the market. Our argument is that the effects of trade must be specified in detail. For Russia, and especially among privatized Soviet firms, exports and imports do not represent the same type of relationship with the world economy. The presence of extractive industries in oil (and oil refining), minerals, or metals makes for relatively more stable and better-paid employment. These firms generate hard currency and do not have the same incentive to operate in barter, with in-kind remuneration, and part-time work, as do enterprises oriented toward the domestic market. Imports, on the other hand, exert strong pressure on domestic manufacturers – especially in a context where Russian industry is less efficient and where the quality of goods is less standardized. High imports in the current economic climate amount to adverse conditions for Russian firms in the local retail market. Hence, we expect imports and exports to have the opposite effect on household informality.

H8: The odds of household participation in the informal sector are positively related to regional imports.

H9: The odds of household participation in the informal sector are negatively related to regional exports.

Clearly these hypotheses and measures are interrelated. The next section describes the dataset and operationalization. The variables are then explored in a series of cross-tabulations, then together in a hierarchical linear regression model with community and individual levels.

Data, measures and analysis

The data are from the Russian Longitudinal Monitoring Survey (RLMS), which conducted face-to-face interviews in 10 rounds between 1992 and 2001. RLMS is a multi-stage probability sample of regions and households. The design attempts to interview all adult members of the household and collect data on all occupants. The design is semi-panel as it follows the same address over time, recruiting new addresses to make up for attrition. The sampling frame was redrawn and a new survey started in 1996:

> First, a list of 2,029 consolidated raions[9] was created to serve as primary sampling units (PSUs). These were allocated into 38 strata based largely on geographical factors and level of urbanization, but also based on ethnicity where there was salient variability. . . . [S]ome remote areas were eliminated to contain costs; also, Chechnya was eliminated due to armed conflict. From among the remaining 1,850 raions (containing 95.6% of the population), three very large population units were selected

> with certainty: Moscow city, Moscow Oblast, and St Petersburg city constituted self-representing (SR) strata. The remaining non-self-representing (NSR) raions were allocated to 35 equal-sized strata. One raion was then selected from each NSR stratum using the method "probability proportional to size." That is, the probability that a raion in a given NSR stratum was selected was directly proportional to its measure of population size.
>
> (RLMS 2000)

The sample is population corrected based on 1989 census data and weighted for non-response.

We operationalize informal participation as those people who have either a first or second job that is unregistered; those who say they have engaged in other, irregular work in the last 30 days; and those who engage in any of the following specific activities outside of their regular employment: raising produce for sale, raising animals for sale, selling items of their own manufacture, reselling goods from local wholesalers, shuttle trading to import goods from abroad, or providing services on an individual basis. Unfortunately, RLMS only collects the detailed breakdown of informal work in 2000 and 2001. For most years, respondents were asked: "Tell me, please, in the last 30 days did you engage in some additional kind of work for which you got paid? Maybe you sewed someone a dress, gave someone a ride in a car, assisted someone with apartment or car repairs, purchased and delivered food, looked after a sick person, sold purchased food or goods in a market or on the street, or did something else that you were paid for?"[10] (RLMS 2000). While that question encompasses most informal work, we will show that there are both temporal and other factors that most likely make it a conservative estimate of the size of the informal labor market.

Figures 8.1 and 8.2 compare the formal and informal labor market over time. These are not restricted to the working-age population, in part because we will investigate the effects of age and retirement on employment. Figure 8.1 shows the result of dramatic decline in formal employment in Russia; the number of those working in registered jobs falls from almost half the population in 1992 to less than 40 percent in 1996. Figure 8.2 shows the growth of informal employment among all respondents, from a little more than 2 percent to more than 8 percent of the population in 10 years. Note that this is the most conservative measure of informal employment, because it only reflects those that answered "yes" to the question cited above and does not include the additional probes or people with unregistered work. The more detailed questions only existed after 2000 in the RLMS surveys.

The description of household budgets and informal participation is taken up in Figure 8.3. Here the line marked with the circles is the aggregate of the individual data in Figure 8.2. It shows the proportion of households with one or more person doing informal work. Informal economic activity

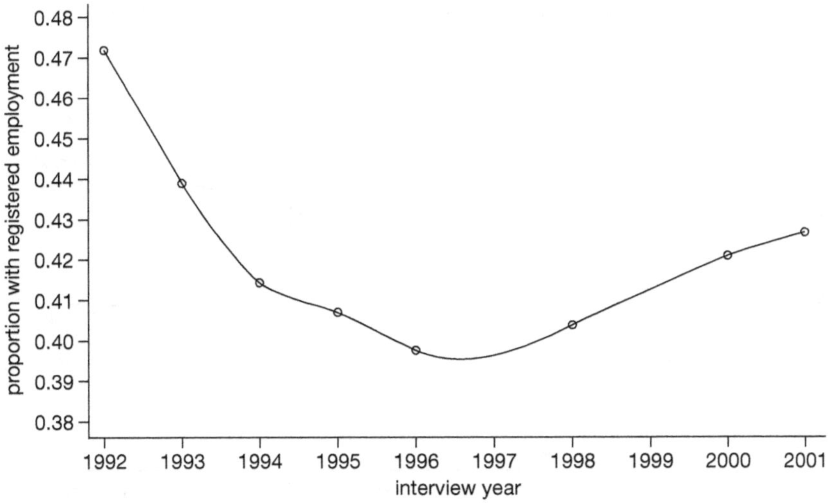

Figure 8.1 Proportion of population with legal registered employment.

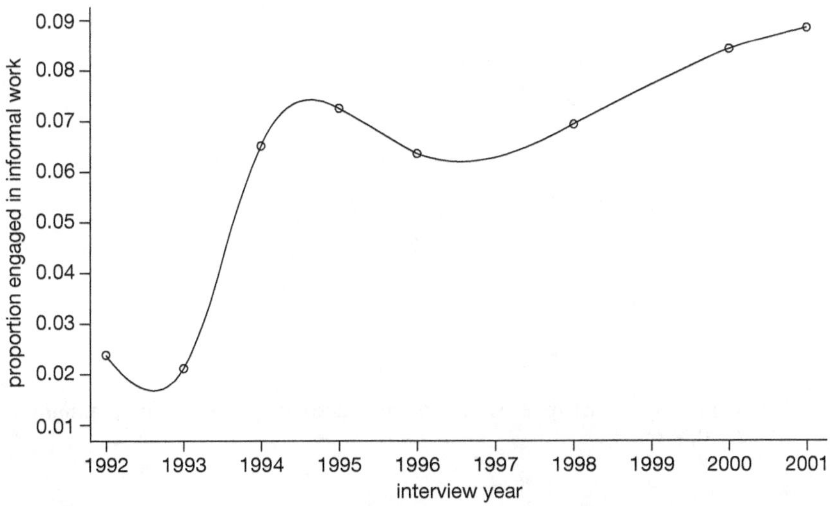

Figure 8.2 Proportion of population with informal employment.

by household grew rapidly from 1992 to 1995 and then experienced gradual growth from 1996 to 2001. The line marked with triangles shows the proportion of household income coming from that informal work. The relative contribution of informal work to the household budget grew rapidly until 1996 and then fell until 2000. While we do not conduct a time-series analysis of these trends in this chapter, it is interesting to note that informal employment grew in 1994 and 1995 while its share of household income

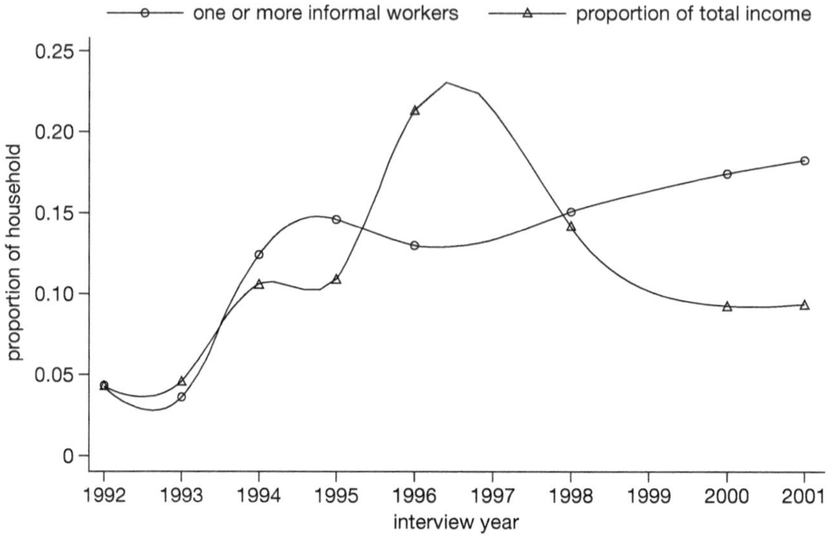

Figure 8.3 Proportion of households with one or more persons doing informal work and proportion of household income from informal activity.

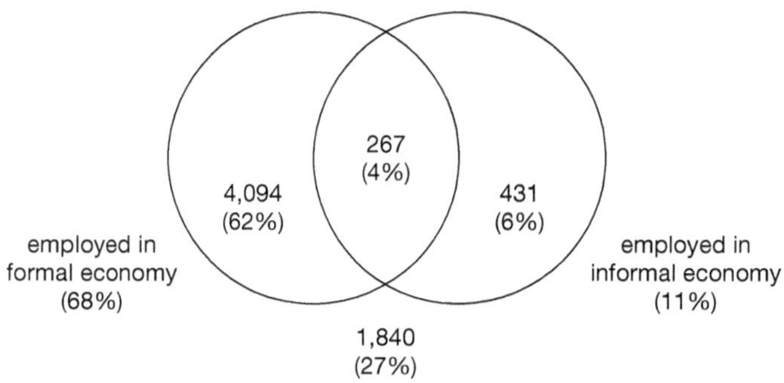

Figure 8.4 Venn diagram of spheres of economic activity (working age population, 2000; = 6632).

remained stable; likewise, it has grown since 1998 while its returns fell and leveled off. Those periods correspond to two severe currency devaluations in 1994 and 1998 (Goskomstat 2001a: 385).

To make sense of the informal sector in Russia, we need to offer some idea of the level of informal employment in other economies. This is made more difficult by the myriad of definitions for informal work and the fact that the OECD prefers to include all self-employment and entrepreneurial activity in the "informal sector." Our argument pertains only to unregistered work and is therefore conservative in its estimation of the size and importance of the informal sector. The informal sector is estimated at 38 percent

Table 8.1 Types of informal work and additional economic activity among population of working age (18–59); data from Round 9 (2000) RLMS

	Mean	*Standard deviation*	*N*
Engaged in informal work last month	0.11	0.31	5346
Unregistered job	0.02	0.15	6285
Extra job	0.12	0.33	5345
Sold produce from garden	0.09	0.28	5349
Sold animal products	0.08	0.28	5347
Sold goods of own manufacture	0.02	0.14	5349
Resold goods	0.03	0.16	5344
Imported goods for sale	0.03	0.16	5346
Rented house, garden, car	0.01	0.09	5344
Provided services	0.06	0.23	5284

of the non-agricultural workforce in Costa Rica (Baez 1996), 20 percent in Tanzania (Ngoi 1996), 36 percent in Nigeria (Ajayi 1996), 9.8 percent in Turkey, 30 percent in Mexico (Winkler 1997), and 32 percent in Chile (Irarrazaval 1997). These estimates come from different years and many of them include employees in various types of small business. If we approximate the less conservative measure used in these studies and include small businesses (with 20 or fewer employees) and those engaged in entrepreneurial activity, our estimate for Russia in 2000 climbs to 57.54 percent of the workforce, higher than any level of such work reported in the literature.

Figure 8.4 shows participation in formal and informal labor markets and those outside the labor market among the working-age population in 2000.[11] Twenty-eight percent of the working-age population is not engaged in either registered work, nor in any of the informal income-earning activities assessed in our survey. The formal economy has 66 percent of the workforce; the informal economy, 11 percent; and 4 percent have both a formal economy job and do some sort of informal work. There is substantial regional and individual variation in participation in the informal economy.

Table 8.1 gives a relative breakdown of the sorts of activities people undertake in the informal sector. These do not total to 100 percent because people often engage in more than one type. Gardening (9 percent), selling animal products such as milk, eggs, or livestock (8 percent), and providing services (6 percent) were the most common answers. This table describes the whole adult population of working age, not just those who reported informal work. The first three lines of the table are for comparison. Eleven percent of the population is employed in the informal economy; 2 percent of the population reports unregistered (and therefore illegal work); and 12 percent report taking some sort of extra job (formal or informal). For purposes of this preliminary analysis, we treat all types of informal work as having something in common.

Table 8.2 Contrast between reporting generally that one engaged in informal labor in the last month versus reporting one or more of the specific informal activities detailed in Table 8.1

	No informal participation last year	*Informal participation last year*	*Totals*
No informal work last 30 days	4323 65.18	1611 24.29	5934 89.48
Informal work last 30 days	0 0.00	698 10.52	698 10.52
Totals	4323 65.18	2309 34.82	6632 100.00

Table 8.2 shows the "informal work" variable used in all 10 RLMS surveys to those who answered yes to any of the activities (except extra job) shown in Table 8.1. Here we want to assess the accuracy of the general informal work question by comparing it to a detailed set of queries about agriculture, service work, reselling, etc. The results show that an additional 24.3 percent of the working-age population engaged in some form of informal economic activity in the last year. Most of them report cash income from that work in subsequent questions. This means that the more general question compared in Figures 8.1–8.4, resulted in substantial under-reporting of informal work in 2000, and that the rate of informal participation in that calendar year was more than three times as high, or 34.8 percent. Thus, all tables really include people engaged in some form of informal activity in the last year. Further work on the specific correlates of informal participation in the two most recent RLMS surveys might provide a model for estimating informal employment in earlier years without the battery of specific queries. We will examine the implications of the measurement of informal participation when we turn to individual-level decisions.

Figure 8.5 assesses the question "Tell me, please, was this incidental work for you or do you often engage in this kind of work and regularly receive money for it?" This is a problematic question as it is double-barreled and confounds regularity with the receipt of cash and, thus, must be read with caution as a likely subset of those doing regular informal work. The up and down tendency of the proportion of the population engaged in regular informal work for cash seems to mirror the household-level participation rate in Figure 8.3. The regularity of this type of work has steadily increased from 1996.

Tables 8.3 and 8.4 test the hypotheses on wages. Counter to expectations, Table 8.3 shows that people of working age who were owed back wages were less likely to participate in informal economic activity than people who were not owed wages. Thirty-eight percent of those with wage debts took on

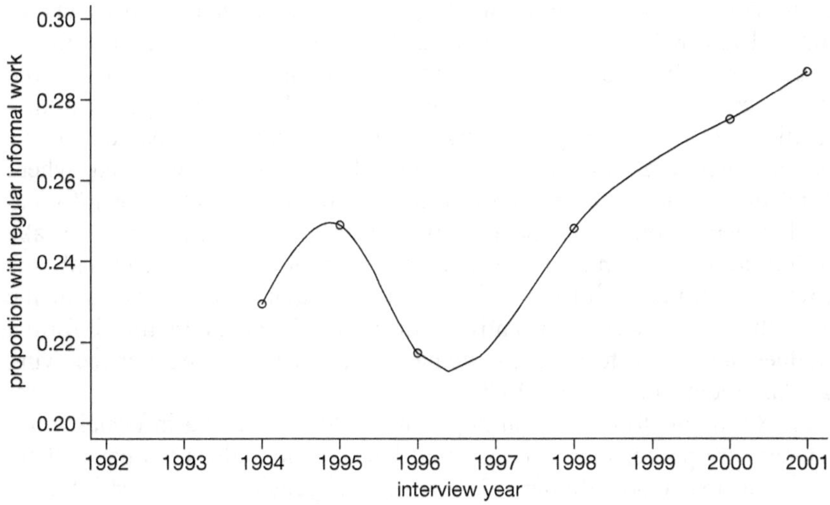

Figure 8.5 Proportion of those reporting regular informal economic activity.

Table 8.3 Respondent owed back wages?

	No	*Yes*	*Totals*
No informal	3570 53.72	753 61.52	4323 54.94
Informal	3075 46.28	471 38.48	3546 45.06
Totals	6645 100.00	1224 100.00	7869 100.00

Note: Pearson $chi^2(1) = 25.3691$; $Pr = 0.000$.

Table 8.4 Respondent paid last month? Effect on broad, yearly definition of informal activity

	No	*Yes*	*Total*
No informal	625 61.21	2742 71.04	3367 68.98
Informal	396 38.79	1118 28.96	1514 31.02
Totals	1021 100.00	3860 100.00	4881 100.00

Note: Pearson $chi^2(1) = 36.4026$; $Pr = 0.000$.

informal work compared with only 46 percent of those not owed wages. In contrast, Table 8.4 shows, as expected, that people who were paid in the proceeding month had a lower rate of participation in informal activity. Table 8.4 has a smaller number of respondents because only the employed, working population can receive wages, whereas Table 8.3 includes those out of the labor force who are still owed wage debts. These results are mixed: where respondents did not receive cash in the last month they opted for informal work, but debts from an unspecified period do not motivate people to take up informal work. Both of these tables were also constructed with the narrower definition of informal employment available for all years in the RLMS; the results were substantively the same. Underestimating informal work does not appear to have a systematic relationship to debts or receiving wages last month in the year 2000.

Table 8.5 points to cash as an important factor in seeking informal work. Pensioners are poorer than average, but that fact alone does not cause them to seek informal work. Rather, 27.4 percent of pensioners opt for informal arrangements while 47 percent of the working population engages in such activities. The security of the regular, albeit meager, pension overrides the necessity for cash. It might be argued that working-age people who have retired early and receive a pension are different from the population as a whole. However, reconstructing this table with the entire population (not just working-age people) yields a substantively identical result.

While the calculus of participation in the informal sector is mixed for individuals, Tables 8.6 through 8.8 suggest that it is clear and related to cash income for households. Table 8.6 shows that households with one or more member who is owed back wages are more likely to have one or more member in informal employment – 68.9 percent of households in which someone was owed wages have one or more members in informal work compared to 51.8 percent among households without wage debts. Table 8.7 shows a similar relationship for households with one or more employees who were not paid last month – 70.7 percent of such households had one or more person in the informal sector compared to 52.4 percent among households where all employees received last month's wages. Table 8.8 shows the effect of having

Table 8.5 Respondent receives a pension? Working-age population

	No	*Yes*	*Totals*
No informal	3758 53.00	565 72.53	4323 54.94
Informal	3332 47.00	214 27.47	3546 45.06
Totals	7090 100.00	779 100.00	7869 100.00

Note: Pearson $chi^2(1) = 108.0801$; $Pr = 0.000$.

Table 8.6 Effect of household owed back wages on having one or more workers in informal sector

	Not owed	*Owed*	*Total*
No informal	1413 48.11	332 31.09	1745 43.57
Informal	1524 51.89	736 68.91	2260 56.43
Totals	2937 100.00	1068 100.00	4005 100.00

Note: Pearson $chi^2(1) = 92.3222$; $Pr = 0.000$.

Table 8.7 One or more household members not paid last month

	Paid	*Not paid*	*Totals*
No informal	1490 47.57	255 29.21	1745 43.57
Informal	1642 52.43	618 70.79	2260 56.43
Total	3132 100.00	873 100.00	4005 100.00

Note: Pearson $chi^2(1) = 93.6398$; $Pr = 0.000$.

Table 8.8 One or more household members receive retirement pension

	No pensioner	*Pensioner*	*Totals*
No informal	594 34.72	1151 50.17	1745 43.57
Informal	1117 65.28	1143 49.83	2260 56.43
Totals	1711 100.00	2294 100.00	4005 100.00

Note: Pearson $chi^2(1) = 95.2443$; $Pr = 0.000$.

a pensioner in the household. Pensions, while subject to delays, are paid more regularly and with less cumulative back debt than wages. Households without pensioners participate in informal economic activity in greater proportion (65.2 percent) than those with a pensioner (49.8 percent).

Next we consider community-level effects on the level of informal employment. We want to know whether trade, bankruptcies, and wage levels create a climate conducive to informal employment. The following section presents logistic regression models of the odds that a household will have one or more member participating in the informal sector in any capacity. With these

Table 8.9 Means and standard deviations of community and household measures

Variable	*Mean*	*Standard deviation*
Household has member in informal sector	0.56	0.50
Household wage	1800.55	2841.78
Household not paid last month	0.22	0.41
Household owed back wages	0.27	0.44
Household has pensioner	0.57	0.49
Median household wage in region	1133.48	1129.67
State firms have gone bankrupt	0.32	0.47
Percentage imports in regional GDP	9.71	8.82
Percentage exports in regional GDP	15.72	13.14

models, we are answering the most basic question: What factors cause households to have someone in informal work? Of course, the nature of informal work could be analyzed in many other ways. We could look at the number of people involved, whether the informal sector provides a primary or secondary job, or what fraction of the household income comes from such work. The details on informal participation will have to await further research. In the present analysis, the models permit a basic look at the relationships presented in the tables thus far, while controlling for their interrelated nature and assessing the effects of the regional economy.

Table 8.9 gives the means and standard deviations of the variables; 56 percent of households have one or more person in the informal sector. The mean total wages from first jobs in the household was 1,800 roubles and the median household income in all regions was 1,133 roubles. Both of these variables are the monthly wages of the respondents' jobs, not the total income, nor necessarily the amount received. The remaining household variables show that 22 percent of households were not paid last month, 27 percent of households were owed back wages (not necessarily from last month), and 57 percent of households had a pensioner. Three other regional level variables (pertaining to the *raion* or site of the RLMS survey) measure the economic conditions in the community of a given household. The first of these shows that 32 percent of communities have had state firms placed in bankruptcy in the last year. As noted above, that is different from closing and does not include the result of the bankruptcy procedure. On average, imports comprise 9.7 percent of regional GNP (Gross Regional Product, or *Valovoi Regional'noi Product, VRP*); exports, 15.7 percent.[12]

Model 1 on Table 8.10 shows the effects of the household variables. The coefficients in the table are odds ratios and reflect the multiplier of the odds due to a particular variable. A value of one does not change the odds, while factions less than one mean that it is less likely for a household to have a member in the informal economy and numbers greater than one mean that it is more likely. All household-level determinants are statistically significant at the 0.5 percent level. Household wages are significant and positive,

Table 8.10 Logistic regression models of household participation in informal economy

	Model 1	*Model 2*	*Model 3*	*Model 4*
Household variables				
Household wage	1.000068			1.00008
	(0.000)*			(0.000)*
Not paid last month	1.719			1.731
	(0.204)*			(0.201)*
Owed back wages	1.485			1.467
	(0.131)*			(0.127)*
Pensioner in household	0.642			0.634
	(0.051)*			(0.050)*
Regional variables				
Median household wage		1.000		1.000
		(0.000)		(0.000)*
Bankruptcies of state firms		0.959		1.074
		(0.129)		(0.150)
Percentage imports			1.002	1.004
			(0.007)	(0.008)
Percentage exports			0.991	0.992
			(0.004)*	(0.004)*
Wald chi-square	110.06*	2.41	5.25	144.30*

Note: Numbers in parentheses are standard errors; * = $p < 0.05$.

although small because they are in rouble units. While we did not present a two-by-two table of household income, this emphasizes that it is not simply the poor or those on low incomes that participate in informal activity. With this crude model, it is not possible to sort out the causal ordering, i.e. whether informality contributed to income or income contributed to informality. The largest single factor, however, is not being paid in the last 30 days. Households where one member was not paid are 1.7 times more likely to take up informal employment. Wage debts are also important: households owed back wages are 1.4 times more likely to have at least one person in the informal sector. Finally, having a retired pensioner at home – meaning that the household receives some small amount of cash – makes informal participation less likely. This last finding needs more exploration, as pensioners would seem to have contradictory connections to the informal economy. On the one hand, they arguably have more time; on the other hand, a greater number of them are not able to work (for example, due to physical limitations). In any case, the model rules out the simple explanation that poor households with retired family members are those in the informal economy.

Model 2 shows that neither median household wages nor the bankruptcy of state firms is related to informal sector participation among households. Both are quite close to one and are not significant. It is not that regions with low-wage households (or particularly well-off families) tend to participate. The bankruptcy procedure against state firms in a region during 1999 does not change family rates of informal participation in 2000.

Model 3 examines the trade variables. While both coefficients are related to household informal participation in the expected direction – imports are positive and exports are negative – both are quite modest and only exports are statistically significant. These variables do not explain much in household decision-making. Regions with a larger export economy are associated with less household-level informality, but regions that consume a relatively large quantity of imports have neither higher nor lower rates of people working in the informal sector.

Finally, Model 4 presents all the variables together. The basic directions and magnitudes of the effects remain the same. Median household wage is a significant net effect of the percentage of exports. This suggests that high-wage households do not participate in the informal economy in geographic areas in which there exists a strong export economy. In areas where exports are relatively small compared to GNP, households with higher wages are taking up informal activities. This finding is quite modest and should be treated as tentative.

Discussion

The individual-level hypotheses about informal participation are partly confirmed. Workers who were not paid last month (H2) and who receive a retirement pension (H3) are less likely to engage in informal work. However, workers who were owed back wages (H1) were also less likely. That contradictory finding was explained by household-level decision-making. While individuals who were owed wages were less likely to opt for informal work, households in which they were a member were more likely (H4). Similarly, and reinforcing that conclusion, households which had members who were not paid last month were more likely to take informal work (H5), but households with at least one pensioner (H6) were not. That wage debts lead households to have some members employed in the informal sector led us to focus the remainder of the analysis on households as the locus of decisions about economic action.

At the level of the community or geographic region, we hypothesized that the bankruptcy of state firms would indicate an atmosphere conducive to informality (H7). Likewise, it was argued that import trade would be associated with poor conditions for domestic firms and, hence, we would witness more informality (H8), while export trade would be associated with their health and reliance on the formal labor market (H9). Only exports as a percentage of regional GDP were significant and negatively related to household informal participation.

Overall, our data shows that informal economic activity has grown, while formal employment shrank. It continues to make up a meaningful form of income-earning activity for households even though its share of household income peaked in the mid-1990s and then leveled off and stabilized in more recent years. Over the past five years, more respondents report informal work in Russia as regular. The main explanation for informal work participation is more specifically a lack of cash and not poverty or general debts, especially for the individual.

At the level of the *oblast'*, *raion*, or *krai*, neoliberal arguments about the market mechanisms eliminating informality are not supported. Export industry participation in the world market has a weak, negative association with household informality, but imports and bankruptcy do not. None of these effects are as important as the economic condition of the household. In short, the economic changes since 1991 do not appear to eliminate informal labor market activity; rather, such work seems to be increasing, if modestly.

Conclusion

The pattern of informal participation suggests several unconventional conclusions about institutional and economic change in Russia. First, contrary to expectations among economic experts and government officials at the time of the collapse of the Soviet Union, it appears that the cash labor market with calculable prices and defined demand has not expanded since then (1992). Expert opinion uniformly expected markets to allocate more resources and to do so according to the logic of price. Where goods and services are not in demand, they should command a smaller price. Firms take that information and reorganize or go bankrupt. However, if people are not paid in cash, demand becomes undefined, the goods produced and used as currency become regional (instead of universal), and price no longer transmits information to enterprises about what to produce or sell. Some other logic must fulfill that role. Informal economic activity is a way for the population and households to garner cash, but it is not one subject to the entrepreneurial planning of the managers of capitalist firms.

Second, informal economic activity is not strictly an "economic survival strategy." That is, this type of work is not taken up by the destitute and unemployed. Instead, it is a response to market failure and it is one among many. Organizations may pay extremely low wages – the median wage considered here is low by Russian standards and in all regions – but that is not enough to push people into the informal sector. Not being paid, not having a pension, being owed back wages – these are the circumstances that send people into the informal economy in search of cash to fill the gap between products provided at work and the subsistence minimum.

Third, and most speculatively, these findings seem to suggest that simply creating the legal infrastructure of capitalism and market – free prices, private property, few government subsidies – is not enough to create a system of market allocation of resources. Instead, people whom standard economic theories expect to engage in job seeking, often opt out of the formal labor market and take up informal activity where they reside rather than relocating to new jobs and new markets. The behavior of displaced post-Soviet workers tends to lend support to those interpretations of globalization that emphasize a multitude of divergent capitalist systems (Dicken 2003; Hall and Soskice 2001; Castells 2000a) rather than those that talk of increased convergence (Barnet and Cavanagh 1994; Reich 1992). This is so even if the pressures resulting in precarious employment, such as increased world competition or IMF-inspired political reforms, are similar across the world's regions (Candland and Sil 2001).

Notes

1 See Simon Clarke's *The Formation of a Labour Market* (1999a) for a thorough account of the labor market in Russia. Burawoy and Krotov (1996: 64) argue that, if capitalism is developing in Russia, then it is developing a form of *merchant capitalism* rather than a form of *bourgeois capitalism*. Burawoy (1999: 5) argues that in fact *involution* – rather than transformation – best describes post-Soviet Russia where "the [market] doctrine was a thin camouflage for the interests of a parasitic 'merchant' class of market intermediaries who squashed production." Hough (2001: 244–5) argues that, in hindsight, reforms needed to begin with agrarian reforms in 1986 and they needed to be implemented more gradually.

2 Based on interview with male vendor, May 9, 2000, St Petersburg, Russia.

3 This is also evident in observations during eight months of research in 2002 in Ukraine between Kiev and Komsomolsk, a small city in Poltava Region.

4 This couple, and their neighbors, lived in a five-story apartment complex in Lebedevka. Consequently, their produce is raised in *ogorod* (the kitchen garden), which is cultivated amongst other residents' gardens. This is a distinctive arrangement of gardens compared to the dacha garden plot or garden plots cultivated at *chastnye doma* (private homes).

5 This interview took place at the residents' home in Lebedevka during a two-month summer visit to Akademgorodok in 2001. Sosnovka, a village located another 30 minutes away by bus from Lebedevka, was also visited during this trip and informal interviews were conducted with a family residing there.

6 In fact, Simon Clarke (1999a: 142) points out that this is why the *trudovaya knizhka* (workbook) is becoming less informative to personnel departments since, "many jobs in the new private sector are not registered and the divergence between the formal and informal characteristics of employment is increasing."

7 Of course, many of the informal institutional arrangements of former Soviet enterprises and governmental offices have not been de-institutionalized (see Schwartz, Chapter 4, this volume).

8 In fact, these activities were not researched by the Soviet state because they were unacceptable (Clarke 2002b: 11). This further complicates gauging empirically the magnitude to which informal activities have increased since the collapse of the Soviet Union.

9 Transliteration of the Russian word for "regions."

10 This is question 56, page 14.J, from the Round 9 codebook. The variable is I9ENGIEA and there is a battery of other questions about this activity, which follow it.

11 The working-age population here is defined as ages 18 to 59. The official retirement age for men in Russia is 59; for women, 55.

12 Import and export figures are from table "24.4 export i import po regionam possiiskoi federatsii v 1998" and Gross Regional Product is from "11.19 Valovoi Regional'noi Product" for 1997 (Goskomstat 2000c). It is less than ideal to compare export/import trade and GNP data from different times than the survey, but such data were not available by region in later years. All currencies are adjusted to billions of 2000 USD.

9 Embeddedness, markets and the state

Observations from Tatarstan

Leo McCann

One of the key purposes of this book is to show how the diverse experiences of Russian economic sectors and regions throw up several challenges for the concept of globalization. On the one hand, much of the evidence confirms the picture of a society rapidly transformed by internationally connected processes of development. On the surface many of the economic and political changes taking place in Russia reflect some sense of global convergence around market democratic norms. Many other Russian features, however, are entirely at odds with this picture. The next step is to attempt to understand why and how these complicated and nonconformist Russian features can be understood in a more general manner. It is not sufficient to say simply that Russia is unique, or that different regions have specific processes and outcomes. This would be an unacceptable slide into subjectivism and description, making further analysis impossible. We need to be able to explain and predict change as well. Instead, it is crucial that divergence is thought about within an overarching framework of postsocialist socio-economics. By examining one region in detail and then attempting to contextualize this region's experiences within a broader context of postsocialist organizational change, some general principles about Russian post-Soviet states and markets can be uncovered.

This chapter focuses on the interplay between state and market in the Republic of Tatarstan, located approximately 500 miles east of Moscow, on the Volga river. The chapter emerges from a larger project (McCann forthcoming 2004) based on qualitative fieldwork and interviewing of key actors (industrial managers, governmental officials and small–medium-sized business entrepreneurs). The Republic of Tatarstan, with a population of nearly four million, is one of the key geo-political players of the Volga region. It is reputed to have a particularly strong and paternalistic regional state apparatus. But what is the nature of the state given the context of neoliberal globalization?

The first three waves of globalization literature have differing views on the future of the state in a global context. The first wave insisted that both the state and bounded national economies are to be swept away in the face of the ruthless efficiency of transnational markets. The second wave argues that states will remain strong and will (to paraphrase Habermas) resist such a 'colonization of its lifeworld' by the transnational market 'system'. These first two positions argue over the comparative agency of the state versus the agency of international markets. The third wave has a different frame of reference. It is less interested in arguing the level of marketization of the world and the level of state retreat from steering of economies. It instead argues that *the global condition has transformed the nature of both states and markets into qualitatively different social features*. Within this context it is inevitable that the comparative sources of agency for states and markets have changed, and the contemporary situation of flux and uncertainty has meant that different regions see different configurations of market and state power. It is the contention of this chapter that the Tatar state fits improperly into the first two models, but fits partially into the third, transformationalist model. I will argue that the nature of the Tatar state is best understood as a partially reformed state, and its markets are best understood as partially formed capitalist markets. The Tatar state and Tatar markets differ considerably from their advanced Western counterparts. Both states and markets must be considered within the context of contradictory and complex changes in the Russian institutional environment, and with some significant global changes.

The local government and large Tatar former state enterprises (FSEs) are dominated by a narrow clique of elite interests. Some of the VIPs of the Tatar economy are literally shared between the state and industrial firms, blurring the distinction between state and market. However, this does not mean that Tatarstan is an 'island of communism'. Instead the Tatar 'transition' reveals some novel organizational forms and processes that contribute to our understanding of the 'varieties of capitalism' (see Hall and Soskice 2001). Elite dominance of the economy and shadowy economic practice may sound familiar given the oligopolistic nature of markets and the corrupt nature of the state in Russia. However, in Tatarstan the process of price liberalization and privatization were done very differently from the rest of Russia. The shares-for-loans scheme did not reach Tatarstan, and local interests (mostly the local government), have managed to retain very large stakes in the key industrial enterprises of the region, such as Tatneft, the oil monopoly that is responsible for over 33 per cent of the Republic's GDP, the KamAZ truck plant and several MIC facilities. This raises an interesting situation regarding the range of possible outcomes for Russian capitalism given the enormous structural constraints place on it by the Soviet legacy.

An appreciation of the specific historical contingencies of Tatarstan's development since *glasnost* is crucial. However, Tatarstan's future also depends to a large extent on the broader Russian environment, and (less so) on the global condition. Political observers of the region often make reference to 'The Tatarstan model' (Khakimov 1999; Walker 1996; Bukhariev 1999). This refers to the limited sovereignty that the region enjoys, following a certain devolution of power from Moscow to the regions. Tatarstan's condition of partial sovereignty makes for an interesting case study. Analysing the political, social and economic configurations in contemporary times and in the recent past allows us to appreciate the diverse impacts of globalization, the reasons why the particular results of asymmetric globalization appeared, and what we can expect to see in the future.

As mentioned in the preceding chapters, globalization claims the following changes. It posits an integrated world market, with increasing development and interdependency, characterized by the rise of international interorganizational linkages (such as global strategic alliances, joint ventures and mergers and acquisitions) and a focus on greater strategic internationalization overseas (such as homogenized global branding; see Ritzer (2000)). The benefits and pitfalls of globalization, and the actual extent of it, are debated ad infinitum (see Frank 2000; Klein 2000; Monbiot 2001; Hutton and Giddens 2000), but most observers agree that globalization is, at the very least, a condition that states and firms are attempting to both stimulate and adapt to.

A key theoretical concept associated with globalization is disembedding – the notion that social systems (particularly transnational firms) become dislodged from their former housing in the nation-state. Gone are the days where a large firm would supply home-produced goods for a domestic market, operating under local laws and regulatory regimes. Whether one agrees that the loosening of national moorings is a welcome or unpleasant development for the world economy, it is rare that one finds material that contradicts this picture. Zygmunt Bauman, who is largely critical of globalization, is especially forceful in his argument that capital has completely deserted nation-state influence. While local restrictions on international capital flows are 'few and far between', Bauman claims that the few restrictions remaining are 'under tremendous pressure to be effaced or just washed out' (1998: 11). But there are several dissenting voices. Altvater and Mahnkopf, for example, are not convinced of the inevitability of disembedding:

> Globalization . . . meets its limits; globalism is never attainable. . . . In contrast to neo-liberal assumptions that more market means less state, market economizations produce an enormous demand for legal regulations. . . . [I]n the transitional economies of Eastern and Central Europe we hear the call for order, for contractual and legal security so that the private 'investors' can make their decisions under conditions of calculable 'risk'. . . . The pure disembedded market is thus a mirage.
>
> (Altvater and Mahnkopf 1997: 320–1)

Hence, far from ushering in a new world of free markets and world integration and its associated benefits and risks, globalization is also associated with increased diversity and complexity of organizational forms and local and regional power configurations. The postsocialist world is an ideal example of such a problematic. After decades of attempted reform within the context of near-total isolation from the Western world, a set of sudden convulsions in the period 1986–91 brought about the death of the Soviet system in a very short period of time. This collapse is described as proof that the inefficiencies of state socialism are impossible to solve (Lockwood 2000; Fukuyama 1992; Castells 2000c). The collapse of the Soviet Union, in theory, is therefore both a result of globalization, and a major contributor to it. In the post-1991 world it was expected that the regions behind the former Iron Curtain would soon be strongly embedded into a newly integrated world system.

But things did not turn out as planned. The postsocialist world is now capitalist, but in a peculiar form. It is connected to 'global capital', but not in the ways anticipated. This confusion reflects the way in which globalization theories are hotly contested. The debate between 'globalists, sceptics and transformationalists' is well-known (Held *et al.* 2000). But the nature of globalization is such that many other debates are continuing elsewhere. Cultural theorists talk of hybridization instead of (or at least alongside) imperialism and homogenization (Bhabha 1994; Hannerz 1992). In organization studies, debates revolve around issues of increasingly divergent firm operation, management structures, collective bargaining agreements and state-firm networks in different societies in the 'varieties of capitalism' literature (Hall and Soskice 2001; Whitley 1999; Katz and Darbyshire 2000; Maurice and Sorge 2000; Hollingsworth and Boyer 1997; Orru *et al.* 1997). It is not always easy to grasp why such differences take place. I would contend that genuine field observation is the best way to understand the true picture of societies in all their different forms. Theorizing the reasons for these differences is therefore the key purpose of such observation. In order to understand the importance of these systems in their unique typologies, it is useful to draw out the commonalities built into these formations. This can be done by considering the roles of action and structure in the region, something that will be attempted towards the end of the chapter.

The interplay between homogenization and heterogenization has to be accounted for with a combination of models. The mainstream, first wave radical model of globalization (see McCann, Chapter 1, this volume), can be thought of as akin to a 'nuclear fission' process. Globalization, conceptualized as a combination of transformative pressures (such as worldwide financial markets, IMF loans and their requisite reform packages, worldwide competition to reduce costs of production and distribution) impact on regions of the world, including national and regional governments, and the business organizations located on their territories. They are then forced to change in such ways that allow for an alignment of the localities with 'the global system' (Sklair 1995). This change then further impacts onto other levels and regions, much like a nuclear chain reaction. The pressures of the global system are continuously fired at nation states until the pressure forces them to split and to transmit the pressures onward to other states.

However, the nuclear fission model is only half of the story. It is too one-sided and reductionist to account for the continuing diversity of regions of the world. This is particularly true of Russia. Even as global pressures cracked open the Soviet Union in 1991, there were a multitude of diverse political actors that resisted change and managed to establish alternative forms of organization. The struggles over Tatar sovereignty at the political and organizational level contributed to different levels of embeddedness and marketization at the local level. Embeddedness and marketization work themselves out at different paces and in different ways (Candland and Sil 2001) in keeping with the varieties of capitalism approach. Hence Russian capitalism has something unique to offer world economics. It is not simply a case of Russia having to change all of its social systems in order to fit into global capitalism. It is also coming up with new forms of governance and embeddedness. These regimes operate simultaneously in different regions. Hence the 'patchwork' metaphor of Stark and Bruszt (1998), which supports the idea of globalization as a combination of external pressures which are met by diverse responses at local levels that never completely align themselves with the intended outcomes of 'transition'-inspired policies. Alongside this 'nuclear fission' model, we have the 'outward growth' model. Even as global pressures build on states and firms, states and firms also contribute new forms of governance and organization to the world. This is 'the structuration of globalization' (Hay and Marsh 2000: 7). Let us begin with a brief overview of Tatarstan's recent history and current prospects.

Introducing the Republic of Tatarstan

The Tatar economy is based heavily on the usual Soviet 'Category A' economy. The largest FSEs are all based in oil extraction, petrochemicals and other forms of heavy industry. Agriculture is largely self-sufficient, although expensive Western packaged foodstuffs are available to those who can afford them. As for the polity, Tatarstan has its own legislature and executive branches of government, including a President, Mintimir Shaimiev, who has been in post for nearly 12 years following the collapse of the Soviet Union. Tatarstan's government initially attempted something of a unilateral economic policy. It attempted to attract FDI and conduct 'foreign economic activity' via tax breaks and Free Economic Zones. However, despite highly favourable risk rankings (at least in Russian terms – Tatarstan was consistently rated between fourth and fifth out of the 89 regions of Russia in terms of low-risk climate by *Ekspert* magazine), what little FDI that was attracted tended to take the form of unsuccessful joint ventures that contributed little or nothing to either party. The Soviet-era plant of the key Tatar enterprises desperately requires updating, but foreign money and equipment is not forthcoming.

The high levels of governmental interference, lack of legal clarity, unfavourable geographic position and low levels of consumer savings, mean that Russian regions are generally not in the minds of Western investors. This helped to encourage a shift in the Republic's thinking. Instead of attempting to link itself directly into global capitalism and in doing so by-passing Moscow, a more measured policy of internally focused growth was pursued (Bukhariev 1999). A key part of this strategy was the so-called 'soft landing' approach, instead of shock therapy. There were no loans for shares in order to support Yeltsin's election, and privatization took place in slower fashion. Industry was subsidized by the local state, and the government retained significant ownership stakes of the large FSEs.

Therefore, the Tatarstan state appears to be running a neostatist economic policy. That is, due to deliberately incomplete disembedding processes, the state retains a considerable amount of managing and coordinating functions, and its regulatory role is limited. How does this relate to the debate on globalization? If the state remains a key economic player, does this mean that globalization is irrelevant to Tatarstan? This question will be developed further in the following sections, when the Tatar story is assessed in full.

Tatarstan is in the rather unique situation of being at once a state with its own legislative and executive branches of government, and a subject of the Russian Federation. It has a flag, a national anthem and two official languages (Tatar and Russian), but it has no army or no currency of its own. Its economy and polity suffer from all of the problems associated with Russian transition. However, the state also maintains a strong presence in the Republican economy. This means that the phrase 'the role of the state' is confused. The Tatar state is both strong and weak. It is weak in its tax-collecting and regulation roles. But it is strong in terms of an informal, steering capacity. The state provides a crucial part of the institutional environment in which Russian enterprises and joint ventures with Western capital operate.

Amid the fallout of August 1998, the phrase 'a return to state control' was frequently heard (Gustafson 1999 is just one example). This took place in a limited fashion in some enterprises across Russia, without ever coming close to a bona fide retreat from general attempts to establish Western-style markets. With continuing high oil prices (Akerman, Chapter 6, this volume) a handful of giant Russian energy companies have managed to develop themselves into enormously strong positions (Schwartz, Chapter 4, this volume). For these organizations, the idea of increased state control makes little sense, as their sheer financial power makes a mockery of the idea. In Tatarstan, however, the largest enterprises remain inherently connected to the local state apparatus.

It has become a cliché to note that 1991 meant the 'triumph' of 'neoliberal ideology' over 'socialist ideology'. With the end of state planning and the new Russia's commitment to building democracy and Westernized economic systems, markets were hailed as the most efficient form available for organizing societies (Sakwa 1999). The death of the Soviet Union took place at a time when neoclassical economics was at the pinnacle of its influence on governments and central banks. The ideas that inspired the shock therapy reforms described in Chapter 2 of this volume were products of a unique time. Of course, in reality all economies are mixed economies, and always have been. The public sectors of all economies are substantial. In the United Kingdom, for example, despite years of privatization and public sector reforms, public sector expenditure has remained at 30–40 per cent of nominal GDP since the Second World War.[1]

A main argument in Western liberal circles is that there is a major absence of effective 'governance' in Russia. According to this view the state needs to rebuild itself along democratic lines. The 'rule of law' is patchy at best, tax collection is a major problem, education and medical services are collapsing, and the governmental bureaucracies, police and armed forces are in corrupt disarray. On the other hand, the state still has some strong steering connections with the economy and the media.

This chapter suggests that the role (both official and unofficial) of the local state is crucial in managing and steering the region's economy. Despite the rhetoric and imagery of globalism being ever-present, there is little evidence of economic forms 'disembedding' themselves from the local and relocating themselves into 'global flows' of investment and partnership. Instead we see a complex system of state management networks that really run the economy, as opposed to the networks of capital and expertise that are supposedly paradigmatic of an effective economy and polity.

As the Communist Party disintegrated in 1991, those in charge of the planning ministries fled the scene, taking whatever political and economic resources they could manage. Theoretically speaking, this should have liberated the giant enterprises from state control, freeing their supposedly innate entrepreneurial ability to reform, seek new markets and innovate. In short, to act like 'normal' business units. However, the absence of the Plan and Party also meant an absence of cash. In this situation, the IMF-inspired rapid reform policies served to impoverish the economy, without creating an impetus to reform organizational dynamics, the labour process or managerial hierarchies. This has resulted in the emergence of a bizarre postsocialist hybrid economy (Gustafson 1999). 'Free market growth' in Russia in 1996–7 was illusory. With hindsight, the problems that led to the financial crash in 1998 had been set in motion with the rapid reform policies of 1992.

The Party and the planning and supply agencies have gone forever. But much of the managerial personnel remains in place. Perhaps more importantly, the physical organizational networks of the socialist economy are still vital to the Russian regions. It is logical for these to be maintained, instead of dismantled according to 'market solutions'. Following the 1998 crash, a large proportion of the labour unions, management and personnel remain in place (Schwartz 2003a). Tatarstan's economy shares the highly politicized nature of other 'late-industrializing countries' (see Candland and Sil 2001).

Despite the debates over the need to develop institutions along with markets, 'free markets' are still overwhelmingly regarded as the best possible means of creating wealth and 'economic equilibrium'. The problem is that economists have become too accustomed to Western-style economies.

They are unused to barter economies, functioning yet bankrupt FSEs, and non-functioning legal spheres (Nekipelov 2000). 'It is therefore the initial theoretical assumptions [of neoliberalism] that are faulty' (Sapir 2000: 489).

There has been something of a backlash against neoliberalism, partly as a response to poor macroeconomic performance in most of the world's regions (with China the obvious exception) since 2000. The 1997 Asian crisis, 1998 Russian crisis, 2002 Argentinian crisis and sluggish growth in the European Union, United States and Oceania have caused much heartache among neoliberals and their critics alike, with both ends of the spectrum calling for capital controls, a 'Tobin Tax', or a general strategic rethink of the policies of the IMF and the IBRD (Gray 1998; Soros 2002; Hutton 2002; Stiglitz 2002). But the market remains the principal organizing paradigm around which contemporary societies are meant to orient themselves.

Tatarstan's strategy, however, continues to emphasize state power. This strategy was formed out of a number of interesting political conditions. Of paramount importance at the time was the objective of establishing and retaining local ownership and control of the Republican enterprises. Both local and Russian political leaders believed that a great deal was at stake politically. There were even rumours of military pressure being threatened.[2]

It was in this context of opposition to the Federal state that the 'soft landing' approach to marketization took place. It was severely criticized at the time by many observers, as representing an 'island of communism' (see Bukhariev 1999). But, following the financial crash of 1998, slower reform strategies are now much more likely to be considered effective by intuitionalists and the now less aggressive neoliberals.

With the FSEs facing numerous challenges, small and medium-sized enterprises (SMEs) may become more important to the regional Russian economy. SMEs have large potential profit margins because of low competition and growing demand. The problems SMEs face are different from those faced by FSEs. They are threatened by the all-encompassing regime of gang crime and protection rackets, and face difficulties arising from a poorly enforced and unclear tax regime, bureaucratic obstruction and confusion. Bribery of government officials is also an essential practice in order to register a new company. Let us examine Tatarstan in more detail and describe the interplay between market and state.

Tatarstan and globalization

Tatarstan was fortunate in that it managed to avoid some of the worst excesses and shocks of the headlong Russian post-1991 reform programme. However, it is still largely unable to attract major foreign capital, nor is it particularly expecting to do so. Its strategy of neostatism has allowed an impressive recovery and stabilization. However, it has so far failed to lead to any major reforms or innovations that might lead to improvements in the market value of the companies. Two of the largest Tatar companies are Tatneft, the oil monopoly at Almetevsk, and KamAZ, the giant truck manufacturer located in Naberizhnii Chelnye. Let us examine these two cases in more detail.

Tatneft is the fourth largest oil company in Russia by production volume, producing half a million barrels a day, with 6.5 billion barrels of oil reserves. However, as an example of a company controlled by vested local government interests, its market capitalization is tiny compared to its Russian competitors. It takes the classical modernist organizational form of a giant pyramid with a huge number of subordinates. The chairman of the board of directors is the Prime Minister of Tatarstan, Rustam Minnekhanov. Tatneft is fundamentally important to the health of the Republic's economy.

The KamAZ truck plant at Naberizhnii Chelnye began production in 1976. It is an enormous, city-forming enterprise that was unfortunate to come on stream just as the Soviet economy began to stumble under Brezhnev. This meant that the enormous costs in labour and personnel vastly outweighed the benefits of establishing the plant (along with an enormous social-sphere infrastructure for its workers and the citizens of the newly built Chelnye). The basic KamAZ model remains largely unchanged since the 1970s, and its noisy and dirty engines do not meet European environmental protection standards. Until the company can get around this situation (attempting to construct new engines at great expense that they largely cannot afford or to import Western replacement engines), KamAZ's customers will remain almost exclusively within Russia and the CIS. Besides, heavy automotive export markets tend to be dominated by higher quality competitors such as Iveco (Fiat), GM, Scania, Mercedes Benz and Isuzu. KamAZ sales nevertheless compare favourably with its Russian competitors in truck manufacturing, such as UAZ and GAZ.

Following the disasters of 1998 and several major restructuring efforts involving the Tatar and Russian state buying large amounts of shares, the ownership of this company has been transformed. The Russian Federal government owns 33.49 per cent of KamAZ's shares, and the Tatar Ministry of Finance owns the remaining 12.39 per cent (KamAZ 1999: 10–13). Sales of the basic KamAZ HGV fell to just 3,273 units in 1998. It has recovered to 22,153 units in 2000, representing 48.3 per cent of Russian market share. Only 7 per cent of the sales are overseas.[3]

KamAZ lost as many as 91,901 employees between 1989 and July 2001 in desperate moves to slash costs.[4] However, in order to survive, cost cutting is necessary, but not sufficient. The need to buy new equipment is absolutely fundamental. The industrial plant should have been retooled in the 1980s. State subsidies protect and incubate the plant, but they tend not to help the plant develop and transform itself. Here again, Tatar neostatism has potential, but is limited in its approach. Tatneft cannot afford to rely only on sales, it must attempt a more diverse approach. It has to embrace a changing world environment, and a changing Russian environment. If it is to hold off the advances of Rosneft, Slavneft, Yukos, Sibneft and the others, it has to offer substantial improvements in its export quality, backed up by larger proven reserves. Exploration and refining are the twin goals it should attempt to pursue. The elites of Tatarstan's economy are (perhaps rightly) fearful of the threat of takeover of their oil reserves by the recent highly aggressive merger and acquisition activity of these massively rich Russian enterprises that were sold to the Russian financial-industrial groups (FIGs) at knock-down prices (see Bedirhanoğlu, Chapter 2, this volume).

As for the other major industrial enterprises, such as Nizhnekamskneftekhim (chemicals), Orgsyntsz (chemicals), Melita (furs), KMIZ (medical instruments), OMZ (optics), KAPO *imeni Gorbunova* (civilian aircraft), Tupolev (civilian and military aircraft) and Kazan Helicopters, they continue to be subsidized by the Tatar government while they desperately attempt to find new customers and create new products. But very little has been done to change the managerial and productive systems of any of these large enterprises. The same is true for the vast majority of Russian FSEs across the Federation (Schwartz, Chapter 4, this volume; Kotkin 2001: 135). Real changes in managerial and organizational practices are negligible. It is more the case that the large monopolies have managed to amass large stocks of capital via external sales and are attempting aggressive takeovers of competitors.

Tatarstan is, so far, resisting them, instead relying on local state protection of industry. It would appear that the large Russian enterprises have managed to become powerful with limited restructuring and reform. So how far has Russian capitalism proceeded down the road of marketization and disembedding? Let us look at a simple model (Figure 9.1). The model is represented by a horizontal axis (production system) and a vertical axis (embedding mechanism). The position of each economy on the axis represents its proximity to the neoliberal goals of a disembedded economy (industry owned by private shareholders located anywhere in the world, not by the local state), and a production system oriented to the needs of free markets, not state planning.

According to transition theory, the state must retreat from managing the economy and become a monitoring system, developing such institutions as a central bank and effective corporate laws. It is not there to provide market coordination, nor to interfere with the general working of the economy. However the RSFSR contained several overlapping regimes of authority. The Tatar political apparatus was able to operate with some degree of autonomy during the chaotic period of the Soviet Union's dissolution. During this period the Tatar state managed to secure a degree of control over the local economy, and followed a slow reform process. Hence, the somewhat different position of Tatarstan in the model.

Here, the state has not retreated to a regulatory position. It is instead a key economic player all by itself. While this is good news for KamAZ and Tatneft, it spells difficulty for SMEs. De novo companies are more able to be marketized. FSEs are less willing and able to do this. But the regulation and protection that SMEs demand are extremely difficult to establish,

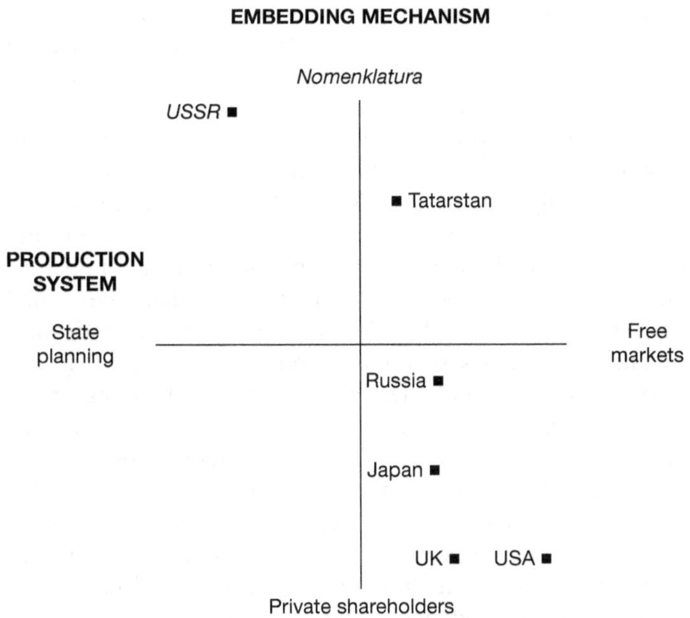

Figure 9.1 Embedding mechanisms and production systems of selected economies.

partly because the Tatar state is effectively in competition with SMEs. There is no political will to offer the same degree of insulation for SMEs as for FSEs.

This is why joint ventures (JVs) are a risk for both parties. The tried and trusted embedding mechanism of the former *nomenklatura* elites is threatened by the influx of Western shareholders. The Western shareholders for their part cannot understand the need to embed the system in the old-style networks. Foreign partners in JVs are inclined to view the situation as 'bureaucracy' and 'power games'. But these dense, politicized networks of influence, barter and exchange existed during the Soviet era as well. The continuation of the use of a similar embedding mechanism helps to explain the continuing bribery, corruption, bargaining, interorganizational debts and network ties to the state. The transition goal of imposing more marketization is extremely difficult to establish because all of the relevant actors are embedded into these a priori existing systems.

The transition goal is to move economies from the top left corner of this model over to the bottom right corner, across both the embedding mechanism and production system axes. So far the Russian economy has shifted across only one axis – production system. This has happened because of the sudden changes to the political sphere in 1992. With the abandonment of the Plan, suddenly Russian enterprises were forced to operate according to market principles, however unprepared for this they may have been. So Russia is located in the middle-right of this model. It has made significant progress down the embedding axis and good progress along the production system axis. Tatarstan has made less progress down towards the goal of disembedding. Tatar enterprises are perhaps even less marketized, as the state is still a large actor and economic coordinator. The state is no longer providing plans and targets, but it is helping to insulate Tatar FSEs from aggressive takeovers. It is also working with local firms to help ameliorate the everyday problems of postsocialism (such as the slum clearance and housing construction programmes, which include participation from a number of Tatneft subsidiaries). The advanced Western economies of Japan, the United States and the United Kingdom are included on the model for comparison.

Hence, Altvater and Mahnkopf's scepticism about the reality of disembedding appears to be correct. Globalization, at least in this region, is best understood as a common set of pressures that impact on diverse regions in different ways. Hence, the collapse of the Soviet system (a major result of, and contributor to, globalization) has not led to uniform change in the governance of the political economy of the regions. In other words, state planning of the economy has disappeared, but the different ways in which the immediate post-Soviet transformation took place led to diverse outcomes in terms of regional embeddedness and marketization, *even within Russia itself.*

If we look at this evidence, it seems that the model of globalization as 'nuclear fission' cannot function effectively as an explainer of Russian regional market development. Instead, the outward growth model seems more accurate. Elements of both exist, but the overwhelming path appears set on the outward growth model. We have capitalism 'Russian style', to go with East Asian, Central European and Anglo-Saxon capitalism. Russian capitalism should eventually be able to contribute to the world economy, but it is unlikely that international JVs in the short term will contribute effectively because of the different embedding mechanisms.

Instead, the Russian future seems to lie with the giant companies that wield enormous power – the oil, energy and metals companies. The key actors in these large enterprises have more power and agency than many sectors of the Russian state, as demonstrated in the continual battles between state and enterprises over non-payment of taxes and utility bills.

As for Tatarstan's own development, it does not have private companies of this size. Tatneft is comparable to a degree, but wields nothing of the trans-regional power of Yukos or Norisk Nickel. Instead, the regional power source lies more with the state. The Tatar state is frightened that its key enterprises will be acquired from outside, via a takeover from one of the Russian giants, or via investment from abroad. So the focus has shifted towards assisting and protecting these companies as much as possible. Much will depend on the behaviour of Shaimiev's successor. The residual state apparatus will still be a major player by virtue of the immense regional power of the established network ties. The Western literature's focus on free-floating concepts of markets and information, symbols and signs is not readily applicable to this region of Russia. The very strong level of local embeddedness of the Tatar economy tends to support the basis of the 'transformationalist', third wave view of globalization, but it does not support its background thesis of total global change and the growth of a globally interconnected, weightless economy. Tatarstan's wealth is not significantly embedded in global networks. Nor is it based on flows of information, or ICT. It remains rooted in the nineteenth century-style, Soviet 'Category A' economy.

Organization theory and Tatar enterprises

The Russian case seems to confirm the picture of the 'varieties of capitalism' literature (Maurice and Sorge 2000; Hall and Soskice 2001; Whitley 1999; Katz and Darbyshire 2000). The diversity and complexity of both Russian organizations and the Russian institutional environment militates against the successful application of 'one size fits all' reform measures. There is little work available that describes how organizations change in a situation of extensive institutional change. This is a major problem for any theory which attempts to assign explanatory power to human action or to social structure. An institutional economics approach to Russia would seem a better approach than a neoclassical one, but still major problems arise. How do we account for why some organizations have survived and some have not? Why is organizational change more extensive in some sectors than in others?

I have attempted to show how understanding the role of the local state in Tatarstan helps us to explain some other organizational situations. The level of embeddedness explains much of the individual organizations' strategies. The interests of large scale FSEs are often closely connected with those of the state. FSE senior management is usually made up of former apparatchiks who had regular contact with the state in Soviet times and continue to do so today. Furthermore, Tatneft and KamAZ *literally share some of the same people*. As we have seen, Tatneft's board of directors is chaired by a senior politician. The chairmen of KamAZ, Tatneft, the Nizhnekamsk oil and chemical facility, and the other major industrial organizations are all well-known public figures who share regular contact with senior Kazan government officials.

SMEs, on the other hand, have very few meaningful ties to the state. In many ways, they have none (taxes are not paid, registrations are difficult to establish). This is why the state is at once strong and weak. The Tatar state has maintained many of its overseeing, 'managing' roles, but has developed few 'regulatory roles'.

Russia is supposedly in the midst of bewildering and totalizing processes of global change. In reality, this change can be rapid or slow in different times and in different sectors, and can be partial and often contradictory.

In the words of Stark and Bruszt (1998: 117), 'Change, even fundamental change, of the social world is not the passage from one order to another, but rearrangements in the patterns of how multiple orders are interwoven.' As with the socialist revolution in 1917, social change did not happen overnight. Indeed it took many years to establish the communist system, and the experience of communism did differ to some extent across the Soviet Union's regions.

The Russian economy is indeed a patchwork of 'interwoven multiple orders' (Stark and Bruszt 1998). The remnants of the old Soviet-style economy face profound difficulties, but are politically vital to the persistence of the regional economy. The newer, more dynamic economy (based to some extent on services and information technology) remains small, and is often untaxed and unregulated. There can be major conflicts of interests between the old Soviet-style economy and the new SME sector. SMEs are in part prone to failure because of barriers to market entry set up by FSEs' inter-organizational ties. For their part, FSEs complain of the unregulated and untaxed operations of SMEs. These conflicts are the result of clashing operation strategies based on different levels of embeddedness. FSEs are highly embedded in local elite networks. SMEs are not so fortunate.

Tatarstan's core enterprises do not so much run on the strength of weak ties (Granovetter 1973), or on structural holes (Burt 1993). The borders between these organizations are somewhat impermeable, except for the extension of personal network ties (McCann 2000, forthcoming 2004: chapter 5). According to institutional theory '[p]ermeable boundaries enable radical change because of the availability of new archetypal solutions' (Greenwood and Hinings 1996: 1030). Again this makes more sense to the developed market economy world than to the 'transition' world. It does not take into account the history of embedding and disembedding, and how the role of the state develops over time. Key actors in regions in Tatarstan operate within a social structure that is radically different from the disembedded markets we have become accustomed to in the Western world since the 1970s.

In other words, Tatar capitalism is more about 'clan' than market (Ouchi 1980). Individual power players have the agency, and the key 'positioning' (see Giddens 1986). Having established the concepts of embedded capitalism and clan power in Tatar development, how can we then locate this discussion within the globalization literature? How can we explain why Tatarstan is operating a rather unique form of embedded capitalism? It is not the case that different regions operate in a vacuum, selecting their own development strategies. Russian regions are interconnected through all kinds of linkages. At a broader level, the Russian economy is also connected in some ways to global capitalism. Given this scenario we would expect less regional divergence. We cannot simply say that different regions have difference systems. A deeper level of explanation can be given. This can be done by examining the role of regional action and structure.

Understanding action and structure

The central question of Tatar embeddedness is as follows: 'To what extent was the Tatar model the result of intentional local policies or the inevitable result of inheriting a bankrupt economy of survival?' It could be argued that the 'soft landing' was simply an easy way for the local elites to maintain control over the region's assets in a monopolistic fashion. On the other hand the policy represents a failure to act. Yet another interpretation is that the problems of the inherited socialist economy meant that there were no alternatives and that inaction was inevitable. This issue raises the question of agency. Shaimiev is often credited as responsible for this effective policy (Bukhariev 1999; Galeev 1999). On the other hand, he and his immediate clan benefited enormously from maintaining their own power structures according to the principles of *nomenklatura* passive revolution (Bedirhanoğlu, Chapter 2, this volume). Shaimiev's electoral success is to some extent dependent on the absence of alternatives (Hutchison and Tegen 2001). It is widely noted that a presidential successor has already been informally selected, not unlike the Yeltsin–Putin power handover in 2000.

The answer, as far as the research presented here appears to show, is that Tatar development was likely to happen in this slower, embedded fashion. The preceding historical configuration certainly pointed in the direction of such a model. Tatarstan has exhibited several clear features since *glasnost*: uncertain, sometimes hostile relations with Russia (into which Tatarstan is landlocked), a legacy of heavy industry and oil extraction, a historically entrenched Tatar Soviet political elite and international isolation that militated against a large-scale FDI-based development leap. In short, Tatarstan possessed very limited economic agency, but plenty of political agency. This is why elite political actors were reluctant to set up free markets, and kept with what they know best – state ownership and steering.

Nothing is inevitable. It is just that certain configurations of socio-historical features create greater or lesser potentialities for the implementation and success of action. The inherited socialist economy lent itself to a persistence of Soviet-type organizational directions. 'Post-Communist Russia would inherit, and grandly privatize, history's largest ever assemblage of obsolete equipment' (Kotkin 2001: 17). Even though technically no longer in state hands, it is naïve to expect that 'the market' would find solutions for the further development and distribution of such worthless 'assets'. This is true for most of Russia, but Tatarstan had other options available, namely the partial continuation of *de facto*, if not *de jure* state control. This does not mean that it had to happen that way, it was just that this path is easiest and most relevant. It is the path of least resistance.

The Western concern with reform and the faith put in free markets reflects a very ethnocentric approach to what markets are. Markets are not necessarily disembedded systems. Given the nature of Tatarstan capital formation and the 'soft landing' it seems that a major divorce of the FSEs from the state apparatus is not forthcoming in the foreseeable future. Tatar capitalism is a particular regional version of the hybrid Russian capitalism that has emerged since 1991. This is because several different economic roads were taken by the Russian regions amid the political battles over the future of the Russian Federation during the Yeltsin era. Different regions' power apparatuses have varying reserves of agency and are located within diverse social structures.

This answer leads us to the conclusion and tentative predictions. A central problem with postsocialist studies is that there are so far no overarching theories that can help us to understand and to integrate the experiences of Russian regional socio-economics. It is hoped that a brief review of Tatarstan within the context of the post-Soviet state versus market debate will shed some light on this issue, and may provide part of a building block towards a more integrative conceptual overview.

Conclusions and predictions

> [I]n the end, restructuring concepts, internationalisation strategies and international trade policies are the result of economic, political and social interaction, i.e. struggles and bargaining processes, and thus the object of social and political choice.
>
> (Ruigrok and van Tulder 1995: 7)

Rather than taking a more residual role as monitors and regulators, post-socialist state regimes can be critical actors in certain geographical areas. The 1998 Russian financial crash gave the Tatar 'soft landing' some political legitimacy. Tatarstan now needs to build some more effective regulatory institutions. This should take place alongside SMEs gradually legalizing themselves over time and generations. Having established these legal standards, however, the state cannot be expected to retreat from 'the market'.

Instead, we can expect to see the Tatar state remain firmly entrenched in FSEs' embedding mechanisms. A unique nexus of personal influence pervades the Russian system, and it is particularly important in the Tatarstan example. Given the nature of the expansion of the large monopolist energy and raw materials companies, we can expect to see a growing level of integration of the regions along monopolistic lines. Although this does not in any way represent a return to state socialism (or state capitalism depending on one's point of view), it does represent a logical progression away from the chaos of the Yeltsin era. The true strength of these giant companies is that they will operate with a similar scale and scope to that of Gosplan and Gossnab. The board of directors of these firms wield similarly political power as the former planning and supply bureaucracies of the pre-1991 age.

What of the Tatar FSEs mentioned in this chapter? We can expect the employee size of KamAZ and the other major industrial production enterprises to eventually shrink further. But, at the moment, labour hoarding is a similar Russia-wide feature. The firms must find new core competencies. KamAZ's products are not available on world markets. The aircraft manufacturers of Tatarstan face major problems. Passenger jet, fighter jet and helicopter markets are saturated by superior (if more expensive) products. The same goes for KamAZ. The domestic market is their only saviour, but for this to bear fruit they have to hope that Western competition from the likes of Iveco (Fiat), GM and Isuzu do not overwhelm them. Of course, Tatarstan itself has a healthy appetite for large-capacity KamAZ vehicles for the state rebuilding and rehousing schemes.

Tatar neostatism has proved to be an effective barrier to external Russian monopoly capitalism. But it has done this by maintaining the Tatar Soviet-style embedding mechanism. The question then arises of whether a state monopoly is preferable to a private monopoly. Given the institutional complexity and haziness of Russian firms and government agencies, the boundaries are often blurred. However, as far as Tatarstan is concerned, the political nature of Russian capitalism is once again highlighted. This confounds the attempts to use free market methods to build free market outcomes. Ultimately if state-embedded capitalism is to be a workable strategy for the future, we have to assume that the Tatar state will spend the oil money appropriately. Encouragingly, Tatneft, not unlike its feared Russian oil-giant competitors is currently making several strategic acquisitions in a multitude of sectors. Investment is the key. In a situation where FDI is not forthcoming, the Tatarstan state must be wise to the task of educating and re-educating its workforce. It must also be willing to spend on projects that will increase living standards. (The slum liquidation project is a worthy task in this regard.)

What of the Russian state itself? The same concentration on the importance of SMEs is crucial. But, with the size of the large oligarchic companies, an active state is less necessary. It shares the less welcome feature of endemic corruption and bribery. It is unlikely that anything constructive will be done to combat this problem. This supports the vision of Castells' 'rise of the fourth world' (2000a: 68–168). The various apparatuses of the Russian federal and local states are capable of managing some areas of their economic affairs. They are less able to deal with other, more pernicious effects. While issues of ownership and control are complex and contested, real change in the management of large-scale enterprises is generally absent throughout the Federation. The main difference between the large Russian oligarchic enterprises and Tatar FSEs is that the former have much larger amounts of capital, and so on a more general level they have more influence in the Russian economy at large. As such they are more likely to view governmental apparatuses as bureaucratic hindrances. Tatar enterprises are smaller and have less cash, and are more dependent on state patronage. This, in turn, protects them from takeover by the larger Russian enterprises.

The Tatar experience reminds us that under no circumstances do the effects of globalizing pressures result in homogenized regional economic practices.

There will always be outliers, as the outward growth model of globalization suggests. It is important to attempt to understand regional structures and agency if we are to predict how these regimes of embedding will be worked out over time. Whether these different forms of governance are able to result in economic growth and development for the long term remains an open question. For the time being, the Tatarstan model looks secure and can be expected to remain in place for some time to come. Its economic performance is comparable to other regions in the locality, but its large enterprises lack the resources of the Russian raw material giants. In this situation, it is logical for us to predict that the local Tatar state will continue its coordinating role over the local economy.

Notes

1 UK Office of National Statistics website (http://www.statistics.gov.uk).
2 It is debatable how serious this threat was. Some claim that Russia was on the edge of invading Tatarstan (Bukhariev 1999), others that the threats from the Kremlin were empty (Walker 1996).
3 http://www.kamaz.net.
4 Figures from author's interview with KamAZ financial director in Naberizhnii Chelnye, July 2001.

10 The development of post-Soviet neo-paternalism in two enterprises in Bashkortostan

How familial-type management moves firms and workers away from labor markets

Caleb Southworth

While many experts on market transition in Russia (Randolph 1994; Åslund 1995; Åslund 2002; Blasi *et al.* 1997; Boycko *et al.* 1995; Barberis *et al.* 1996; Shleifer and Vasiliev 1996) expected firms which were converted into joint-stock companies (*aktsionernoe obshchestvo*) to be governed by the profit motive and produce for the market, the situation in the first decade since large-scale private ownership was established is less than clear (Schwartz, Chapter 4, this volume). Many enterprises use family-like, paternalistic practices[1] in both the determination of what is produced and in their relationship with employees. There was a strong tradition of paternalism in Soviet industrial relations. This tradition has not been completely de-institutionalized by global market forces. Surviving paternalistic relationships with factory workers often include provision of housing subsidies, food, and garden space, typically through barter with municipalities and the firm's clients (Southworth 2001a; Lefèvre 2001). Paternalistic choices about what to produce and in what volume are commonly the result of the enterprise director's desire to maintain connections with clients, employees, and regional state officials.

This chapter describes the market situation in Russia during 1998, when the employees of many manufacturing enterprises, particularly those outside of Moscow, worked for long periods of time without being paid regular wages (Clarke 2002b; Earle and Sabirianova 2002; Dasn 1998). The empirical project involves ethnographic evidence from two Soviet-era brick factories in the Republic of Bashkortostan that were converted into private joint-stock companies. One of them, referred to as Red Brick in this chapter, is located in Ufa, the capital city of the Republic. The other, White Brick, is located in a provincial "workers' outpost" (*rabochye posyolok*) 200 kilometers to the south. The central questions are conceptual: How did directors in these firms hire, fire and discipline employees? How are the assets of such newly privatized enterprises invested? What sort of bookkeeping do these firms utilize?

Are they able to compute profits in the partly cash, partly barter economic environment? And what have been the results of the attempts to reform these organizations into firms that are more likely to succeed in globalized capitalism?

This chapter suggests that capitalism exists in a variety of forms. Max Weber argued that, while modern capitalism involves industrial production monitored with double-entry bookkeeping, the form of capitalist production in any given society varies widely (Weber 1981: 275). Some regions of an economy may be capitalistically organized, while others follow handicraft or manorial patterns. The analysis here of two Soviet-era industrial firms that were converted into private property in the early 1990s seems to support the notion of diversity of capitalist arrangements. While many social scientists (Åslund 1995; Boycko *et al.* 1995; Eyal *et al.* 1998; Blasi *et al.* 1997) have declared the expansion of product markets and the end of state planning a "transition to capitalist, market economy," actual practice in post-Soviet firms exhibits a mixture of forms. Moreover, it is difficult to conclude on the basis of the labor relations and profit calculation present inside post-Soviet enterprises that they are in a period of "transition" toward the sort of rational accounting, investment, and profit-making that Weber identified as the crucial components of Western capitalism.

To foreshadow the main point, I conclude that factory directors maintain a paternalistic relationship with their employees, one in which general responsibilities for workers' well-being is substituted for cash wages. This paternalism intercedes into the management of assets, frequently used as the director's personal wealth, and into the "calculation" of "profit" that occurs in an environment where cash prices are frequently absent and each worker's employment represents a subsidy to the firm rather than a cost.[2] This paternalism is not simply a continuation of the paternalistic practices of the Soviet state (Kornai 1980, 1986), where firms appealed to their specific production ministry for resources or to make up financial shortfalls. Such subsidies no longer exist. Instead, the locus of paternalism has shifted from between firm and ministry, to between firm and workforce.

Theories of capitalist management

In a capitalist economy, human needs are provided by enterprise, by private business seeking a profit; what Schumpeter called the "simple economic system, where economic activity goes on by private initiative for private profit" (1991: 300). For Weber, the ideal type of a capitalist economy was developed in contrast to economies where exchange was motivated by forced contributions or traditionally defined gifts or rituals. The extent of capitalist development in a given society was a matter of degree measured by the scope of legal-rational authority in governing private exchange for gain and the organization of labor within enterprises.

Within a firm, Weber outlined a set of conditions for "rationalized capitalism," which can be compared with the actual practices of the two factories in Bashkortostan. "[A] rational capitalistic establishment, is one with capital accounting, that is, an establishment which determines its income yielding power by calculation according to the methods of modern bookkeeping and the striking of a balance" (Weber 1981: 275; Collins 1980). Specifically, five factors were found to arise in a constellation creating the competitive dynamics of capitalism described by Marx. First, there must exist private appropriation of the means of production under the control of entrepreneurs:

> Land, buildings, machinery, and materials must all be assembled under a common management, so that decisions about their acquisition and use can be calculated with maximal efficiency. All these factors must be subject to sale as private goods on an open market.
>
> (Collins 1980: 928)

Many analysts believed this condition – the sale of the assets of the Soviet state, placing them in private hands – to be fundamental for creating a capitalist market economy. There is a double-edged tension with the private nature of assets and their control by entrepreneurs. That is, capital could be "privatized" without necessarily putting entrepreneurs in charge. This was a common occurrence in Russia during the 1990s. Likewise, state managers sometimes adopt an entrepreneurial spirit, attempting to expand market share and increase efficiency and profits. (This was observed even during the Soviet period, cf. Bettelheim 1975; Berliner 1957.)

The second factor in the complex of capitalist economic relations is industry's reliance on technology in production; this enables the calculation of value added and efficiency of many individual tasks in production. Collins notes that "mechanization is most significant for the organization of large-scale capitalism" (1980: 928). Seventy years of Soviet socialism mechanized industry, but did it leave manufacturing firms in the 1990s in a position to use mechanization for accounting?

Third, labor must be free and mobile. To have a functioning capitalist labor market, employees need to able and willing to switch jobs and geographic markets, and be compelled to participate in some kind of labor market, the stimulus behind job seeking. Fourth, trading on the market must not be restricted by irrational, non-economic limits on trade. Although trade is frequently regulated in capitalist societies, religious or traditional strictures cannot prevent the factory's output from being sold. Direct restriction on trade was not a problem faced by the management of the two brick factories. Finally, the most important factor in capitalist production is the calculation of profit and the reorganization of the factors of production based on profit calculations. These amount to the "commercialization of economic life," such that it is possible "to conduct the provision for needs exclusively on the basis of market opportunities and the calculation of net income" (Weber 1981: 277–8).

Factories typically have some authority regime in order to collectively organize production, create a division of labor, and distribute their product. The wage-labor contract, in which wages are exchanged for workers following orders during work hours on the factory grounds, is a common form in Western capitalism. Weber called the form of authority present with the conditions outlined above "legal-rational authority." Productive enterprises in antiquity have also been organized with traditional or patrimonial authority. Walder, in his study of China, identified the authority of the party-state in Chinese factories as neo-traditional because the party-state legitimated the authority of the director, replacing the "age-old rules" but keeping the personal loyalty to the organization and discretion of the superior that Weber argued was the basis for traditional authority (Walder 1986; Weber 1981: 226–7).

I argue that these two post-Soviet factories are run with "neo-paternalistic authority," a variant of traditional authority. The paternalistic relationship resembles that between parent and child, where the parent provides resources and the child is subject to family discipline in all areas of life. The relationship is semi-contractual in that workers are formally employed and voluntarily surrender control over their own actions. Unlike the authority of the entrepreneur over employee, the dominance of the paternalistic employer extends beyond the workplace into the household on a sustained and regular basis. Neo-paternalism resembles traditional authority in that the director exercises personal control, staff and personnel are loyal to the management, and financing of operations is in kind with irrational systems of law and taxation. Moreover, workers are not fully separated from the means of subsistence and have meaningful household production in addition to whatever goods and wages they receive from the firm. It is "neo" paternalism because paternalistic relations typically fade away as a competitive labor market develops, but here paternalism has arisen after the competitive labor market of the Soviet Union collapsed (cf. Granick 1987). The case of Bashkir labor markets illustrates how supposedly "global" capitalism operates in different ways in different regions. Indeed, if globalization is to be considered a process of change, it must be said that it impacts differentially on societies and regions because of important differences in previously existing institutional arrangements.

Data and methods

This study is a comparison of ethnographic data on two cases – two different Bashkortostan brick factories. The goal is to interrogate each case to develop concepts for the analysis of market behavior in a postsocialist society and to compare variation between the two enterprises in order to show causal connections. It is not the intention of this chapter to generalize from the contextual information from my observations and interviews in each plant, nor the differences between the firms. Much more can be learned from detailed information on a small number of cases by comparing the strong assertions from economic and sociological theories of capitalist development to conditions which *must be present.*

I spent one month in each factory during the summer of 1998. In one factory, I performed a menial job; in the other, I was permitted to spend unlimited time in the mechanical section of the plant and tour others, although I was not employed. I talked informally with workers from all sections of both firms and took field notes each evening. Once I had an outline picture of the situation, I interviewed the director or his deputy on the economic environment and their business plan. Because I had a month to conduct such interviews, I could cross-check the stories of both employees and management. This meant, for example, that when the director told me that employees always received payment in full (*polnyi raschet*), implying cash wages each month, I was able to ask why the workers of specific sections claimed only to have been paid in goods (*natural'nyi obmen*). The director then elaborated his story and said that the firm accounted for products and goods paid in kind as though they were cash (*zaima za chyot*). This highlights a strength of intensive interviews with few firms as opposed to a greater number of interviews: while a larger set of interviews can assess the frequency of a specific relationship, it is extremely difficult to validate the information received (Burawoy 1991).

These two firms are part of a larger study of six enterprises in Bashkortostan (Southworth 2001b). The central questions of that study are: What sort of authority relationship has replaced the organizing role of the party and state planning ministries within post-Soviet factories? How are relations between managers and workers structured so that enterprises can produce? How do authority relations secure a workforce for the firm? The intent was to ascertain why workers labor and why firms produce in the economic crisis of the late 1990s in Russia.

Although these data come from observations on only two firms, each enterprise contains many sets of relationships, i.e. between firm and employees of different types, between director and resellers, between firm and clients, etc. Each of these can take on a more or less capitalistic, calculating, or entrepreneurial character. Analysis of a particular complex of these relationships against the backdrop of the ideal type of capitalist development illuminates commonalities in the economic behavior of Russian enterprises and those in other historical situations. This is an alternative to the assumption that Russia is indeed experiencing a capitalist development, albeit of particular form.

The economic situation in Bashkortostan, 1998

The factories described here are located in the Russian Republic of Bashkortostan, located in the eastern Urals; it is the easternmost edge of the

European part of Russia. The republic has its own government, which negotiates the flow of resources through taxes and federally funded projects with Moscow. The Republican government is substantially independent from Moscow and has had strong political disagreements with the federal government over elections, the broadcast content of ORT (the state television channel), and the amount of taxes owed by various large firms in the region.

Ufa is the cultural, political, and economic center of the Republic and is the only city with greater than one million population (1,080,003 in 1997). Industrialization began in 1922 with the construction of a large motor plant which produced engines for Soviet cars and military vehicles. In that year the republic was proclaimed the Bashkirian Autonomous Soviet Socialist Republic (*Aftonomnyi Sovetskii Sotsiolisticheskii Respublik*, or ASSR), a status with greater independence and local governmental power than an *oblast'* (administrative region), but less significant than an Independent Republic (*Nezavisimyi Sovetskii Sotsiolisticheskii Respublik*) such as Kazakhstan. Within the next five years, oil was discovered in Bashkiria and development began of what would become a large oil refining and chemical industry. By the time of World War II, Ufa was already a large industrial center; the Soviet government moved many strategic military industries to the republic to keep them away from the front lines. Ufa became a "closed city," to which foreigners were prohibited from traveling for security reasons.

As the focal point of railroads, highways, and airplane routes to the region, Ufa quickly experienced the opening of the Soviet markets in the early 1990s. Diverse stores and kiosks have opened in the city and the central market now teems with imported goods and foodstuffs from all over the former Soviet Union and abroad. For those who can afford it, as of 1998 Ufa has supermarket shopping – where, as in the West, all manner of groceries are for sale in one store where the customer selects them, instead of several stores where the clerks control the inventory (the Soviet-era norm). The labor market, however, has experienced a decline over the last five years and the number of unemployed has increased. Unemployment has climbed dramatically while the population of the city has declined. In the capital, unemployment increased from 2.5 percent in 1996 to 14.7 percent in June 1998. Joblessness, combined with the growing wage delays, particularly in heavy industry and education, meant that many of the citizens of Ufa did not enjoy the fruits of the new commerce. Workers with jobs have a strong incentive to remain employed regardless of working conditions and pay.

The ethnic makeup of the territory is approximately 22 percent Bashkir, 27 percent Tatar, 39 percent Russian, and residual other ethnicities. Bashkir is the titular nationality and with recent reforms the second official government language. Being a native speaker of Bashkir is a formal requirement for the presidency.

In factories, most work, food preparation, negotiation of benefits from foodstuff to free cigarettes, and particularly swearing, is done in Russian. Tatar and Bashkir workers occasionally use a mix of these Turkic languages and Russian amongst themselves, but switch to Russian in the presence of Russian speakers. It is more common for ethnic managers and directors to use Bashkir or Tatar (which are mutually intelligible) to make trade deals and cut Russian speakers out of conversations held in their offices. There is also a tension between the two groups: historically, Tatars were urban and Bashkirs rural. The Soviets created a written language for Bashkirs, something that did not exist before the revolution, in an effort to keep Bashkiria and Tatarstan separate. While this leads to many jokes on the shop floor about the arrival of a "wild Tatar" (a Bashkir), there is no noticeable ethnic animosity or prejudice in the allocation of tasks or conduct in the workplace. Within the cities and towns, Bashkir, Tatar, and Russian peoples are not residentially segregated; friendships and marriages commonly cross ethnic lines and different ethnic groups interact together in the market and at work.

At present, Bashkirian gas and oil are nearly exhausted and the republic imports oil for refinement. Timber, agriculture, construction materials, and auto manufacturing are other important industries in Bashkortostan. The republic has strong export links to other Russian republics and is ranked fifth in overall goods and services produced in 1997.

With the spring thaw in May and the first snows in November, Bashkortostan has a long growing season, compared to northern areas of Russia, and most cities and factories have municipal gardens for their workers. These are plots of approximately half an acre which workers can use as they please. While rural land has not been privatized – it is technically leased from the municipality – plots can be easily bought and sold and often remain in families for generations.

Comparison of work and finance in two brick factories

This section describes the nature of private ownership, technology in production, profit calculation, and labor markets in both factories. The two enterprises are discussed together because, although they differ in crucial respects highlighted in the next section, they exhibit a common pattern of market averse behavior and reliance on barter.

The Red Brick Factory's main product is red, reinforced bricks. These are high-strength building materials for the construction of multi-story buildings. The firm has a sideline in bat and board insulation, but lack of raw materials often closes this section. It is located in a small town with chemical and gas refining about 200 km from Ufa. Managers own 7 percent of the stock; workers, 28 percent; and a state holding company, 65 percent. The economic situation at the firm is cashless but stable. There are substantial payments in kind despite wage delays of around three years, and employment is stable at around 600 workers on three shifts.

The White Brick Factory produces, likewise, red bricks for general construction, reinforced red bricks for foundations and tall buildings, and ceramic white bricks for facades. It is located in a large city with many construction firms and substantial housing construction, the main market for its products. Five percent of its stock is owned by management; 38 percent by workers; and 57 percent by a state holding company. The economic situation at this factory is troubled: wage delays are over two and a half years, management has difficulty making payments on worker housing, and they often lack the money to purchase raw materials or gasoline for deliveries. Employment here has declined over the last five years from 840 to 720 in 1998.

Privatization, the conversion of state-owned enterprises into joint-stock companies, occurred at both firms during 1994. Stock was distributed to employees through a voucher system with all current employees receiving a fixed number of shares and an additional number proportionate to the number of years worked. Management received additional shares. According to the workers and managers at both plants, there was an initial period of interest in trading or selling the stock, and a small dividend amounting to a few dollars for the average worker was paid in the next year. After that time no further dividends were paid. The transfer of stock is also strictly limited by the director who holds the registration book in his office safe. Without the director's permission, stock cannot be transferred or sold.

Both firms underline the distinction between a *privately held, joint-stock company* of the sort created by privatization programs in Russia and *private property*, meaning property in the hands of entrepreneurially minded individuals. Privatization created the legal infrastructure for the existence of private ownership. Many former state companies were transferred into private hands. An even greater number of small businesses were created by entrepreneurs. It would be a mistake, however, to equate the creation of the legal form of OAO and ZAO[3] with the expansion of private capital per se. Further evidence is required. In line with the classical concepts of Weber (1981) and the later writings of the New Economic Sociology authors (such as Granovetter 1985; Hall and Soskice 2001) there is a variety of types of ownership within diverse forms of capitalism.

Another salient difference between the conversion of state socialist enterprises into joint stock companies and the creation of public corporations from privately held ones in Western capitalism is capitalization. In Western capitalism, the creation of a joint-stock company takes place either through an initial purchase of stock or through the organization of bank or venture capital into a new public enterprise. Both involve substantial cash transfer or investment: the previous owners of a firm "going public" are paid for their interest or stock; the management of a newly created public firm receive start-up capital from banks, venture capitalists, or other investors.

According to their directors and the head of the state holding company with a majority interest in both firms, neither Red Brick nor White Brick received any investment at the time of their privatization. The stock was literally given away to the employees. Privatization did not result in new capital for the firm, meaningful profit sharing, or any important legal indemnity for the new owners – all of which are important rationales for creating joint-stock companies in Western capitalist economies. This fact highlights the *political* nature of postsocialist ownership transformation (see Bedirhanoğlu, Chapter 2, this volume). Privatization has been forced onto these enterprises, rather than being done out of the choice of senior management, as we might expect to be the case in the West, where companies frequently embark on internal transformations and innovations in order to keep up with competition or cut costs.

Given this peculiar path of reform, one might reasonably ask: Did the brick factories undergo a restructuring of their assets as a result of privatization? Substantial restructuring did occur between privatization and my observations during 1998. During this period, Red Brick turned the apartment buildings housing the majority of its workforce, and which had been constructed under the firm's direction since World War II, over to the municipality. Both enterprises had also curtailed health care, educational, child care, and vacation benefits they formerly provided their workers. While the director made such adjustments based on an assessment of the resources available, such decisions were not the sort of rational calculation linked to opportunities to produce profits in the relevant commodity markets. Instead, the director at Red Brick, for example, cut vacation benefits – the factory formerly paid for workers' month-long visits to a holiday resort – because the factory could no longer pay and was unable to strike a barter deal with the resort's director. Other cuts, such as the transfer of apartment buildings or elimination of a day care center, were at the direction of the state holding company and followed the economic fads of the day. These were not cuts made by an entrepreneur in an effort to improve the efficiency of the firm or lower labor costs. Both directors expressed regret at the turnover of these assets and suggested that "if it were possible" they would like the firm to provide such services as a way of retaining employees. It is only through planning in relation to measured efficiency and market prices that such actions take on the legal-rational authority Weber identified with the private property owner in the West.

Decisions made within the firm do not follow the pattern of stock ownership. The director makes all decisions within the firm and his word is final. There is a general director of the state holding company and majority stock holder. The general director hires and fires the directors of the firms in which the state holds stock; but he cannot challenge the individual decisions of the director. Interestingly, despite holding approximately one-third of the stock and being nearly 100 percent unionized, workers have no voice in decisions and cannot attend or vote in shareholders' meetings held at the state holding company. Workers at both plants reported that anyone who made trouble, either through the union or through the courts, would be shown the door, even if they were successful in pressing one particular grievance. Workers filing suits for back wages was fairly common among employees who had left the firm or been fired.

Calculation is perhaps the most important factor considered here. The directors of both firms said that a higher volume of output was better and more profitable. They were disappointed with declines in production in recent years. The changes in production cannot be said to result from planning or reaction to market forces or profit opportunities on the part of the management. The expectation of many experts was that, with the sell off of state firms, quantity and quality of output would be altered in response to effective demand. The problem with this proposition, however, is the same for the analyst as it is for the directors if they want to adjust output to demand: in the Russian economic environment of 1998, the demand for goods such as bricks is undefined. Demand is the relationship between the quantity of a commodity that buyers wish to purchase per period of time and the price of that commodity. The difficulty in this calculation begins with the absence of a cash price. Goods are given nominal prices in roubles in a given barter exchange, but the value of those roubles is unclear.

Hyperinflation and massive currency devaluations complicate all financial calculations. During the currency devaluations of August 1998, the value of the rouble fell by a factor of four in four days. How much it fell varied by region. Moreover, directors at the firms I visited did not adjust their prices in response, as the prices were based on the cost of production plus a percentage "profit." The cost of production was met through barter, and commodities obtained in this way were used to reimburse the workforce and suppliers. But inflation alone was not the most serious impediment to calculation.

How did the sale of bricks and construction materials occur? One route involved the firm seeking buyers or clients. The marketing department faxed its price list to construction firms. The director drove personally to cities all over Bashkortostan three to four days a week, meeting private construction companies and state ministries with large building projects. Of this trade, which constituted the vast majority of the brick factory's output, 80 percent was conducted in barter for other goods. Quantities of goods to be exchanged are often assigned a nominal rouble or even dollar value. The directors of both firms said that they would prefer to calculate prices based on the nominal values of their inputs (also priced similarly) plus a fixed percentage profit. Before privatization, the firms marked up their products 20 percent over the cost and distributed them according to a marketing plan. In the negotiations with clients that I witnessed, it was clear that the buyers knew that the factory had to barter and that the nominal cost-plus-20-percent price was just a starting point. In a context where the market offered clear prices for substitute goods or the same goods from other suppliers, prices would be set relative to the money values of other goods. But, just as the factory's inputs were largely valued in barter in the economic environment of the late 1990s, so was the vast majority of other goods. Some key goods, such as electricity, had no real price in Bashkiria at this time. They were obtained by industry on a barter basis and only in extremely rare circumstances would a major productive enterprise be cut off. Many bankrupt firms made some attempt to deliver goods to municipal electric stations and received power without having paid their bills for more than a year. In short, when the cash price of the most important inputs is missing, materials such as bricks cannot be assigned a market price either through assessment of the cost of production nor through comparison to the price of other goods on the market.

In bookkeeping terms, no number can be entered into the debit column of a sale because the sale is not banked. Likewise, what figure should be credited to the sales account is not fixed by money changing hands. These goods can be valued in nominal roubles, but the value assigned could differ by an order of magnitude. With price undefined, a trial balance of the type Weber envisioned in the calculation of profit is impossible. The figures used to arrive at the balance would be entirely arbitrary.

The missing commodity price is only half of the problem, as the price of labor is also undefined, and possibly even negative. A negative price for labor would mean that each additional worker represented a subsidy to the firm. What sort of wages do workers receive? Workers had not received regular cash wages at Red Brick in three years and at White Brick in two and a half years. They were issued a receipt on pay day that indicated their pay in nominal 1996 roubles, not indexed to the rate of inflation. They could take food stuffs, housewares, clothing, and other goods from the company store. The costs for these items, obtained by the factory through barter, were deducted from their balance. Management also took responsibility for other bills, such as lights, gas, and maintenance, on their employees' apartments. The firm bartered with the municipality and utility companies to pay these expenses.

The price of labor has no clear monetary value. What is more, the *otel' kadrov* (personnel department) of both enterprises was actively trying to hire particularly skilled laborers. Directors and their marketing departments in these firms both wanted to produce the largest volume of output possible. Adding additional workers gave them more resources to operate the plant closer to its capacity. While there were no cash wages, and management did complain about the constant trading necessitated by paying in kind, mid-level managers, such as the *master tsekha* (or director of the company store), said that the firm had no difficulty providing in-kind payments to additional workers.

Whereas the exploitation of wage labor for Marx was predicated upon the conversion of money into capital and back into money with the realization on the sale of the product (M – C – M′), here there is no such conversion. Wage labor involves exploitation in Marx's theory because the value realized through the sale of the commodities greatly exceeds the value in wages (and other inputs) used in production. In the non-monetary environment of post-Soviet industry of the late 1990s, the workforce effectively advances the firm a subsidy by working without cash payment and in exchange for fewer bricks (in barter) than they produce on the assembly line.

This difference alters the entire authority relationship between managers and employees in the firm.

Weber saw calculation as the most important consequence of the use of money. In a money economy, "goods are more or less systematically compared, whether for consumption or for production, with all potential future opportunities of utilization or of gaining a return, including their possible utility to an indefinite number of other persons" (1968: 81).

The equipment used to produce bricks at both Red Brick and White Brick dated from the 1950s, with some of the electric trolleys for loading the bricks in ovens, and milling machines for making metal components, dating to the 1970s. Both factories had assembly lines for the different products and separate sections or buildings for a machine shop, an electrical shop, a garage, a mixing area, drying ovens, and a loading yard. White Brick, with a similar but slightly more modern line for producing construction bricks, had a single mixer and former that deposited wet clay bricks onto metal trays, which were then rolled by hand on a conveyer and put into a cart that would be mechanically loaded into a gas oven. The foreman of the section knew the counts of bricks per shift and the frequency with which the machinery broke down and idled his crew. Likewise, the clay mixture of metal, sand, and mud that made up the unbaked bricks was strength-tested in a laboratory in the section. These tests let the managers know if the mixture was too wet or too dry and whether sufficient heat was added to the mix. Spare parts and repairs were a constant problem; many parts had to be fabricated by the factory machine shop. In all, there was nothing to prevent the management from making basic efficiency calculations concerning how many units could be produced given the amount of labor utilized. This is a calculation that both directors said they did not make.

The technical means for calculation were in place, but the main goal of the directors was extensive production. That is, adding workers and shifts to produce the *largest possible number of bricks*, rather than a concern with how many bricks were produced by how much labor. The latter would be a concern with cost. In a barter economy, the more volume you have to trade, the more goods you can receive. In capitalist production governed by legal-rational authority, there is a diminishing return to each additional unit of labor brought to the line. Where that return is too low, managers will not employ workers or will make them redundant. Further, managers wanted to avoid antagonizing workers with efficiency reviews or restructuring. With cash wages, the foreman would have had much more latitude in disciplining workers and reorganizing production than in the environment of the late 1990s, where such factories could not hire all the labor needed.

Lastly, the free mobility of labor is central to capitalist planning. While in Russia there are legal restrictions tying workers to their current employer and residence, these have been extremely weak even since Gorbachev. Workers can and do take jobs at other firms, in other labor markets, even in other cities (Southworth and Hormel, and Busse Spencer, Chapters 10 and 7, this volume). The main limit on their mobility, particularly in areas of provincial Russia, stems from the lack of a cash economy and the non-tangible nature of their assets and wages.

Workers at these factories have a fixed guarantee with their current employer in their current village. Workers received some medical, dental, and day care, partly subsidized by the factory. The factory maintained a small clinic for routine matters and minor injuries that workers could use free of charge. This facility had a full-time nurse and a doctor who visited on an irregular, as-needed basis. A dentist visited the clinic once a month and regularly had a full schedule of fillings, extractions, and other basic dental care. The plant had its own preschool and subsidized attendance for workers' children. Full-time day care cost 50–80 roubles or approximately $8–12 per month for children less than six years old.

Red Brick has made efforts to expand the health and comfort facilities for the workers. In 1992, they began a project to increase the capacity of lockers and changing rooms. As of 1998, management still planned for each section of the plant to have its own sauna and shower facilities, although at the time of writing only the sauna for the insulation section has been completed. The workers had ready access to a large health club with weight equipment, ping-pong, and areas for stretching and martial arts.

Some workers, notably an electrician, a skilled maintenance worker, and a machinist, had received one year or more of technical training (at a regional *professional'no-tekhnicheskoe uchilishchie*, or *PTU*) at the company's expense. Training its own workers was one way for the factory to supply itself with skilled workers.

The provision of housing in company-owned buildings, subsidy of rent and bills in other living accommodations, and the promise of future housing in a partly constructed apartment building were all vital components of the neo-paternalistic exchange centered on living space. These three components – direct provision of housing, subsidy of rent and utilities, and the pledge to construct new units – were at the core of the transaction between workers and managers at Red Brick. Almost a third of the workforce lived in the "workers' dormitory," a three-story building with one- and two-room apartments.

Most workers lived in one of two arrangements: privatized apartments which they or their relatives owned or in individual single-story houses. The so-called *otdel'nyi dom* (separate house) typically had central heating and plumbing, and was occupied by either a family that had a long history in the region (if the house was old) or a worker who received a factory sponsored loan to purchase a plot and build his or her own home. This latter option was part of a factory program from the 1970s to build single family homes in the nearby countryside to help alleviate the housing shortage for employees.

Construction of new housing was a contentious issue among workers at Red Brick. The factory had a large, seven-story apartment building partially completed. The frame of the building, floors, stairway, and elevator housing were all complete. Construction, however, had come to a near standstill in 1993 and no work at all had occurred since 1996. Despite the fact that there was no heating, no plumbing, no electricity and the units lacked windows, doors, and basic interior carpentry, workers desperately wanted these apartments. They spent a good deal of time during their shifts worrying about their place in the queue. They argued over strategies to improve their chances of getting housing. The company trade union controlled the queue and the deputy director for social affairs could influence people's rank on the list. This was a management function carried out by the trade union.

In addition to housing, long-standing arrangements with the workers at Red Brick provided them with garden space, almost all of which was located on the territory of the factory. Gardens and dachas became popular in Russia with the expansion of land available to the public through the enterprise under Brezhnev. Judging by the reports of the workers at Red Brick, however, such arrangements had been expanded over the past five years. According to my survey data (see Southworth 2001b), 40 percent of the workers at Red Brick reported that they survived the non-payment of wages with the help of vegetables which they grew for family consumption. A full 83 percent had garden plots, 56 percent had additional separate plots just for potatoes, and 44 percent had relatives in the nearby countryside with even larger gardens. Workers reported receiving meat, milk, eggs, and fruits and vegetables from their rural relations. The majority of the gardens were just within the factory grounds ahead of a long road to the main gate. This meant that workers finishing either the morning or night shift walked out the main gate, down the road, and into their gardens. With the long summer days, they could often be seen working in the garden until 10.30 or 11 p.m. at night. Those on the afternoon shift, which finished around 10 p.m., came back to their gardens to work in the early morning. Principal tasks involved weeding and watering, the latter accomplished with the help of small electric pumps used to draw water through hoses from a nearby common well. A full 40 percent of the workers said that this was an important means of surviving long periods without wages.

To preserve potatoes and other produce for winter, workers need a cellar, basement, or other underground storage, as it is not practical to refrigerate such large quantities in a small apartment. Sixty three percent of Red Brick's population had a garage with a cellar, although only 33 percent had a car. The construction of garages with 12-foot-deep cellars was the single largest construction project at Red Brick. The director said his goal was to encircle the entire territory of the factory with garages.

The subsistence guarantee through generations living in the same community, garden space, storage, and other benefits received through the employer, plus goods in kind, meant that workers in these brick factories had a substantial reason to stay where they were. Although workers routinely said that residency permits (required to be in one's passport) and registration (required for employment) were problems they would face if they left for a larger city or other employment, nearly all said those problems could be surmounted. The main reason cited for not moving was the belief that other factories were in similar straits and that they would lack the resource base of garden, garage, and apartment that had been negotiated in their present situation. The lack of movement would seem to support the arguments of theorists such as Castells (2000a), Sassen (1998), and Bauman (1998), who claim that globalization is highly selective in its connections. Mobility becomes a key feature of those who are connected to global capital (Urry 2000). Immobility is the result for those unfortunate enough to be disconnected.

Management, market position and barter relations compared

The evidence presented thus far has shown that, despite the creation of private property and private owners, Russian industry has not begun to provision everyday wants through the market for private gain. Instead, the major forces Weber identified for the development of capitalism in the West are missing or incomplete. This leaves open the main questions for these economic enterprises: Why do firms produce? The profit potential from the market is largely unmeasurable and the enterprises themselves are bankrupt and inefficient. Why do employees work? Wages are extensively delayed and the work is arduous. Immigration and self-reliance are real alternatives.

This section attempts to answer those questions through a comparison of the two firms. While the firms are more similar than different, the management style, market position, and success in setting up workable barter arrangements vary in a pattern that might explain the degree to which the labor contract is paternalistic and the workforce is satisfied with the arrangement.

Table 10.1 shows that Red Brick and White Brick are similar in terms of their stock structure, labor relations, while market position, worker satisfaction, and acceptance of the paternalistic labor contract differs. At Red Brick the workforce was stable. Workers held on to their employment, and were accepting of the goods they received in kind. The workers at White Brick, in contrast, were disgruntled, ready to leave for other employment, and had struck twice in the last two years, forcing the director to make a cash payment on back wages each time.

The director at White Brick had been there since the mid-1980s and believed that it was the state's job to provide resources to solve the plant's technical and labor problems. At Red Brick, in contrast, the director had been appointed in 1996 after a long tenure in the administration of the factory, and stated repeatedly that no aid was forthcoming from the regional government or anywhere else. "We're bankrupt," he said. "And so? Where to from here? Can society really exist without construction materials?" This led to a basic difference in their management styles. The director of White Brick made frequent trips to see the director of the state holding company and to

Table 10.1 Comparison of selected components of two brick factories in Bashkortostan, Russia, 1998

	Red Brick	*White Brick*
Labor relations		
Wage delay (years)	3	2.5
Food in kind	Yes	Yes
Workforce housed (%)	34	17
Future housing	Yes	No
Retail barter	Yes	Yes
Market structure		
Barter delivery (%)	80	90
Workforce size	Stable	Shrinking
Property relations		
State ownership (%)	65	57
Worker ownership (%)	28	38
Management ownership (%)	7	5
Outside shareholder (%)	0	0

the regional capital to ask the government of Bashkortostan to intervene and provide funds for housing, wages, and health care. None of these appeals was answered. The director of Red Brick spent his time meeting with potential clients, despite being frequently dismissed, and arranging partial, in-kind payments for the factory's bills.

The barter arrangements at Red Brick were much more successful than at White Brick. Meat, chicken, and milk appeared weekly in the company store. In White Brick, the one day that chickens were delivered to the store, everyone left work and queued up in the hope of getting one. A deputy director of the plant managed a trade for a large quantity of flour, but this turned out to be rancid and it sat in a hallway for two weeks without being returned or distributed. A major complaint of the workers in the company dormitory involved a dispute between the director of White Brick and the municipal electric company. With the electric bill unpaid for months, the municipality cut off power to the dormitory leaving the workers in the dark for two days. The paternalistic contract was being fulfilled to a greater degree at Red Brick than at White Brick.

Long-term prospects appeared better for workers at Red Brick. The factory had started construction on a medium-sized apartment building in the 1980s. Although little progress had been made in recent years, the structure of the building was basically complete and there was a solid prospect of apartments being distributed to employees at low cost in the next year. While White Brick had a plan for a similar building that had been approved in the late 1980s, there were no funds to start construction, nor any prospect of any during the summer of 1998. Housing is one of the most important reasons, historically and at present, that people have sought employment in Russia.

Finally, there is a substantial difference in access to garden space and transportation at the two plants. Workers at White Brick had gardens and grew their own produce, but these agricultural plots were a train ride away from the firm. This meant their use required travel time and some small cash for the *elektrichka* ticket. The gardens for the workers at Red Brick were on the factory grounds. When their shift ended in the summer months, they went directly to work on their plots. The director also organized additional potato plots through a barter deal with a nearby collective farm. A free factory bus took workers to these plots on the weekends.

The terms of the neo-paternalistic labor contract were fulfilled to a greater degree at Red Brick. Workers received more benefits that applied to their general welfare, health, and family than at White Brick. The efforts of the director to accept the non-cash economy and the absence of support from the state made the paternalistic labor contract function.

Conclusions: a shift in the locus of paternalism

It might be argued that what is called neo-paternalism is merely a continuation of Soviet-era economic organization in which the firm took responsibility for a number of aspects of employee welfare, including housing, vacations, sometimes education, and child care. However, we can see in the comparison of these two enterprises that the reorganization for social welfare benefits happens *after the firms are privatized* and in the opposite relationship to the management style that such an argument would expect. Red Brick, the more paternal of the two, and the firm endeavoring to construct housing that in Soviet times would have been built by the factory with the aid of the Ministry of Construction of the Republic of Bashkortostan, *expanded* its social welfare benefits *after privatization*. That is, after wage arrears became a serious problem in 1995 the director began to look for ways to provide additional benefits, child care supplements, and educational funds, and to build bath facilities, gardens and garages on the premises. The temporal ordering would have these facilities already existing during Soviet times if the economic arrangement were that of "old wine in a new bottle." Without cash wages these forms of provision became more important. "Globalization," far from liberating Soviet workers, has tied them to the locality.

The director at White Brick, on the other hand, would have liked to continue Soviet-era forms of funding. The director, however, was reluctant to engage in social organization of welfare benefits – such as nearby garden space, company transportation, or housing – for his employees.

The difference between the firm providing such benefits during the latter years of the Soviet Union and similar remuneration in the 1990s is the financing. Whereas a firm, in conjunction with regional party officials and its relevant planning ministry, would be allocated funds to construct an apartment building, Red Brick was now entirely responsible for the construction of such housing. It received no aid from the state, and, therefore, the management style of its director became all important.

Soviet socialism treated firms paternalistically; the relationship between the firm and the state was paternalistic. When the Soviet firm had a shortfall in output, could not obtain sufficient raw materials, or overspent its budget, the state made up the differences through resource transfers or by adjusting the plan targets. In a neo-paternalist factory regime, the workforce ends up supplying the firm with free labor; this partly takes the place of the fatherly beneficence of the state. Of course, the Russian state plays an important role in creating conditions for neo-paternalistic labor relations. It has tax laws that discourage directors from earning income in cash; it restricts currency in order to limit inflation, in so doing limiting the amount of cash in circulation that can be used to value output, and it does not enforce the labor code or bankruptcy laws in any meaningful way. But neo-paternalism is dependent on the ideology and strategy of the enterprise leadership, not on relations with the state per se. This shift in location of paternalism from state to workforce has important implications for class formation within the workplace. The globalization-inspired reform of privatization has limited the short- to medium-term prospects for economic development for Bashkir industry. It has, however, increased the diversity of responses to crisis, creating new forms of capitalist labor relations.

Note

1 "Paternalism" within a firm refers to management practices that merge the private, home sphere with payment and disciplinary relationships at work. Paternalistic labor relations involve managers overseeing workers' housing, education, child care, and other institutional arrangements. In Russia in the 1990s, managers were involved in providing food, housing payments, and services that in a capitalist economy would typically be mediated by the market and with cash. While paternalistic relations are more common in pre-industrial or industrializing societies, they have also been seen with the cradle-to-grave employment policies in post-war Japan.

2 I refer to these terms here in quotation marks because the concepts of calculation and profit in a part-barter, part-cash economy in which the value of the currency and rate of inflation vary wildly are tenuous and have little resemblance to their meaning inside Western capitalist firms.

3 OAO is *Otkrytoe Aktsionernoe Obshchestvo* (Open Joint-Stock Company). ZAO is *Zakrytoe Aktsionernoe Obshchestvo* (Closed Joint-Stock Company).

Part III
Theoretical reflections

11 Russia and globalisation

Concluding comments

Richard Sakwa

This book has questioned the degree to which globalisation can claim to be the new 'grand narrative' of the social sciences. Globalisation suggests the universal application of a certain dynamism that is rooted in the socio-technical and cultural reorganisation of capitalism as a universal global system. As Michael Mann puts it, 'The term "globalization" refers to the extension of social relations over the globe' (2001: 51). The whole world becomes embroiled in a single set of social relations. When applied to the former communist countries this suggests the universal applicability of some sort of integral 'transition' process where the shift to the market is accompanied by a common set of economic and social norms. It also has political effects, and the assumption is that the creation of a liberal democratic order is 'the best possible shell' for capitalism, as Lenin put it.

The evidence presented in this book suggests that Russia after the fall of communism did indeed become part of common globalising processes, in the sense suggested above. However, the version of globalisation that suggests that a uniform transformatory process is at work everywhere and with equal intensity is questioned by the empirical studies presented in this volume. Globalisation in a country such as Russia is in practice tempered by more local processes. This is not to deny the importance of the political practices represented by globalisation. The evidence presented in this book does not argue that the effect of capitalism as a global system is not important, but that its impact is fragmented and often contradictory. This is a finding consonant with most other research on the question.

Russia beyond the East: North or South?

Globalisation is both a programme to be fulfilled and a phenomenon that can be empirically tested. To what degree has the Russian economy now become implicated into the world economy? What have been the qualitative changes associated with this? In the post-Stalin era the Soviet/Russian economy entered the global system and the autarchic model of development was gradually eroded. During the era of détente in the 1970s the country became ever more dependent on Western loans and grain imports, while at the same time building up its energy export base, above all natural gas, to the West European market. A pattern of mutual dependency emerged that with the turn to the market became even more intense. Today about half of Russia's economy is based on trade with the European Union alone, by far its largest trade partner. However, the end of the state socialist path of alternative modernity and modernisation has brought the question of developmental paths firmly back into focus. Although the rhetoric and reality of 'transition' occludes debates and imbues the post-communist trajectory of the region with a sense of closure and choicelessness, the question of optimal strategies for development and modernisation has certainly not disappeared.

One of the salient features of globalisation is that certain regions are left out. Exclusionary processes take place on a global scale, but they are also marked within a single country. Russia, as the world's largest state territorially, is particularly prone to such exclusionary processes. While Moscow city is forging ahead, having increased its population by 16 per cent between the two censuses of 1989 and 2002, the rest of the country is *losing* population. Although Moscow contains only 6 per cent of the country's population, it contains over half of the country's banking activity, over a fifth of its retail trade, and one-third of its wholesale trade. Its per capita income is much higher than in any of the other 88 regions, and is more than double that of its closest competitor, St Petersburg (O'Laughlin and Kolossov 2002: 161). Moscow has become a 'world city', while the rest of the country remains firmly national.

What is clear is that any strong version of globalisation theory that suggests that capitalism in the post-cold war era has become transnational, that is, undermines the borders and boundaries between states and eliminates state autonomy, should be approached with caution. However, those theories of globalisation that suggest that it is more a cultural phenomenon have a strong case, although culture here can mean no more than superficial obeisance to certain Westernised (primarily American) consumption patterns. In their daily lives, as this study amply shows, Russians still live in a world of their own. Indeed, individual communities in patterns of daily life and work live isolated from each other and generate patterns of interaction with market-oriented norms that are singular and shaped by local conditions. Strategies are primarily based on survival. In other words, while the spread of globalising processes may well be universal, their impact is strongly mediated by local conditions.

Thus globalisation fragments as much as it unites. It fragments at the local level, and it fragments at the level of the international system. The world is marked by growing disparities, with the 'global' culture on one side and with the excluded on the other; an exclusion that takes new, and sometimes more intensive, forms as a result of globalisation. Russia's position in this new pattern of centre and periphery is profoundly ambiguous. The deconstruction of a world centred on a bipolar East–West axis has given way to one in which North–South divisions become ever more accentuated. This is a division that cuts across Russia, containing elements of both the North and the South. Moscow and certain leading regions are largely part of the globalised North, but Russia's own periphery finds itself trapped in a new type of third world South. Just as the old East and West were not strictly geographical, so too today the South can be found anywhere, with large parts of northern Russia suffering depopulation and chronic economic decline because of its climatic marginality. Northern-style integration into the international economy can be found in various regions in Russia, parts of China and India, and many other countries that are making the geo-economic shift from the South to the North. As Mann puts it, 'economic "globalization" is mostly Northernization, integrating the advanced countries but excluding much of the world's poor' (Mann 2001: 54).

The national context of globalisation remains a stubborn reality, despite the arguments of some of globalisation's more ardent partisans. There is a distinctive style to capitalism in Russia, characterised above all by the dominance of a small number of financial-industrial conglomerates headed by powerful 'oligarchs' (Zudin 1999: 45–65). In 1996 the oligarchs had played a crucial role in re-electing Boris Yeltsin for a second term, and Boris Berezovsky, the brashest of all the oligarchs for whom business was only a means to engage in politics, had bragged about the power of the '*semibankirshchina*' (rule of the seven banks) and their ownership of half of the Russian economy. A study in 2002 found that the eight largest conglomerates controlled 85 per cent of the shares in the country's top 64 firms.[1] The emergence of these companies in the oil and gas sectors is analysed by Ella Akerman in this volume (Chapter 6), noting the powerful trend for these groups to 'go global' as they become ever more integrated into international energy markets, and indeed gradually become key economic actors in the global economy. There is no single term used to describe these huge new economic players, in the energy sector and beyond. Yakov Pappe (2000), for example, uses the term 'industrial-business groups' (IBGs), while Dynkin and Sokolov (2002: 78–95) talk of 'integrated business-groups' (also IBGs). The term 'financial-industrial conglomerates' (FICs), used by Sergei Kolmakov (2003: 15–17) and others, most effectively captures their essence, including the concentration of capital balanced by the ramshackle nature of many of these emergent corporations. Under Yeltsin the oligarchs had become part of the power system, and, although Putin tried to maintain 'equidistance' from them, he could not ignore them.[2] The top eight FICs in 2002 employed 1.76 per cent of Russia's workforce of 64.3 million, yet provided a quarter of the country's exports and provided a third of the country's tax revenues (Dynkin and Sokolov 2002: 90).

At the same time, by the time of the rouble crisis of August 1998 Russian GDP had fallen by 42 per cent. The economy returned to growth in 1997, but the economic crisis of 1998 showed how fragile the recovery had been. The government was unable to collect sufficient taxes to cover its expenditure as the budget deficit rose to about 8 per cent of GDP. The shortfall in tax revenues resulted in part from the enormous subsidies still paid to loss-making enterprises; the government had not been able adequately to cut its expenses, even though it collected (although arbitrarily and incompetently) some one-third of GDP in tax revenues, similar to the US level. The shortfall was covered by issuing government bonds at ever-rising interest rates until the whole pyramid collapsed in the partial default of 17 August 1998 (Tikhomirov 1999). Many foreign banks had their fingers burnt in Russia's financial meltdown (discussed by a number of authors in this book), which in part had been provoked by the contagion effect of the crisis since Autumn 1997 in East Asia, but the partial default of August 1998 was a crisis mostly 'made in Russia'. The crisis demonstrated that Russia was indeed part of the global economy, but that national factors were primary in shaping the particular forms that the crisis would take.

Russia's entry into the world of globalised capitalism was thus a traumatic one. If in the last years of the Soviet Union its GDP per capita ranked at number 43 in the world, by the time Putin came to power in 2000 Russia ranked at number 135, rubbing shoulders with countries such as Costa Rica. A large proportion of the population was impoverished by the shift to the market, and inequality had risen dramatically. By March 2003 Russia could boast of 17 billionaires, most of whom had made their money in the energy sector,[3] while at that time the average monthly income was 3,868 roubles (about $110), with some 30 million people (22 per cent of the population) gaining less than the minimum living wage of just under 2,000 roubles.

The relationship of FICs and the state bureaucracy changed with Putin's arrival. One aspect was the establishment of an oligarchy–state alliance regulated by new rules of the game. A type of 'social contract' was established whereby the oligarchs were to keep out of politics, and in return they would be allowed to enjoy their acquisitions in the 'wild East' phase of privatisation in the 1990s. Another aspect was that the FICs were to invest in the 'real' economy. A notable case was the involvement of Oleg Deripaska's Russian Aluminium company in the purchase and subsequent restructuring of the Gorky Automotive Works (GAZ). In a globalising world the power of states is reckoned to be eroding, while that of transnational corporations is growing, but in Russia under Putin a distinctive system appeared to emerge where the FICs themselves provided the state with resources for its industrial policy, and in general acted as substitute sinews of the state. Old-fashioned *dirigisme* now gave way to an original form of neo-corporatism. The interests of big business and the state did not always coincide, of course, and the peculiar development of the state and Russian capitalism was characterised by numerous political contradictions. These came to the fore in the pressure that factions in the Kremlin brought to bear against Mikhail Khodorkovsky and his Yukos oil company in 2003. It appeared that Khodorkovsky's generous support for a number of political parties and his open political ambitions had breached the terms of the 'social contract'.

Globalisation and Russia's regions

Following the 1998 crisis big business actively extended its influence in Russia's regions, spreading out of Moscow, St Petersburg and the energy producing areas to establish a genuinely national capitalist system. In the 1990s regional corporatism had been widespread. The average four-firm concentration ratio (the total of the market share of the four top companies) was about 95 per cent.[4] Newcomers found it extremely difficult to break into these markets.[5] Under Putin, however, a more aggressive type of capitalism emerged, breaking up the cosy relationships between governors and regional businesses. Yevgeny Nazdratenko's regime in Primorsky *krai* had been a classic case of a regional political and business elite joining together to exclude outsiders for mutual benefit, leading to the establishment of a corrupt, protectionist and authoritarian system in which the consumers suffered (Kirkow 1995). Putin had forced Nazdratenko to resign, and his successor, Sergei Darkin, opened the region up to Moscow business interests. The seven presidential plenipotentiaries (*polpredy*) also helped break up regional clientelist development models.

The FICs gradually extended the scope of regional coverage and penetration. If in 1993 Lukoil operated in 5 regions, by 2000 it was active in 21; over the same period Vladimir Potanin's Interros group's coverage rose from 1 to 23, and Alfa-group from 2 to 37 regions; while the primordially Moscow-centric Sistema by 2001 operated in 42 regions (Dynkin and Sokolov 2002: 87–8). While political elites were concerned to diversify the main economic players in their region, they also tended to oppose the intrusion of economic interests that they could not control; that is, whose provenance was not from the region itself.[6] Under Putin the FIC's strengthened their hold on the regions, particularly the ones where they had investments and holdings (Yorke 2003). Gubernatorial elections sometimes became open contests for power between competing oligarchic groups, notably in the Krasnoyarsk election of 22 September 2002 to replace Alexander Lebed, after the latter's death on 28 April 2002. Here Interros supported the former director of its Norilsk Nickel plant and former governor of Taimyr *autonomous okrug*, Alexander Khloponin, who had begun his career as a financier in Moscow. They were pitted against Alexander Uss, the speaker of the regional legislature supported by Russian Aluminium and the 'family', the colloquial term for the combination of favoured oligarchs, insider politicians, political advisers, and some of Yeltsin's blood family members. The official political parties were hardly to be seen. Khloponin was declared the winner, following the Kremlin's intervention, after desperate attempts by the Uss camp to have the election declared invalid. Elsewhere, Komi Republic appeared to have become a satrapy of Lukoil, while its legislature was dominated by business interests.[7] The election of Roman Abramovich as governor of Chukotka autonomous *okrug* rendered the dominance of Sibneft complete there, complementing its 'ownership' of Omsk. Big business was now certainly making its presence felt at the regional level.

Russia had attracted relatively little FDI for most of the 1990s, and indeed had been a net capital exporter through 'capital flight' to such safe havens as Cyprus. It was only midway through Putin's first term as president that the tide began to turn, symbolised by the $6.75 billion link-up between BP-Amoco and the Tyumen Oil Company (TNK) in 2003. However, even before this there was evidence that a region could use globalisation to its advantage. The case of Novgorod the Great is exemplary in this respect. The regional leadership here from the early 1990s, led by the governor Mikhail Prusak, had circumvented Moscow and pitched straight into the world economy. The results were impressive for such a relatively small and backward region (its area is roughly that of Ireland, but it has a population of only 710,000), with no natural resources to speak of. The region pursued an aggressive strategy of wooing foreign investment, offering local tax holidays until the foreign investment turned a profit, help in negotiating the bureaucracy and legal guarantees framed by foreign accounting firms. The results were spectacular, with over 200 foreign firms investing well over half a billion US dollars by the end of the 1990s, employing nearly 20,000 workers, producing two-thirds of regional industrial output, and generating over 40 per cent of regional budget revenues (Petro forthcoming 2004: ch. 2). Notable investors included the Danish Stirol chewing gum manufacturer and Cadbury-Schweppes. This foreign involvement was long-term manufacturing investment that transformed the quality of production and had enormous knock-on effects, including political ones. Payments to pension and social funds meant that, in this region, welfare payments and wages have been paid on time. If in many regions capitalism is regarded with suspicion and became a profoundly alienating experience, in Novgorod capitalism has become far more benignly embedded in local social relations. Although the local branch of the Communist Party is numerically the largest, it has failed to win more than a handful of seats in the regional and local legislatures. More than that, survey evidence suggests the emergence of a vigorous and self-confident middle class; on income levels alone, over a quarter of the population in the region would fall into this category. The Novgorod case suggests that, although all regions and the country as a whole are faced with structural constraints, the scope for purposive developmental and political strategies framed by specific actors has not disappeared. Globalisation is not such a highly over-determined project that it can entirely wipe out the scope for 'agency'.

Theory and practice in life

Globalisation is often seen to be one of the factors that led to the fall of the communist regimes in the late 1980s (Brooks and Wohlforth 2001). According to Lockwood (2000), the Soviet Union could no longer withstand the pressure to conform to the logic of capital accumulation. This has had a major effect on the way that we study the region (Segbers and Imbusch 2000).

The evidence presented in this book is as fragmented as its subject. There is some evidence to support the view of those who suggest that globalisation is a myth (Hirst and Thompson 1999; Veseth 1998). Certainly, the argument of Colin Hay and others that globalisation is as much a programme to be fulfilled as an objective structural process is confirmed (Hay and Marsh 2000: 1–17). The debate over globalisation is as much an ideological one as a question of technical changes in the world economy. Above all, the relationship between global economic processes and territorially based democracies remains under-theorised.[8] One response has been to suggest new forms of transnational citizenship as the counterpart for the growing weight of transnational corporations.[9]

The changing relationship between state and capital to a degree subordinates the state to the needs of international capitalism. This is one of the key arguments of the 'third way' school of thinking, which argues that Keynesianism in one country or region is no longer realistic (Giddens 2000), while at the same time propounding a rather linear and certainly authoritarian ideology of 'modernisation' at a time when such grand narratives of social progress in an age of postmodernity are considered to be anachronistic. Although traditional demand-led Keynesianism is challenged by the fluidity of contemporary capitalism, there remains considerable scope for the way that the national state can mediate between the global and the local.[10] Predictions about the end of the nation state have been exaggerated (for example in Guehenno 1995). Structural arguments have long suggested that the state is little more than an instrument of capital accumulation operating on a global scale,[11] but recent thinking in the globalisation debate has suggested a less deterministic approach based on the idea of the emergence of the 'competition state' locked into a process (rather than a teleologically determined structure) of historically determined changes, which involve both state and non-state actors (Rhodes 1998; Esping Anderson 1996; Cerny 1997). A type of 'competitive corporatism' emerges, in which globalising processes are internalised by the national state, and to a degree can even enhance the role of the state as the manager of globalising processes. Some of its old autonomy is lost, and probably the scope for democratic intervention in welfare, labour and other issues is weakened, yet globalisation remains, paradoxically, a nationally managed process. The adaptation of national economies (and societies) to the demands of globalisation is tempered by the intervention of the state in shaping the direction and nature of globalisation. Globalisation is indeed only the latest phase of 'the great transformation' identified by Polanyi long ago (Polanyi 1944/2001). It is neither a natural nor a spontaneous process.

This is brought out most clearly in studies of Russia. In a volume edited by Klaus Segbers, the 'patchwork' and fragmented nature of this great transformation in the era of globalisation is brought out most forcefully, and in particular the distinctive patterns that emerge in the interaction of Soviet legacies and international pressures (Segbers 2001). The free trade policies associated with globalisation have intensified uneven development and increased regional disparities in levels of development and incomes. The degree to which these effects have been exogenously driven or are a product of particular choices made by Russian elites is at the core of the issues discussed in this book. It is clear that the liberal reformers who came to power in the early 1990s had a particular vision of the world that they sought to impose on Russia's complex and stubborn realities. To that extent, Russia's journey to the market was ideologically driven, and it is for this reason that Russia's liberal reformers have been called 'Bolsheviks of the market' (Reddaway and Glinsky 2001).

At the same time, the scope for institutional innovation and policy choice was to a large extent circumscribed by the harsh realities of a country on the verge of bankruptcy. It has now become common to criticise Russia's early reformers for their neglect of the state, above all their failure to root the shift to the market in stronger institutions and a more forceful normative and legal environment. Pınar Bedirhanoğlu (Chapter 2 in this volume) draws on the neo-Gramscian approach to argue that elites in the early 1990s were caught between the grand narrative of liberal transformation and the concrete interests of specific groups, and in the event encouraged a pell-mell rush to the market. The failure to take a more cautious approach that would have allowed institutions and the rule of law to have developed at the same pace as the development of the market allowed a criminalised neo-*nomenklatura* elite to consolidate its power and undermine genuine liberalism and democracy. The counter-factual argument is always a dubious one (although never less than tempting and interesting), and we can never know how an alternative economic policy may have fared in Russian conditions. There was no shortage of alternative plans, notably that devised by Grigory Yavlinsky at the head of the Yabloko party, which called for macroeconomic stabilisation and demonopolisation before embarking on mass privatisation.

For Yegor Gaidar and other architects of Russia's reform, this was simply a non-starter. As far as Gaidar was concerned, Russia had little choice but to proceed in the way that it did because of the lack of financial, personnel and institutional resources (Gaidar 1996). For Anatoly Chubais, the main thing was to disburse state property as quickly as possible to ensure the creation of a class interested in the continuation of market transformation. Although fears of a communist *revanche* may appear exaggerated now, at the time they were real. Although the core of the new ruling elite was drawn from the old Soviet *nomenklatura*, studies show that at least two-thirds of the 'new class' are newcomers. The model that suggests that the old Soviet ruling elite simply transformed itself into a new capitalist class leaves much out of the picture, above all the emergence of a new class of entrepreneurs. Equally, although the global capitalist order did exert considerable pressure on Russia, this did not remove all scope for institutional choice. The reassertion under Putin of state autonomy (from the oligarchs and regional bosses) and state capacity suggests that the much-vaunted weakening of the Russian state in the 1990s was as much to do with Yeltsin's personal characteristics and style of rule as with structural factors.

The ability of nations to forge their own destinies is one of the points brought out by Anastasia Nesvetailova in her study of the 1998 crisis (Chapter 3, this volume). Although, paradoxically, the partial default showed Russia at its weakest, the jolt that it provided allowed the country to continue its path to the market along a somewhat different route. The chapter suggests that globalisation does not intrinsically mean the capitulation of weaker economies to the predations of the strong. A stronger state role, above all in curbing the appetites of the oligarchs, meant that, in the years following 1998, Russia pursued the model of developing a 'competition state', and thus the point made by Pınar Bedirhanoğlu is confirmed. Although the state was weakened, it was not 'stolen',[12] and it retained the potential for revival. Similarly, the culturalist arguments about Russia cited in Nesvetailova's chapter (for example, 'the mentality of Russians remains anti-market') have already been falsified by developments in Novgorod and elsewhere. In the event, the 1998 crisis demonstrated less the inability to implant 'Western civilization' in Russia than the pressures to do so in a more logically consistent and 'Western' way. And the only way to do that, as Putin realised, was not to try to find some distinctive 'Russian path' to modernity but to embrace existing Western modernity more forcefully and coherently. This does not mean a return to state ownership, but a more robust and effective state regulatory system and the functional differentiation of the political and economic spheres.

The case of Novgorod demonstrates the complex interaction between domestic sources of policy innovation and the opportunities opened up by a capitalist world hungry to extend its reach to new regions of investment with new markets to exploit. The policies pursued by Prusak in Novgorod can be seen not so much as part of a 'competition state' strategy as reflecting attempts to create a 'competition region' that pre-dated Putin's moves in the direction of competitive corporatism by nearly a decade.[13] The regional leadership was able to take advantage of the temporary weakness of the centre. With the onset of Putin's policy of 'gathering the state', the scope for Novgorod to innovate and experiment was dramatically reduced. At the same time, the central government continued to pursue policies intended to integrate Russia even more firmly into the global economy. The aim was to join the World Trade Organisation, even though the date of entry was much later than originally intended. Regions still struggled to attract FDI and to break into world markets, but their capacity to innovate politically, economically and institutionally was sharply reduced by Putin's state-building efforts. This only confirms, however, the centrality of the nation state as the predominant mediating force between localities and the globalising world.

Regionalism, however, could take distinctive forms, as Sarah Busse Spencer shows in this volume (Chapter 7). In Novosibirsk dominant actors adopted a different strategy based above all on exploiting the new freedom of action for short-term gain. The 'agency' element here, although constrained by similar structural factors as the leadership in Novgorod, adapted differently to the situation. Failure to create an attractive environment for foreign investment reinforced the region's relative failure to achieve a coherent model of competitive regionalism. The attempt to mediate globalisation through a vigorous macro-regional framework – the Siberian Accord organisation bringing together the regions of Siberia – proved to be a non-viable strategy. This was reflected at the local level by the growth of the informal sector and an economy marked by various shades of greyness. The work of Caleb Southworth and Leontina Hormel presented here (Chapter 8) demonstrates that a negative strategy of removing impediments to the development of a capitalist labour market, such as removing price controls, subsidies and state ownership, is perhaps a necessary but a far from sufficient condition to the creation of capitalist economic relations. In the event, the labour process in the region became more archaic. It was on the basis of this sort of evidence that arguments have been made that Russia was not creating a capitalist market but an oriental bazaar. While some regions were becoming 'Northernised', others were joining the South.

A third model of regional development, between Novgorod's competitive regionalism and Novosibirsk's anarcho-capitalism, was pursued in Tatarstan. Here a very different strategy of regional adaptation was in evidence, although some of the points made in connection with Novgorod are applicable here too. The role of the regional state was crucial in managing the local economy, but, instead of generating a viable model of a globalising competition region, the corporatist model that was applied here was less than competitive. Instead of an outward-looking competitive neo-corporatism, a rather more traditional and somewhat ethnicised model of closed corporatism emerged. The power elite in this republic not only undermined the free operation of competitive party and representative politics,[14] but also sought to substitute for the operation of the market. As Leo McCann shows in this volume (Chapter 9), Tatarstan could not stand aside from the challenges posed by developments in international political economy, but the region was able to mediate them in a distinctive way. As elsewhere, the complex and sometimes surprising inter-relationship between the state and the market forces us to abandon any simplistic preconceived deterministic notions and to draw modified conclusions from real-life processes. The globalised capitalist enterprise, even if part of a global transnational corporation, is forced to adapt to local conditions, giving rise to multiple patterns of embeddedness. At the same time, regions react to the challenges of globalisation in different ways, and it is on the coherence of these reactions that the success or failure (in economic terms) of the region depends. All economies are political, despite the nostrums of the neo-liberals, and nowhere more so than in Russia and its regions.

Relations between enterprises, the government and regional authorities in post-communist Russia are equally politicised, as Gregory Schwartz demonstrates (Chapter 4). He argues that enterprise management has been most creative in devising survival strategies, and that this forces us to re-examine some of our textbook theories on how enterprises should behave. Too often the argument has been made that Russian reality has failed to live up to expectations; whereas clearly it is our theoretical models that need to be re-examined in the light of emerging realities. The traditional Soviet enterprise was far more than just an economic unit but was also at the heart of welfare and social life in general. This social embeddedness is challenged by neo-liberal theory, and, while many plants have indeed divested themselves of many of their social functions (above all, with housing transferred to municipal authorities), the Russian enterprise is still a complex economic and social player whose rationality far exceeds the narrow limitations of textbook economics. Paradoxically, the shift to the market has in many respects reinforced the solidarity of the labour collective and management in the face of regional and national government; while the challenges of globalisation have reforged the collective interests of all four in the face of international challenges.

These general findings are confirmed by Caleb Southworth's study of the development of neo-paternalism in two enterprises in Bashkortostan (Chapter 10). Just as the Soviet order by the end had degenerated into an extended patronage system, at the micro level of the enterprises extended paternalistic relations had become prevalent. The shift to the market only reinforced, in new ways, these relations, blurring the boundaries of public and private, state and collective, and individual and community. Far from this being a postmodern celebration of the collapse of modernity's striving to differentiate and segregate, these are pre-modern responses to the challenges of a not very effective capitalist modernity. As in China, post-communist Russia has assumed aspects of neo-traditionalism where personal ties take pre-eminence over impersonal authority patterns. As always in Russia, however, there is an enormous diversity in responses to the challenges of post-socialism. This is reflected in the life patterns of the social subjects of globalising post-communism, as detailed in Olga Shevchenko and Yakov Schukin's thoughtful study of six individuals coming to terms with the new conditions (Chapter 5). Although tempered by Russian conditions, much in the tension between national identity and yearnings for aspects of global culture could be replicated in France, Portugal or any other country trapped uncomfortably between international representations of progress and the values represented by tradition.

The world is changing as a result of global economic transformations, but at the same time states and sub-national regions are forging a new role as the mediators of these changes. The question then becomes, as this volume has shown, not so much whether globalisation (however defined) exists, but how the social subjects of globalisation adapt to the challenges of the new era. Here, the experience of Russia suggests that a wide variety of responses are possible, and in this respect at least the structural determinants of globalisation have not yet entirely done away with agency and choice. Globalisation represents a bundle of policy processes and practices, and it has its agents and its opponents. As hitherto peripheral countries join the capitalist metropole they do not simply reproduce existing practices in their own societies or leave the extant capitalist world the same as a result their joining, but a two-way process of change, adaptation and learning takes place that transforms both while modifying the very definition of space and territoriality. For Russia this is both a challenge and an opportunity, and allows the concept of *krizis* to return to its original Greek meaning: a time of reflection in the life of the community.

Notes

1 *Moscow Times* 23 August 2002.
2 See Peter Rutland (ed.), *Business and State in Contemporary Russia* (Boulder, CO, Westview, 2001); Peter Rutland, 'Putin and the Oligarchs', in Dale R. Herspring (ed.), *Putin's Russia: Past Imperfect, Future Uncertain* (Oxford, Rowman & Littlefield, 2003), pp. 133–54. For an overview of Russian politics under Putin, see Richard Sakwa, *Putin: Russia's Choice* (London and New York, Routledge, 2004).
3 *Forbes Magazine*, 17 March 2003.
4 *Russian Regional Report*, Vol. 7, No. 23, 22 July 2002.
5 A well-known case was the dominance of the Tyumen Oil Company (TNK) in the petrol retail market in Kursk *oblast*. Attempts by Yukos to break into the market failed, and entry costs became even higher once the Kursk governor Alexander Mikhailov established friendly relations with TNK president Semen Kukes.
6 For analysis of regional-business relations, see Rostislav Turovsky (ed.), *Politika v regionakh: gubernatory I gruppy vliyanie* (Moscow, Tsentr Politicheskikh Tekhnologii, 2002); S. Peregudov, N. Lapina and I. Semenenko, *Gruppy interesov I rossiiskoe gosudarstvo* (Moscow, editorial URSS, 1999), ch. 5.
7 *Russian Regional Report*, 14 March 2003.
8 As authors like Naomi Klein point out, the rise of the 'anti-globalisation' movement is a response to the perceived irrelevance of electoral party politics in the world of global corporations, fluid capital and immobile labour. Naomi Klein, *Fences and Windows: Dispatches from the Front Lines of the Globalisation Debate* (London, Flamingo, 2002).
9 For example, Andrew Linklater, *The Transformation of Political Community* (Cambridge, Polity Press, 1998). For a good presentation of the ideas of the 'cosmopolitan democracy' school of thought, see D. Archibugi and D. Held, 'Editors' Introduction', in D. Archibugi and D. Held (eds), *Cosmopolitan Democracy* (Cambridge, Polity, 1995).
10 For a useful discussion, see Shampa Biswas, 'W(h)ither the Nation-state?: National and State Identity in the Face of Fragmentation and Globalisation', *Global Society*, Vol. 16, No. 2, 2002, pp. 175–98.
11 Drawing on the Wallerstein and Milliband traditions, Hugo Radice presents an updated and stark version of the structuralist argument. H. Radice, 'Globalisation and National Capitalisms: Theorising Convergence and Differentiation', *Review of International Political Economy*, Vol. 7, No. 4, 2000, pp. 719–42.
12 Cf. Stevel L. Solnick, *Stealing the Soviet State: Control and Collapse in Soviet Institutions* (Cambridge, MA, Harvard University Press, 1998).

13 The neo-corporatist elements were identified by Natalia Dinello, *What's So Great About Novgorod-The-Great: Trisectoral Cooperation and Symbolic Management* (Washington, DC, National Council for Eurasian and East European Research, Title VIII Program, 2001).

14 See *Osobaya zona: vybory v Tatarstane* (Ul'yanovsk, 2000); *Chto khotel by znat' izbiratel' Tatarstana o vyborakh (no ne znaet gde eto sprosit')* (Kazan', GranDan, 2002).

Bibliography

Abalkin, L. (2000) *Trydy Volnogo Ekonomicheskogo Obshchestva Rossii*, Moscow: Ekonomika.

Abed, G.T. and Davoodi, H.R. (2000) *Corruption, Structural Reforms, and Economic Performance in the Transition Economies*, IMF Working Paper, Fiscal Affairs Department, International Monetary Fund.

Ajayi, O.O. (1996) 'Problems of surveying the informal sector: the case of Nigeria', in Bohuslav Herman and Wim Stoffers (eds) *Unveiling the Informal Sector: More Than Counting Heads*, Brookfield, VT: Avebury.

Alasheev, S. (1995) 'On a particular kind of love and the specificity of Soviet production', in S. Clarke (ed.) *Management and Industry in Russia: Formal and Informal Relations in the Russian Industrial Enterprise*, Cheltenham: Edward Elgar.

Allison, G. and Yavlinsky, G. (1991) *Window of Opportunity: The Grand Bargain for Democracy in the Soviet Union, 1991*, Harvard University, John F. Kennedy School of Government Strengthening Democratic Institutions Project, USA/Center for Economic and Political Research (EPCENTER), USSR, New York: Pantheon.

Altvater, E. and Mahnkopf, B. (1997) 'The world market unbound', in A. Scott (ed.) *The Limits of Globalization*, London: Routledge.

Amin, S. (1996) 'The challenge of globalization', *Review of International Political Economy* 3(2): 216–59.

Aminzade, R. (1993) *Ballots and Barricades: Class Formation and Republican Politics in France, 1830–1871*, Princeton, NJ: Princeton University Press.

Andrle, V. (2001) 'The buoyant class: bourgois family lineage in the life stories of Czech business elite persons', *Sociology* 35(4): 815–33.

Andrusz, G.D., Harloe, M. *et al.* (eds) (1996) *Cities After Socialism: Urban and Regional Change and Conflict in Postsocialist Societies*, Oxford: Blackwell.

Anonymous (1997) 'Russia approves plan to privatize Rosneft', *Oil and Gas Journal* 95(48): 36.

Anonymous (2000) 'Vital statistics: oil, natural gas and energy in Russia', *Drillbits & Tailings* 5(15), 19 September, available on-line at http://www.moles.org/ProjectUnderground/drillbits/.

Appadurai, A. (1990) 'Disjunction and difference in the global cultural economy', *Theory, Culture and Society* 7: 295–310.

Arnason, J.P. (1993) *The Future That Failed: Origins and Destiny of the Soviet Model*, London: Routledge.

Arnot, B. (1988) *Controlling Soviet Labour: Experimental Change from Brezhnev to Gorbachev*, London: Macmillan.

Ashwin, S. (1996) 'Forms of collectivity in a non-monetary society', *Sociology* 30(1): 21–39.

—— (1998) 'Tattered banners: labour, conflict and corporatism in postcommunist Russia', *Work, Employment and Society* 12(1): 175–6.

—— (1999) *Russian Workers: The Anatomy of Patience*, Manchester: Manchester University Press.

Aslanova, T.O. and Pashkova, I.I. (1997) 'Problems of correlating liberalism with protectionism in Russia's foreign economic policy', *Studies on Russian Economic Development* 8(2), March/April: 158–63.

Åslund, A. (1995) *How Russia Became a Market Economy*, Washington, DC: Brookings Institution.

—— (1998) 'Russia's financial crisis: causes and possible remedies', *Post-Soviet Geography and Economics* 39: 6.

—— (2002) *Building Capitalism: The Transformation of the Former Soviet Bloc*, New York: Cambridge University Press.

—— and Dmitriev, M. (1999) 'Economic reform versus rent seeking', in A. Åslund, and M. Olcott (eds) *Russia After Communism*, Washington, DC: Carnegie Endowment for International Peace.

Atal, A. (1999) *Poverty in Transition and Transition in Poverty*, Paris: UNESCO.

Atkinson, P., Coffey, A. and Delamont, S. (2001) 'A debate about our canon', *Qualitative Research* 1(1), April: 5–21.

Baez, M.M. (1996) 'Surveying the informal sector, statistical pitfalls: the case of Costa Rica', in B. Herman and W. Stoffers (eds) *Unveiling the Informal Sector: More Than Counting Heads*, Brookfield, VT: Avebury.

Barberis, N., Boycko, M., Shleifer, A. and Tsukanova, N. (1996) 'How does Russian privatization work? Evidence from the Russian shops', *Journal of Political Economy* 104: 764–90.

Barnet, R.J. and Cavanagh, J. (1994) *Global Dreams: Imperial Corporations and the New World Order*, New York: Simon & Shuster.

Bauman, Z. (1998) *Globalization: The Human Consequences*, Cambridge: Polity.

Beck, U. (1992) *Risk Society*, London: Sage.

—— (2000) *What is Globalisation?*, Cambridge: Polity.

Beneria, L. (2001) *Changing Employment Patterns and the Informalization of Jobs: General Trends and Gender Dimensions*, Geneva: International Labour Office.

Berger, P.L. and Luckmann, T. (1967) *The Social Construction of Reality: A Treatise in the Sociology of Knowledge*, London: Allen Lane.

Berliner, J.S. (1957) *Factory and Manager in the USSR*, Cambridge, MA: Harvard University Press.

Bettelheim, C. (1975) *Economic Calculation and Forms of Property*, New York: Monthly Review Press.

Bhabha, H.K. (1994) *The Location of Culture*, London: Routledge.

Bilenkin, V. (1996) 'Russian workers under the Yeltsin regime: notes on a class in defeat', *Monthly Review* 48(6), November.

Blanchard, O., Boycko, M., Dabrowski, M., Dornbusch, R., Layard, R. and Shleifer, A. (1993) *Post-Communist Reform, Pain and Progress*, Cambridge, MA: MIT Press.

Blankenagel, A. (1993) 'Where has all the power gone?', *East European Constitutional Review* 2(1), Winter: 26–9.

Blasi, J.R., Kroumova, M. and Kruse, D. (1997) *Kremlin Capitalism: Privatizing the Russian Economy*, Ithaca, NY: Cornell University Press.

Böröcz, J. (1993) 'Simulating the great transformation: property change under prolonged informality in Hungary', *Archives Européennes de Sociologie* 34(1): 81–107.

—— and Southworth, C. (1998) '"Who you know": earnings effects of formal and informal social network resources under late state socialism in Hungary, 1986–87', *Journal of Socio-Economics* 27: 401–25.

Boswell, T. and Chase-Dunn, C. (2000) *The Spiral of Capitalism and Socialism*, London: Lynne Rienner.

Bourdieu, P. and Wacquant, L. (1992) *An Invitation to Reflexive Sociology*, Chicago, IL: University of Chicago Press.

Boycko, M., Shleifer, A. and Vishny, R. (1995) *Privatizing Russia*, Cambridge, MA: MIT Press.

Bradley, H., Erickson, M., Stephenson, C. and Williams, S. (2000) *Myths at Work*, Cambridge: Polity.

Brekhuniov, A.M., Zolotov, A.N., Rezunenko, V.I. *et al.* (2001) 'West Siberia to remain the main oil and gas producing province of Russia in the XXI century', *Petroleum Geology* 35(4): 388–91.

Breslauer, G.W. and Dale, C. (1997) 'Boris Yel'tsin and the invention of a Russian nation-state', *Post-Soviet Affairs* 13(4): 303–32.

——, Brada, J., Gaddy, C.G., Ericson, R., Saivetz, C. and Winston, V. (2000) 'Russia at the end of Yel'tsin's presidency', *Post-Soviet Affairs* 16(1): 1–32.

Bridger, S. and Pine, F. (eds) (1998) *Surviving Postsocialism: Local Strategies and Regional Responses in Eastern Europe and the Former Soviet Union*, New York: Routledge.

Brooks, S. and Wohlforth, W.C. (2001) 'Power, globalization and the end of the Cold War', *International Security*, Winter 2000–1.

Brown, W. (1963) *Piecework Abandoned: The Effect of Wage Incentive Systems on Managerial Authority*, London: Heinemann.

Browning, G. (1997) *Russia and the Restored Gospel*, Salt Lake City, UT: Deseret Book Company.

Brudny, Y.M. (1993) 'The dynamics of "democratic Russia," 1990–1993', *Post-Soviet Affairs* 9(2): 141–70.

Bryson, J.R. and Daniels, P.W. (eds) (1998) *Service Industries in the Global Economy*, Cheltenham: Edward Elgar.

Buchs, T. (1999) 'Financial crisis in the Russian Federation', *Economics of Transition* 7(3): 687–715.

Buci-Glucksmann, C. (1979) 'State, transition and passive revolution', in C. Mouffe (ed.) *Gramsci and Marxist Theory*, London: Routledge & Kegan Paul, pp. 207–36.

Bukhariev, R. (1999) *The Model of Tatarstan*, London: Curzon.

Bukovskii, V. (1981) *Pis'ma Russkogo Puteshestvennik*, New York: Chalidze.

Bunce, V. (1999) *Subversive Institutions: The Design and the Destruction of Socialism and the State*, Cambridge: Cambridge University Press.

Burawoy, M. (1985) *The Politics of Production: Factory Regimes under Capitalism and Socialism*, London: Verso.

—— (1996) 'The state and economic involution: Russia through a China lens', *World Development* 24(6): 1105–17.

—— (1998) 'The extended case method', *Sociological Theory* 16.

—— (1999) 'The great involution: Russia's response to the market'. Manuscript.

—— (ed.) (2000) *Global Ethnography: Forces, Connections, and Imaginations in a Postmodern World*, Berkeley, CA: University of California Press.

—— and Krotov, P. (1996) 'The Soviet transition from socialism to capitalism: worker control and economic bargaining in the wood industry', in S. Clarke, P. Fairbrother, M. Burawoy and P. Krotov (eds) *What About the Workers? Workers and the Transition to Capitalism in Russia*, New York: Verso.

——, —— and Lytkina, T. (2000) 'Involution and destitution in capitalist Russia', *Ethnography* 1(1): 43–65.

Burbach, R., Kagarlitsky, B. and Nunez, O. (1997) *Globalization and Its Discontents*, London and Chicago, IL: Pluto Press.

Burlatsky, F. (2001) 'Change of elite', *Nezavisimaya Gazeta*, March 13.

Burt, R.S. (1993) 'The social structure of competition', in R. Swedberg (ed.) *Explorations in Economic Sociology*, New York: Russell Sage Foundation.

Busch, A. (2001) 'Unpacking the Globalization Debate: Approaches, Evidence and Data', in C. Hay and D. Marsh (eds) *Demystifying Globalization*, London: Palgrave.

Busse Spencer, S. (2001) 'Strategies of daily life: social capital and the informal economy in Russia'. Forthcoming in *Sociological Imagination* 38 (2/3) (Special issue on Informal Economy).

Calhoun, C. (1982) *The Question of Class Struggle: Social Foundations of Popular Radicalism During the Industrial Revolution*, Chicago, IL: University of Chicago Press.

Callinicos, A. (2001) *Against the Third Way: An Anti-Capitalist Critique*, Cambridge: Polity.

Callon, M. (ed.) (1998) *The Laws of the Markets*, Oxford: Blackwell.

Cambell, R.W. (1968) *The Economics of Soviet Oil and Gas*, Baltimore, MD: Johns Hopkins Press.

—— (1976) *Trends in the Soviet Oil and Gas Industry*, Baltimore, MD: Johns Hopkins Press.

Candland, S. and Sil, R. (eds) (2001) *The Politics of Labor in a Global Age: Continuity and Change in Late-industrializing and Post-socialist Economies*, Oxford: Oxford University Press.

Cannell, M. and Wood, S. (1992) *Incentive Pay: Impact and Evolution*, London: Institute of Personnel Management and National Economic Development.

Caplan, P. (ed.) (2000) *Risk Revisited*, London: Pluto Press.

Cappelli, O. (1993) 'The Short Parliament 1989–91: political elites, societal cleavages and the weakness of party politics', *Journal of Communist Studies* 9(1), March (Special issue entitled *The Soviet Transition From Gorbachev to Yeltsin*): 109–30.

Carnoy, M. *et al.* (1993) *The New Global Economy in the Information Age*, Philadelphia, PA: Pennsylvania University Press.

Castells, M. (1989) *The Informational City: Information Technology, Economic Restructuring, and the Urban-Regional Process*, Oxford: Blackwell.

—— (2000a) *The Rise of the Network Society*, 2nd edn, Oxford: Blackwell.

—— (2000b) *The Power of Identity*, 2nd edn, Oxford: Blackwell.

—— (2000c) *End of Millennium*, 2nd edn, Oxford: Blackwell.

—— (2000d) 'Materials for an explanatory theory of the network society', *British Journal of Sociology* 51(1), January/March: 5–24.

—— and Portes, A. (1989) 'World underneath: the origins, dynamics, and effects of the informal economy', in A. Portes, M. Castells and L.A. Benton (eds) *The Informal Economy: Studies in Advanced and Less Developed Countries*, Baltimore, MD: Johns Hopkins University Press.

Cawthorne, P. (2001) 'Identity, values and method: taking interview research seriously in political economy', *Qualitative Research* 1(1): 65–90.

Center for Strategic & International Studies (1998) 'Bankruptcy in Russia', *New Global Economy Monitor*, Washington, DC, available on-line at http://www.csis.org/nge/nge16.html.

Cerny, P. (1997) 'Paradoxes of the competition state: the dynamics of political globalisation', *Government and Opposition* 32(1): 251–74.

Charvat, F.J. (1961) *Supermarketing*, New York: Macmillan.

Cheru, F. and Gill, S. (1997) 'Structural adjustment and the G-7: limits and contradictions', in S. Gill (ed.) *Globalization, Democratization and Multilateralism*, Tokyo, New York and Paris: Macmillan and UN University Press.

Chervyakov, V. (1995) 'The Russian national economic elite in the political arena', in K. Segbers and S. de Spiegeleire (eds) *Post-Soviet Puzzles, Mapping the Political Economy of the Former Soviet Union, Volume I: Against the Background of the Former Soviet Union*, Baden-Baden: Nomos Verlagsgesellschaft, pp. 205–82.

Child, J. and McGrath, R.G. (2001) 'Organizations unfettered: organizational form in an information-intensive economy', *Academy of Management Journal* 44(6): 1135–48.

——, Faulkner, D. and Pitkethly, R. (2000) 'Foreign direct investment in the UK 1985–1994: the impact on domestic management practice', *Journal of Management Studies* 37(1): 141–66.

Clark, W.A. (1989) *Soviet Regional Elite Mobility After Khrushchev*, New York: Praeger.

Clarke, S. (1993a) 'Privatisation and the development of capitalism in Russia', in S. Clarke, P. Fairbrother, M. Burawoy and P. Krotov (eds) *What About the Workers? Workers and the Transition to Capitalism in Russia*, London and New York: Verso, pp. 199–241.

—— (1993b) 'The contradictions of "state socialism"', in S. Clarke, P. Fairbrother, M. Burawoy and P. Krotov (eds) *What About the Workers? Workers and the Transition to Capitalism in Russia*, London and New York: Verso.

—— (1996) 'The enterprise in the era of transition', in S. Clarke (ed.) *The Russian Enterprise in Transition*, Cheltenham: Edward Elgar.

—— (1998a) 'Trade unions and the non-payment of wages in Russia', *International Journal of Manpower* 9(1): 68–94.

—— (1998b) 'Structural adjustment without mass unemployment? Lessons from Russia', in S. Clarke (ed.) *Structural Adjustment Without Mass Unemployment? Lessons from Russia*, Brookfield, VT, and Cheltenham: Edward Elgar, pp. 9–86.

—— (1999a) *The Formation of the Labour Market in Russia*, Cheltenham: Edward Elgar.

—— (1999b) *New Forms of Employment and Household Survival Strategies in Russia*, Coventry: Centre for Comparative Labour Studies.

—— (2000) 'Contradictions and class conflict in Russia in transition', paper presented to the ICCEES Conference, Tampere, Finland, August.

—— (2002a) 'Market and institutional determinants of wage differentiation in Russia', *Industrial and Labor Relations Review* 55(1): 628–48.

—— (2002b) *Making Ends Meet in Contemporary Russia: Secondary Employment, Subsidiary Agriculture and Social Networks*, Cheltenham: Edward Elgar.

—— and Donova, I. (1999) 'Internal mobility and labour market flexibility in Russia', *Europe-Asia Studies* 51(1): 213–43.

—— and Kabalina, V. (1995) 'Privatisation and the struggle for control of the enterprise', in D. Lane (ed.) *Russia in Transition: Politics, Privatisation and Inequality*, London and New York: Longman, pp. 142–58.

——, Fairbrother, P., Borisov, V. and Bizyukov, P. (1994) 'The privatisation of industrial enterprises in Russia: four case-studies', *Europe-Asia Studies* 46(2): 179–214.

——, ——, Burawoy, M. and Krotov, P. (1996) *What About the Workers? Workers and the Transition to Capitalism in Russia*, New York: Verso.

Coates, D. (2000) *Models of Capitalism*, Cambridge: Polity Press.

Cohen, S. (2001) *Failed Crusade: America and the Tragedy of Post-Communist Russia*, London: W.W. Norton.

Collins, R. (1980) 'Weber's last theory of capitalism: a systematization', *American Sociological Review* 45: 925–42.

Commander, S. and Jackman, R. (1993) 'Providing social benefits in Russia: redefining the roles of firms and government', EDI Policy Research Working Paper WPS 1184, Washington, DC.

—— and Mummsen, C. (2000) 'The growth of non-monetary transactions in Russia: causes and effects' in P. Seabright (ed.) *The Vanishing Rouble*, Cambridge: CUP.

—— and Tolstopiatenko, A. (1996) 'Why is unemployment low in the former Soviet Union? Enterprise restructuring and the structure of compensation', EDI Policy Research Working Paper WPS 1617, Washington, DC.

——, Dhar, S. and Yemtsov, R. (1996a) 'How Russian firms make their wage and employment decisions', in S. Commander, Q. Fan and M.E. Shaffer (eds) *Enterprise Restructuring and Economic Policy in Russia*, Washington, DC: The World Bank.

——, Fan, Q. and Schaffer, M.E. (eds) (1996b) *Enterprise Restructuring and Economic Policy in Russia*, Washington, DC: The World Bank.

——, Lee, U.J. and Tolstopiatenko, A. (1996c) 'Social benefits and the Russian industrial firm', in S. Commander, Q. Fan and M.E. Schaffer (eds) (1996) *Enterprise Restructuring and Economic Policy in Russia*, Washington, DC: The World Bank.

Cox, R. (1999) 'Civil society at the turn of the millennium: prospects for an alternative world order', *Review of International Studies* 25(1).

Current Digest of the Post-Soviet Press (1992–1999).

Dallago, B. (1987) 'The underground economy in the West and the East: a comparative approach', in S. Allessandrini and B. Dallago (eds) *The Unofficial Economy: Consequences and Perspectives in Different Economic Systems*, Brookfield, VT: Gower.

Dasn, P. (1998) 'Wage arrears in Russia', *Economic and Political Weekly* 33(35).

Deaton, A. (1997) *The Analysis of Household Surveys: A Microeconometric Approach to Development Policy*, Baltimore, MD: Johns Hopkins University Press for the World Bank.

Delbridge, R. and Lowe, J. (eds) (1998) *Manufacturing in Transition*, London: Routledge.

Department of Economic and Social Affairs (1997) *The Russian Gas Industry*, New York: United Nations.

Dicken, P. (1998) *Global Shift: Transforming the World Economy*, London: Paul Chapman Publishing.

—— (2003) *Global Shift: Reshaping the Global Economic Map in the 21st Century*, London: Sage.

Dienes L. and Shabad T. (1979) *The Soviet Energy System: Resource Use and Policies*, Washington, DC: V.H. Winston & Sons.

DiMaggio, P. (1994) 'Culture and economy', in N. Smelser and R. Swedberg (eds) *The Handbook of Economic Sociology*, Princeton, NJ: Princeton University Press.

—— and Powell, W.W. (eds) (1991) *The New Institutionalism in Organizational Analysis*, London: University of Chicago Press.

Doeringer, P.B. and Piore, M.J. (1985) *Internal Labour Markets and Manpower Analysis*, Armonk, NY: M.E. Sharpe.

Drucker, P.F. (1990) *Managing the Non-profit Organization*, New York: HarperCollins.

Duma (1999) 'Zakluchenie Vremennoi Komissii Soveta Federatsii po rassledovaniy prichin, obstoyatelstv i posledstvii prinyatiya reshenii pravitelstva Rossiiskoi Federacii i Centralnogo banka ot 17 Avgysta 1998 goda'.

Dynkin A. and Sokolov A. (2002) 'Integrirovannye biznes-groupy v rossiyskoy ekonomike', *Voprosy Ekonomiki* 4: 78–95.

Earle, J.S. and Sabirianova, K. (2002) 'How late to pay? Understanding wage arrears in Russia', *Journal of Labor Economics* 20(3): 661–707.

East European Constitutional Review (1992–2001).

EBRD (1998–2002) *Transition Report*, London: EBRD.

Economist, The (2000) 'Putin the great unknown', 8 January: 19.

Eichengreen, B. (1999) *Towards a New Financial Architecture: A Practical Post-Asian Agenda*, Institute for International Economics, available on-line at http://www.stern.nyu.edu?#nroubini/asia/AsiaHomepage.htm.

Eisenstadt, S.N. and Roniger, L. (1984) *Patrons, Clients and Friends: Interpersonal Relations and the Structure of Trust in Society*, Cambridge: Cambridge University Press.

Elliott, L. and Atkinson, D. (1999) *The Age of Insecurity*, London: Verso.

Elster, J., Offe, C. and Preuss, U. (1997) *Institutional Design in Post-Communist Societies: Repairing the Ship at Sea*, Cambridge: Cambridge University Press.

English, R.D. (2000) *Russia and the Idea of the West: Gorbachev, Intellectuals, and the End of the Cold War*, New York: Columbia University Press.

Ershov, M. (2000) *Valytno-Finansovye Mekansimy v Sovremennom Mire*, Moscow: Ekonomika.

Esping Anderson, G. (ed.) (1996) *Welfare States in Transition: National Adaptations in Global Economies*, London: Sage.

Evangelista, M. (1999) *Unarmed Forces: The Transnational Movement to End the Cold War*, Ithaca, NY: Cornell University Press.

Eyal, G. *et al.* (1997) 'The theory of post-communist managerialism', *New Left Review* 222.

——, Szelenyi, I. and Townsley, E. (1998) *Making Capitalism Without Capitalists*, London: Verso.

Femia, J.F. (1987) *Gramsci's Political Thought*, Oxford: Clarendon Press.

Filtzer, D. (1986) *Soviet Workers and Stalinist Industrialization: The Formation of Modern Soviet Production Relations, 1928–1941*, London: Pluto Press.

—— (1994) *Soviet Workers and the Collapse of Perestroika: The Soviet Labour Process and Gorbachev's Reforms, 1985–1991*, Cambridge: Cambridge University Press.

Financial Times (2000) 'Survey of Russia', 10 May.

Fish, M.S. (1995) *Democracy From Scratch: Opposition and Regime in the New Russian Revolution*, Princeton, NJ: Princeton University Press.

Flaherty, P. (1991) 'Perestroika and the neo-liberal project', in R. Miliband and L. Panitch (eds) *Communist Regimes: The Aftermath, Socialist Register*, London: The Merlin Press, pp. 128–67.

Forgacs, D. (ed.) (1988) *A Gramsci Reader, Selected Writings 1916–1935*, London: Lawrence & Wishart.

Fortune (2002) *Russian Oil Report*, 13 May: 30–7.

Frank, T. (2000) *One Market Under God*, London: Secker &Warburg.

Freeland, C. (2000) *Sale of the Century: The Inside Story of the Second Russian Revolution*, London: Little, Brown & Company.

French, R.A. and Hamilton, F.E.I. (eds) (1979) *The Socialist City: Spatial Structure and Urban Policy*, Chichester, NY: Wiley & Sons.

Frienkman, L.M. and Haney, M. (1997) *What Affects the Propensity to Subsidize: Determinants of Budget Subsidies and Transfers Financed by the Russian Regional Governments, 1992–1995*, Washington, DC: World Bank.

—— and Starodubrovskaya, I. (1996) 'Restructuring of enterprise social assets in Russia: trends, problems, possible solutions', EDI Policy Research Working Paper WPS 1635, Washington, DC.

Fruchtmann, J. (2001) 'Putin's approach to economic policy: changes in style and content', paper presented at the BASEES Annual Conference, Cambridge, UK, 6–9 April.

Fukuyama, F. (1993) *The End of History and the Last Man*, London: Penguin.

Gaddy, C.G. and Ickes, B. (1998) 'Russia's virtual economy', *Foreign Affairs* 77(5): 53–67.

—— and —— (1999) 'An accounting model of the virtual economy in Russia', *Post-Soviet Geography and Economics* 40(2).

Gafyrov, S. (1997) 'Is a rectifying crisis plausible in Russia?', *Rynok Cennyh Bymag* 19.

Gaidar, Y. (1996) *Dni prozhenii i pobed*, Moscow: Vagrius.

Galeev, M. (1999) 'Ekonomicheski i politicheski problemy adaptatsii Rossii k mirovomu rinku', in R. Khakimov (ed.) *Ekonomika Tatarstana polse 17 Avgusta*, Kazan: Panorama-Forum.

Garcelon, M. (1997) 'The estate of change: the specialist rebellion and the democratic movement in Moscow, 1989–1991', *Theory and Society* 26(1): 39–75.

Gerber, T.P. (2002) 'Labor market transitions in Russia in the 1990s', *American Sociological Review* 67(5): 629–59.

—— and Hout, M. (1998) 'More shock than therapy: market transition, employment, and income in Russia, 1991–1995', *American Journal of Sociology* 104: 1–50.

Germain, R. (ed.) (2000) *Globalization and its Critics*, London: Macmillan.

Giadar, Y. (1996) *Istoricheskie sud'by radikalnoi ekonomicheskoi reformy*, Prague: Laguna.

Giddens, A. (1986) *The Constitution of Society*, Cambridge: Polity.

—— (1990) *The Consequences of Modernity*, Cambridge: Polity.

—— (1991) *Modernity and Self-Identity*, Cambridge: Polity.

—— (1998) *The Third Way: The Renewal of Social Democracy*, Cambridge: Polity.

—— (1999) *The Runaway World: How Globalisation is Reshaping Our Lives*, London: Profile.

—— (2000) *The Third Way and its Critics*, Cambridge: Polity.

—— and Pierson, C. (1998) *Conversations with Anthony Giddens: Making Sense of Modernity*, Cambridge: Polity.

Gill, G. and Markwick, R.D. (2000) *Russia's Stillborn Democracy? From Gorbachev to Yeltsin*, Oxford: Oxford University Press.

Gill, S. (1999) 'The geopolitics of the Asian crisis', *Monthly Review* 50: 10.

Glaziev, S. (1998a) *Genocide*, Moscow: Terra.

—— (1998b) 'Stabilisation of the Russian economy', *Belarussian Economic Journal* 3.

—— (2000) 'Vozmozhen li v Rossii novyi finansovyi krisis?, *Voprosy Ekonomiki*, March.

—— (2001) 'O vybore strategii budushego razvitiya', *Svobodnaya Mysl* 2: 4–23.

Gordon, L.A. and Pliskevich, N.M. (1995) 'Crossroads and pitfalls of the transition period', *Russian Politics and Law, A Journal of Translations* 33(5), September/October: 5–24.

Gordon, R.J. (1999) 'Has the "New Economy" rendered the productivity slowdown obsolete?', 14 June, available on-line at http://www.econ.northwestern.edu.

Gorst, I. (1991a) 'Russia: what price export liberalization?', *Petroleum Economist* 58(12): 36.

—— (1991b) 'Soviet Union: oil export shrinks', *Petroleum Economist* 58(1): 17.

—— (1992a) 'Russia: who will be the local Rockfeller?', *Petroleum Economist* 59(3): 19.

—— (1992b) 'Russia: reasons to be cheerful', *Petroleum Economist* 69(2): 10.

—— (1992c) 'Gas colossus seeks new bearings', *Petroleum Economist* 59(6): 5.

—— (1993) 'Russia: carry on corporizing', *Petroleum Economist* 60(6): 72.

Goskomstat (1996) *Trud i zanyatost' v Russii*, Moscow: Goskomstat Rossii.

—— (1998) *Rossiiskii statisticheskii yezhegodnik*, Moscow: Goskomstat Rossii.

—— (1999a) *Ekonomicheskoe polozhenie Possii, January–March*, Moscow: State Committee on Statistics.

—— (1999b) *Rossiia v tsyfrakh*, Moscow: Goskomstat Rossii.

—— (2000a) *Rossiia v tsyfrakh*, Moscow: Goskomstat Rossii.

—— (2000b) *Rossiiskii statisticheskii yezhegodnik*, Moscow: Goskomstat Rossii.

—— (2000c) *Sotsial'no-ekonomicheskoe polozhenie Rosii, 2000 god*, Moscow: Goskomstat Rossii.

—— (2000d) *Sotsial'noye polozheniie i uroven' zhyzni naseleniia Rossii*, Moscow: Goskomstat Rossii.

—— (2001a) *Rossiia v tsyfrakh*, Moscow: Goskomstat Rossii.

—— (2001b) 'Zatraty na rabochuyu silu, zarabotnaya plata rabotnikov', in Goskomstat (ed.) *Trud i zanyatost' v Rossii*, Moscow: Goskomstat Rossii.

Gow, D. (2003) 'Russian buys 5% of Corus', *The Guardian*, 15 May, available on-line at http://www.guardian.co.uk/business/story/0,3604,956217,00.html.

Gowan, P. (1999) *The Global Gamble: Washington's Faustian Deal for World Domination*: London: Verso.

—— (1996) 'Eastern Europe, Western power and neoliberalism', *New Left Review* 216.

Grabher, G. and Stark, D. (eds) (1997) *Restructuring Networks in Post-Socialism*, Oxford: Oxford University Press.

Gramsci, A. (1971) *Selections from the Prison Notebooks*, trans. Q. Hoare and G.N. Smith, New York: International Publishers.

Granick, D. (1960) *The Red Executive: A Study of the Organization Man in Russian Industry*, Garden City, NY: Doubleday.

—— (1987) *Job Rights in the Soviet Union: Their Consequences*, Cambridge: Cambridge University Press.

Granovetter, M. (1973) 'The strength of weak ties', *American Journal of Sociology* 78: 1360–80.

—— (1985) 'Economic action and social structure: the problem of embeddedness', *American Journal of Sociology* 91(3): 481–510.

—— and Swedberg, R. (eds) (1992) *The Sociology of Economic Life*, Oxford: Westview.

Granville, B. (1999) 'Bingo or fiasco? The global financial situation is not guaranteed', *International Affairs* 75(4): 713–28.

Gray, J. (1998) *False Dawn: The Delusions of Global Capitalism*, London: Granta.

Gregory, P.R. (1990) *Restructuring the Soviet Economic Bureaucracy*, Cambridge: Cambridge University Press.

Grossman, G. (1977) 'The "second economy" of the USSR', *Problems of Communism* 26: 25–40.

—— (1989) 'Informal personal incomes and outlays of the Soviet urban population', in A. Portes, M. Castells and L.A. Benton (eds) *The Informal Economy: Studies in Advanced and Less Developed Countries*, Baltimore, MD: Johns Hopkins University Press.

Guehenno, J.M. (1995) *The End of the Nation-State*, Minneapolis, MN: University of Minnesota Press.

Guillen, M.G. (2001) 'Is globalization civilizing, destructive or feeble? A critique of five key debates in the social science literature', *Annual Review of Sociology* 27: 235–60.

Gustafson, T. (1999) *Capitalism Russian Style*, Cambridge: Cambridge University Press.

Hahn, J.W. (ed.) (1996) *Democratization in Russia: The Development of Legislative Institutions*, Armonk, NY: M.E. Sharpe.

Hall, P.A. and Soskice, D. (eds) (2001) *Varieties of Capitalism*, Oxford: Oxford University Press.

Hann, C. (2002a) 'Dimensions of inequality', in C. Hann (ed.) *Postsocialism: Ideas, Ideologies and Practices in Eurasia*, London and New York: Routledge.

—— (2002b) 'Farewell to the socialist "other"', in C. Hann (ed.) *Postsocialism: Ideas, Ideologies and Practices in Eurasia*, London and New York: Routledge.

Hannerz, U. (1992) *Cultural Complexity*, New York: Columbia University Press.

Hanson, P. (1986) *The Serendipitous Soviet Achievement of Full Employment: Labour Shortage and Labour Hoarding in the Soviet Economy*, New York: New York University Press.

—— (2002) 'Barriers to long-run growth in Russia', *Economy and Society* 31(1): 62–84.

Hardt, M. and Negri, A. (2000) *Empire*, Cambridge, MA: Harvard University Press.

Harvey, D. (1989) *The Condition of Postmodernity*, Oxford: Basil Blackwell.

Hausner, J., Jessop, B. and Nielsen, K. (eds) (1995) *Strategic Choice and Path-dependency in Post-Socialism*, Cheltenham: Edward Elgar.

Hay, C. and Marsh, D. (eds) (2000) *Demystifying Globalization*, London: Palgrave.

Hedlund, S. (1999) *Russia's 'Market' Economy: A Bad Case of Predatory Capitalism*: London: UCL Press.

—— (2000) 'Path dependence in Russian policy making: constraints on Putin's economic choice', *Post-Communist Economies* 12: 4.

Heertz, N. (2001) *The Silent Takeover: Global Capitalism and the Death of Democracy*, London: Heinemann.

Held, D., McGrew, A., Goldblatt, D. and Perraton, J. (2000) *Global Transformations*, Cambridge: Polity.

Herzfeld, M. (1992) *The Social Production of Indifference: Exploring the Symbolic Roots of Western Bureaucracy*, Chicago, IL: University of Chicago Press.

Hirst, P. and Thompson, G. (1999) *Globalization in Question,* 2nd edn, Cambridge: Polity.

Hoffman, D.E. (2002) *The Oligarchs: Wealth and Power in the New Russia*, London: PublicAffairs.

Hollingsworth, J.R. and Boyer, R. (eds) (1997) *Contemporary Capitalism: The Embeddedness of Institutions*, Cambridge: Cambridge University Press.

Holmstrom, N. and Smith, R. (2000) 'The necessity of gangster capitalism: primitive accumulation in Russia and China', *Monthly Review* 51(9): 1–15.

Hough, J.F. (2001) *The Logic of Economic Reform in Russia*, Washington, DC: Brookings Institution Press.

Humphrey, C. (1995) 'Creating a culture of disillusionment: consumption in Moscow; a chronicle of changing times', in D. Miller (ed.) *Worlds Apart: Modernity Through the Prism of the Local*, London: Routledge.

—— (1999) 'Traders, "disorder," and citizenship regimes in provincial Russia', in M. Burawoy and K. Verdery (eds) *Uncertain Transition: Ethnographies of Change in the Postsocialist World*, New York: Rowman & Littlefield Publishers.

—— (2002) *The Unmaking of Soviet Life: Everyday Economies After Socialism*, Ithaca, NY: Cornell University Press.

Hutchison, D. and Tegen, G. (2001) 'Republic of Tatarstan presidential election through the eyes of international observers', paper presented at the BASEES Annual Conference, Cambridge, UK, 6–9 April.

Hutton, W. and Giddens, A. (2000) *On the Edge: Living With Global Capitalism*, London: Jonathon Cape.

International Energy Outlook (2002) Energy Information Administration, US Department of Energy, March.

International Monetary Fund (IMF) (1998–2000) *World Economic Outlook*, Washington: IMF.

——, World Bank, OECD and EBRD (1991) *A Study of the Soviet Economy*, Washington, DC: International Monetary Fund.

Irarrazaval, I. (1997) 'Learning from the informal sector', in O. Lippert and M. Walker (eds) *The Underground Economy: Global Evidence of its Size and Impact*, Vancouver: The Frasier Institute.

James, H. (1996) *International Monetary Cooperation since Bretton Woods*, Washington, DC: International Monetary Fund; and New York and Oxford: Oxford University Press.

Jessop, B. (1999) 'Reflections on globalisation and its (il)logic(s)', in K. Olds *et al.* (eds) *Globalisation and the Asia-Pacific: Contested Territories*, London: Routledge.

—— (2000) 'The crisis of the national spatio-temporal fix and ecological dominance of globalizing capitalism', Department of Sociology, Lancaster University, available on-line at http://www.comp.lancaster.ac.uk/sociology/soc043rj.html.

Johnson, J. (1997) 'Russia's emerging financial-industrial groups', *Post-Soviet Affairs* 13(4): 333–65.

Johnson's Russia List. Various issues available at: http://www.cdi.org/russia/johnson/default.cfm.

Joyce, P. (1980) *Work, Society and Politics: The Culture of the Factory in Later Victorian England*, Hassocks: Harvester.

—— (1991) *Visions of the People: Industrial England and the Question of Class, 1848–1914*, Cambridge: Cambridge University Press.

Kabalina, V. (1998) 'Predpriiatie kak sotsial'no-ekonomicheskii institut sovetskogo i postsovetsogo obshchestva', *MEiMO* 2: 34–7.

—— and Sidorina, T. (1999) 'Predpriiate – gorod: transformatsiia sotsial'noi infrastruktury v period reform', *Mir Rossii* 1–2: 167–98.

Kagarlitsky, B. (1995) *Restoration in Russia*, London: Verso

—— (1999) *New Realism, New Barbarism*, London: Pluto Press.

Kalb, D. (2002) 'Afterword: globalism and postsocialist prospects', in C. Hann (ed.) *Ideas, Ideologies and Practices in Eurasia*, London and New York: Routledge.

Kaldor, M. (1999) 'The new ideas that freed Europe', *The Independent*, 22 October.

KamAZ (1999) *Godervii Ocherk* (*Annual Report*).

—— (2002) 'Marketing i prodazhi', available on-line at http://www.kamaz.net.

Kambakis, J. (1997) 'The Communist Movement in Russia in the period of 1991–92', Ph.D. Colloquium paper presented at Lancaster University, Department of Sociology, 11 December.

Katz, H.C. and Darbyshire, O. (eds) (2000) *Converging Divergences: Worldwide Changes in Employment Relations*, Ithaca, NY: Cornell University Press.

Keister, L.A. (2000) *Wealth in America: Trends in Wealth Inequality,* New York: Cambridge University Press.

Kellner, D. (2002) 'Theorizing globalization', *Sociological Theory* 20: 285–305.

Khakimov, R. (ed.) (1999) *Ekonomika Tatarstana polse 17 Avgusta*, Kazan: Panorama-Forum.

Kirkow, P. (1995) 'Regional warlordism in Russia: the case of the primorskii krai', *Europe-Asia Studies* 47(6): 923–47.

Kirsch, L.J. (1972) *Soviet Wages: Changes in the Strucutre and Administration since 1956*, Cambridge, MA: MIT Press.

Klein, N. (2000) *No Logo*, London: Flamingo.

Klugman, J. (ed.) (1997) *Poverty in Russia: Public Policy and Private Responses*, EDI Development Studies, Washington, DC: The World Bank.

Knox, K. (2001) 'Russia: economy rebounds from 1998 slide', *Radio Free Europe/Radio Liberty*, Prague, 20 August.

Kolmakov, S. (2003) 'The role of financial industrial conglomerates in Russian political parties', *Russia Watch* 9, January: 15–17.

Kommersant (1998) 'Kredit IMF yshel k G Sorosy', 29 July.

Koopman, J. (1992) 'The hidden roots of the African food problem: looking within the rural household', in N. Folbre, B. Bergman, B. Agarwal and M. Floro (eds) *Women's Work in the World Economy*, New York: New York University Press.

Kornai, J. (1980) *Economics of Shortage*, Amsterdam: North-Holland Publishing Company.

—— (1986) 'The soft budget constraint', *Kyklos* 39: 1–30.

Kotkin, S. (2001) *Armageddon Averted*, Oxford: Oxford University Press.

Koumakhov, R. and Najman, B. (2001) 'La question des sureffectifs en Russie: une explication en terms de competences', *Revue Economique* 52(4): 915–41.

Kravchenko, A. (1999) 'Tri kapitalisma v Rossii', *Voprosy Ekonomiki* 2.

Krylov, N.A., Bokserman, A.A. and Stavrovsky, E.R. (eds) (1998) *The Oil Industry of the Former Soviet Union: Reserves and Prospects, Extraction, Transportation*, Amsterdam: Gordon & Breach Science Publishers.

Laguerre, M.S. (2000) *The Global Ethnopolis: Chinatown, Japantown and Manilatown in American Society*, New York: St Martin's Press.

Lane, D. (1986) *Labour and Employment in the USSR*, London: Wheatsheaf Books.

—— (ed.) (1995) *Russia in Transition: Politics, Privatization, and Inequality*, London: Longman.

—— and O'Dell, F. (1978) *The Soviet Industrial Worker*, Oxford: Martin Robertson.

Lavigne, M. (1995) *The Economics of Transition*, London: Macmillan.

Lazear, E.P. (ed.) (1995) *Economic Transition in Eastern Europe and Russia: Realities of Reform*, Stanford, CA: Hoover Institution Press.

Ledeneva, A.V. (1998) *Russia's Economy of Favours:* Blat, *Networking and Informal Exchange*, Cambridge: Cambridge University Press.

—— (2000) 'Shadow barter: economic necessity or economic crime?', in P. Seabright (ed.) *The Vanishing Rouble: Barter Networks and Non-monetary Transactions in Post-Soviet Societies*, Cambridge: Cambridge University Press.

Lefèvre, C. (2001) 'La municipalisation complexe de la "sphère sociale" des enterprises Russes: un aspect important et méconnu de la transition économique et sociale', *Revue d'études comparative Est-Ouest* 32(4): 125–51.

Leitzel, J. (1995) *Russian Economic Reform*, New York: Routledge.

Leksin, V. and Shvetsov, A. (1999) *Novye problemy rossiiskikh gorodov. Munitsypalizatsyia sotsyal'nykh obyektov: pravovye i finansovye resheniia*, Moscow: TACIS.

Lempert, D.H. (1995) *Daily Life in a Crumbling Empire: The Absorption of Russia into the World Economy*, Boulder, CO: East European Monographs.

Levy-Livermore, A. (ed.) (1998) *Handbook on the Globalization of the World Economy*, Northampton, MA: Edward Elgar.

Levyveld, M. (2002) 'Russia: little progress made towards free market', *Radio Free Europe/Radio Liberty*, Boston, 31 May.

Lewis, N. (1997) 'Capitalism's modern mystics', *Living Marxism* 93.

Lippert, O. and Walker, M. (eds) (1997) *The Underground Economy: Global Evidence of its Size and Impact*, Vancouver: The Frasier Institute.

Lipton, D. (1998) 'Testimony before the House banking General Oversight and Investigations Subcommittee on Russia', *US Treasury News.*

Lockwood, D. (2000) *The Destruction of the Soviet Union: A Study in Globalization*, London: Macmillan.

Lohr, E. (1993) 'Arkadii Volsky's political base', *Europe-Asia Studies* 45(5): 811–29.

Lynch, A. (2002) 'Roots of Russia's economic dilemmas: liberal economics and illiberal geography', *Europe-Asia Studies* 54(1): 36–7.

McAuley, A. (1979) *Economic Welfare in the Soviet Union: Poverty, Living Standards, and Inequality*, Madison, WI: University of Wisconsin Press.

McCann, L. (2000) 'The informal economy and the informal state in Tatarstan, Russia', *International Journal of Sociology and Social Policy* 20(9–10): 5–36.

—— (forthcoming 2004) *Economic Development in Tatarstan: Global Markets and a Russian Region*, London: RoutledgeCurzon.

McCauley, M. (2001) *Bandits, Gangsters and the Mafia: Russia and the CIS since 1991*, London: Longman.

McChesney R.W. *et al.* (eds) (1998) *Capitalism and the Information Age: The Political Economy of the Global Communication Revolution*, New York: Monthly Review Press.

McFaul, M. (1995) 'State power, institutional change, and the politics of privatization in Russia', *World Politics* 47, January: 210–43.

McGovern, P. (2001) 'Review of Bradley *et al.* (2000) *Myths at Work*', *British Journal of Industrial Relations*, December: 627–9.

Maillet, L.L. (2001) 'Gushers for some . . .', *East/West Letter* 1(2), Spring.

Mandel, E. (1975) *Late Capitalism*, London: Humanities Press.

Mann, M. (2001) 'Globalization and September 11', *New Left Review*, 2nd series 11, November/December.

Mariotti, F. and Delbridge, R. (2002) 'A portfolio of ties: managing knowledge transfer and learning within network firms', paper presented at the Academy of Management Conference, Denver, CO.

Martin, R. (1998) 'Central and Eastern Europe and the international economy: the limits of globalisation', *Europe-Asia Studies* 50(1): 7–26.

Mastepanov A.M. (2002) *Energy Strategy of the Russian Federation to the Year 2020*, Ministry of Energy of the Russian Federation, May.

Mattera, P. (1985) *Off the Books: The Rise of the Underground Economy*, New York: St Martin's Press.

Mau, V. (1995) 'Perestroika: theoretical and political problems of economic reforms in the USSR', *Europe-Asia Studies* 47(3), May: 387–411.

—— (1996) *The Political History of Economic Reform in Russia, 1985–1994*, Bury St Edmunds: St Edmundsbury Press.

Maurice, M. and Sorge, A. (eds) (2000) *Embedding Organizations*, Amsterdam and Philadelphia, PA: John Benjamins.

May, R., Bormann Young, C. and Ledgerwood, D. (1998) 'Lessons from Russian human resource management experience', *European Management Journal* 16(4): 447–59.

Meiksins Wood, E. (1996) 'Modernity, postmodernity, or capitalism?', *Monthly Review*, July/August.

—— (1997) '"Globalization" or "Globaloney"?' *Monthly Review*, 2, February.

Menjivar, C. (2000) *Fragmented Ties: Salvadoran Immigrant Networks in America*, Berkeley, CA: University of California Press.

Mestrovic, S. (1998) *Anthony Giddens: The Last Modernist*, London: Routledge.

Meyer, J.M., Boli, J., Thomas, G.M. and Ramirez, F.O. (1997) 'World society and the nation-state', *American Journal of Sociology* 103: 144–81.

Mickiewicz, E. (1999) *Changing Channels: Television and the Struggle For Power in Russia*, Durham, NC: Duke University Press.

Mies, M. (1998) *Patriarchy and Accumulation on a World Scale: Women in the International Division of Labour*, New York: Zed Books Ltd.

Mikhailov, N. (2001) *Overview of the Russian Oil and Gas Sector*, available on-line at http://www.bisnis.doc.gov.

Monbiot, G. (2001) *The Captive State: The Corporate Takeover of Britain*, London: Macmillan.

Montaigne, F. (2001) 'Russia rising', *National Geographic* 200(5), November: 2–31.

Morrison, C. (2003) 'Labour and technological discipline: chaos and order in a Russian textile company', *Research in Economic Anthropology* 22(1).

—— and Schwartz, G. (2003) 'Managing the "labour collective": wage systems in Russian industrial enterprises, *Europe-Asia Studies* 55(4): 553–74.

Moscow Times, The (1994–2001) available on-line at http://www.themoscowtimes.ru.

Murrell, G.D.D. (1997) *Russia's Transition to Democracy: An Internal Political History, 1989–1996*, Brighton: Sussex Academic Press.

Nalivkin, V.D. (1998) 'Prediction for development of the oil and gas industry of Russia', *Petroleum Geology* 32(3): 309–18.

Nekipelov, A. (2000) 'The Washington Consensus and Russian economic policy', *International Social Science Journal* 116: 467–77.

Nelson, L.D. and Kuzes, I.Y. (1995a) *Radical Reform in Yeltsin's Russia: Political, Economic and Social Dimensions*, London: M.E. Sharpe.

—— and —— (1995b) 'Privatisation and the new business class', in D. Lane (ed.) *Russia in Transition: Politics, Privatisation and Inequality*, London: Longman.

Ngoi, G. (1996) 'Data collection and policy-oriented analysis: the case of Tanzania', in B. Herman and W. Stoffers (eds) *Unveiling the Informal Sector: More Than Counting Heads*, Brookfield, VT: Avebury.

Nove, A. (1964) 'Social welfare in the USSR', in A. Nove (ed.) *Was Stalin Really Necessary? Some Problems of Soviet Political Economy*, London: George Allen & Unwin.

Novodvorskaja, V. (2000) *Dialogi: A. Panikin i V. Novodvorskaja*, Moscow: Solidarnost'.

O'Connor, J. (1987) *The Meaning of Crisis*, Oxford: Blackwell.

OECD (1997) *Labour Market Dynamics in the Russian Federation*, Paris: Center for Co-operation with the Economies in Transition.

Ohmae, K. (1994) *The Borderless World, Power and Strategy in the Interlinked Economy*, London: HarperCollins.

O'Laughlin, J. and Kolossov, V. (2002) 'Moscow as an emergent world city', *Eurasian Geography and Economics* 23(3): 161–270.

Ong, A. (1999) *Flexible Citizenship: The Cultural Logics of Transnationality*, Durham: Duke University Press.

Oommen, T.K. (ed.) (1997) *Citizenship and National Identity: From Colonialism to Globalism*, Thousand Oaks, CA: Sage.

Otsu, S. (1992) *Sovetskii rynok truda*, Moscow: Mysl'.

Pappe, Y.S. (2000) *'Oligarkhi': Economicheskaya Khronika 1992–2000*, 2nd edn, Moscow: Gosudarstvennyi universitete Vysshaya sckola ekonomiki.

Park, R.E. and Burgess, E.W. (1925) *The City: Suggestions for Investigation of Human Behavior in the Urban Environment*, Chicago, IL: University of Chicago Press.

Parsons, T. (1960) *Structure and Process in Modern Societies*, Glencoe: Free Press.

Petras, J. and Veltmeyer, H. (2001) *Globalization Unmasked: Imperialism in the 21st Century*, London: Zed Books.

Petro, N. (forthcoming 2004) *Jump-Starting Democracy: The Novgorod Model of Rapid Social Change*, Ithaca, NY: Cornell University Press.

Petroleum Economist. Various issues available at: http:// www.petroleum-economist.com/contents/publications/petel.

Pickles, J. and Smith, A. (eds) (1998) *Theorising Transition: The Political Economy of Post-Communist Transformations*, London: Routledge.

Pilkington, H. (1994) *Russia's Youth and its Culture*, London: Routledge.

PlanEcon (1998) *Review and Outlook for the Former Soviet Republics*, Washington, DC, October: 24.

Plyshevskii, B. (2000) 'Sistemnost investitsionnogo krizisa', *Nezavisimaya Gazeta* 20, June, available on-line at http://politeconomy.ng.ru/research/2000–06–20/6_system_crisis.html.

Polak, J.J. (1997) 'The World Bank and the IMF: a changing relationship', in D. Kapur, J.P. Lewis and R. Webb (eds) *The World Bank: Its First Half Century, Volume 2: Perspectives*, Washington, DC: Brookings Institution Press, pp. 473–521.

Polanyi, K. (1944/2001) *The Great Transformation*, Boston, MA: Beacon Press.

Pop, L. (2001) 'From naive communism to "popular capitalism" in Eastern Europe? A case of selective participation in the global market place', paper presented at the PSA Annual Conference, Manchester, April.

Popov, V. (2001) 'Currency crisis in Russia in a wider context', in D. Dasgupta *et al.* (eds) *Capital Flows Without Crisis?*, London and New York: Routledge.

Portes, A. (1994) 'The informal economy and its paradoxes', in N. Smelser and R. Swedberg (eds) *The Handbook of Economic Sociology*, Princeton, NJ: Princeton University Press.

—— and Böröcz, J. (1988) 'The informal sector under capitalism and state socialism: a preliminary comparison', *Social Justice* 15(3–4): 17–28.

—— and Sassen-Koob, S. (1987) 'Making it underground: comparative material on the informal sector in Western market economies', *American Journal of Sociology* 93(1), July: 30–61.

Poser, J.A. (1998a) 'The interrelationship between inter-enterprise arrears and macroeconomic aggregates in post-Soviet economies', *Communist Economies and Economic Transformation* 10(1): 35–47.

—— (1998b) 'Monetary disruptions and the emergence of barter in FSU economies', *Communist Economies and Economic Transformation* 10(2): 157–77.

Prakash, A. (2001) 'The East Asian crisis and the globalisation discourse', *Review of International Political Economy* 8(1): 119–46.

Protopopov, A.O. (1996) 'Church–state relations in the Russian Federation', *Brigham Young University Law Review* 4: 853–71.

Pugliaresi, L. (1993) 'Russia grappling with economic and political challenges', *Oil and Gas Journal* 91(31): 58.

Randolph, R.S. (1994) 'Economic reform and private sector development in Russia and Mexico', *The Cato Journal* 14(1).

Ray, L.J. (1996) *Social Theory and the Crisis of State Socialism*, Cheltenham: Edward Elgar.

Reddaway, P. and Glinsky, D. (2001) *The Tragedy of Russia's Reforms: Market Bolshevism against Democracy*, Washington, DC: United States Institute of Peace.

Reich, R. (1992) *The Work of Nations*, New York: Vintage Books.
Remington, T.R. (1994) 'Representative power and the Russian state', in S. White, A. Pravda and Z. Gitelman (eds) *Developments in Russian and Post-Soviet Politics*, Hampshire and London: Macmillan, pp. 57–87.
Rhodes, M. (1998) *The European Welfare State: A Future of Competitive Corporatism?*, in M. Rhodes and Y. Meny (eds) *The Future of the European Welfare State*, Basingstoke: Macmillan.
—— and Meny, Y. (eds) (1998) *The Future of the European Welfare State*, Basingstoke: Macmillan.
Ritzer, G. (1999) *The McDonaldization Thesis*, London: Sage.
—— (2000) *The McDonaldization of Society*, Thousand Oaks, CA: Pine Forge Press.
Roberts, J. and Hite, A. (eds) (2000) *From Modernization to Globalization*, Oxford: Blackwell.
Robertson, R. (1992) *Globalization, Social Theory and Global Culture*, London: Sage.
Rodrik, D. (1997) *Has Globalization Gone Too Far?*, Washington, DC: Institute for International Economics.
Rose, R. (1999) 'Living in an antimodern society', *East European Constitutional Review* 8(1–2): 68–75.
—— (2000) 'Uses of social capital in Russia: modern, pre-modern, and antimodern', *Post-Soviet Affairs* 16(1): 33–57.
—— (2001) 'When government fails: social capital in antimodern Russia', in B. Edwards, M.W. Foley and M. Diani (eds) *Beyond Tocqueville: Civil Society and the Social Capital Debate in Comparative Perspective*, Hanover: Tufts University Press, pp. 55–69.
Rosenberg, J. (2001) *The Follies of Globalisation Theory*, London: Verso.
Ruigrok, W. and van Tulder, R. (1995) *The Logic of International Restructuring*, London: Routledge.
Russian Economic Trends. Various issues available at: http://www.blackwell publishing.com/ruet
Rutland, P. (1994) 'The economy: the rocky road from plan to market', in S. White, A. Pravda and Z. Gitelman (eds) *Developments in Russian and Post-Soviet Politics*, London: Macmillan, pp. 131–61.
Sabirova, E. (2001) 'Sakhalin oil and gas update Summer 2001', *Oil and Gas Timeline*, available on-line at http://www.bisnis.doc.gov.
Sachs, J.D. (1992) 'Privatization in Russia: some lessons from Eastern Europe', *American Economic Review* 80: 43–8.
Sakwa, R. (1990) *Gorbachev and His Reforms, 1985–1990*, New York: Prentice Hall.
—— (1996) *Russian Politics and Society*, 2nd edn, London, Routledge.
—— (1999) *Postcommunism*, Buckingham: Open University Press.
—— (2000) 'State and society in post-communist Russia', in N. Robinson (ed.) *Institutions and Political Change in Russia*, London and New York: Macmillan.
Sampson, S. (2002) 'Beyond transition: rethinking elite configurations in the Balkans', in C. Hann (ed.) *Postsocialism: Ideas, Ideologies and Practices in Eurasia*, New York: Routledge.
Sapir, J. (2000) 'The Washington Consensus and the transition in Russia: history of a failure', *International Social Science Journal* 116: 479–91.
Sassen, S. (1988) *The Mobility of Labor and Capital: A Study of International Investment and Labor Flow*, New York: Cambridge University Press.

—— (1991) *The Global City: New York, London, Tokyo*, Princeton, NJ: Princeton University Press.

—— (1994) *Cities in a Global Economy*, Thousand Oaks, CA: Pine Forge Press.

—— (1998) *Globalization and its Discontents*, New York: New Press.

—— (2000) *Cities in a World Economy*, Thousand Oaks, CA: Pine Forge Press.

Schaeffer, R. (1997) *Understanding Globalization*, London: Rowman & Littlefield.

—— (2002) *Understanding Globalization: The Social Consequences of Political, Economic, and Environmental Change*, Oxford: Rowman & Littlefield.

Schaffer, M.E. (1995) 'Should we be concerned about the provision of social benefits in transition firms?', *Economics of Transition* 3(2): 247–66.

Schröder, H. (1999) 'El'tsin and the oligarchs: the role of financial groups in Russian politics between 1993 and July 1998', *Europe-Asia Studies* 51(6): 957–88.

Schumpeter, J. (1991) *The Economics and Sociology of Capitalism*, Princeton, NJ: Princeton University Press.

Schwartz, G. (2003a) 'Employment restructuring in Russian industrial enterprises: confronting a "paradox"', *Work, Employment and Society* 17(1): 23–40.

—— (2003b) 'Recasting the "labour collective": employment, wages and the labour process in Russia', Ph.D. Thesis, Department of Sociology, University of Warwick.

SCISC (1999) *Siberian Civic Initiatives Support Center: Making a Difference . . .*, Novosibirsk: SCISC.

Scott, A. (ed.) (1997) *The Limits of Globalization, Cases and Arguments*, London: Routledge.

Scott, W.R. (1987) 'The adolescence of institutional theory', *Administrative Science Quarterly* 32: 491–511.

Seabright, P. (ed.) (2000) *The Vanishing Rouble: Barter Networks and Non-monetary Transactions in Post-Soviet Societies*, Cambridge: Cambridge University Press.

Segbers, K. (ed.) (2001) *Explaining Post-Soviet Patchworks, Volume 1: Actors and Sectors in Russia Between Accommodation and Resistance to Globalization*, Cheltenham: Ashgate.

Semenenko, I. (2003) 'Yukos powers ahead with Sibneft merger', *The Moscow Times*, July 8, available on-line at http://www.moscowtimes.ru/stories/2003/07/08/041.html.

Semler, D. (1993–4) 'The end of the First Russian Republic', *East European Constitutional Review*, Fall 1993/Winter 1994 (Focus: Crisis in Russia): 107–14.

Sewell, W.H. (1980) *Work and Revolution in France: The Language of Labor from the Old Regime to 1848*, Cambridge: Cambridge University Press.

Shekshnia, S. (1998) 'Western multinational's human resource practices in Russia', *European Management Journal* 16(4): 460–5.

Shevtsova, L. (1995) 'The two faces of postcommunist Russia', *Journal of Democracy* 6(3): 56–71.

—— (1997) *Yeltsin's Russia: Challenges and Constraints*, Moscow: Carnegie Moscow Centre.

Shiller, R. (2000) *Irrational Exuberance*, Princeton, NJ: Princeton University Press.

Shipps, J. (1985) *Mormonism: The Story of a New Religious Tradition*, Urbana, IL: University of Illinois Press.

Shiva, V. (2000) 'The world on the edge', in W. Hutton and A. Giddens (eds) *On The Edge: Living With Global Capitalism*, London: Jonathon Cape.

Shleifer, A. and Treisman, D. (2000) *Without A Map*, Cambridge, MA, and London: MIT Press.

—— and Vasiliev, D. (1996) 'Management ownership and Russian privatization', in B. Frydman (ed.) *Corporate Governance in Central Europe and Russia*, Oxford: Oxford University Press.

Siegelbaum, L.H. and Walkowitz, D.J. (1995) *Workers of the Donbass Speak: Survival and Identity in the New Ukraine 1989–1992*, Albany, NY: New York University Press.

Silverman, B. and Yanowitch, M. (1997) *New Rich, New Poor, New Russia: Winners and Losers on the Russian Road to Capitalism*, Armonk, NY: M.E. Sharpe.

Simonov, V. and Kyharev, A. (1998) 'The perspectives of the development of the Russian government debt market', *Voprosy ekonomiki* 11.

Sitaryan, S.A. and Krasnov, L.V. (1995) 'Russia's foreign economic relations during the formation of an open market economy', *Studies on Russian Economic Development* 6(6), November/December: 523–35.

Sklair, L. (1995) *Sociology of the Global System*, 2nd edn, London: Prentice Hall.

—— (2001) *The Transnational Capitalist Class*, Oxford: Blackwell.

—— (2002) *Globalization, Capitalism and its Alternatives*, Oxford: Oxford University Press.

Slider, D. (1994) 'Privatization in Russia's regions', *Post-Soviet Affairs* 10(4): 367–96.

Smirnov, P. (1999) 'L'goty i sotsial'naya sfera predpriiatii: formy kompensatsii za trud vne zarabotnoi platy', Moscow: IE RAN.

Smith, J. and Johnston, H. (eds) (2002) *Globalization and Resistance: Transnational Dimensions of Social Movements*, Oxford: Rowman & Littlefield.

Smitienko, B.M. and Karaeva, L.U. (1994) 'The formation of financial-industrial groups in Russia', *Studies on Russian Economic Development* 5(4), July/August: 315–19.

Sokolov, B.A. and Khain, V.Y. (1995) 'Theory and practice of oil and gas exploration in Russia: results and tasks', *Petroleum Geology* 29(9/10).

Solnick, S. (1998) *Stealing the State: Control and Collapse in Soviet Institutions*, Cambridge, MA: Harvard University Press.

Sonin, C. and Zhuravskaya, E. (2001) 'Bankruptcy in Russia: away from creditors' protection and restructuring', *Russian Economic Trends* 1.

Southworth, C. (2001a) 'Implications of Russian enterprises' reliance on neo-paternalism for economic development: evidence from six factories in Russia', in R.T. Nasibullin, A.A. Baimbetov and F.G. Khairullin (eds) *Sotsiologiya v Menyaushchemsya Sotsiume*, Ufa, Russia: Ufa Aviation State Technical University.

—— (2001b) 'How Russian industry works: worker and firm survival strategies in six enterprises in Bashkortostan', Ph.D. dissertation, Department of Sociology, University of California at Los Angeles.

Spagat, M. (1994) 'The disintegration of the Russian economy', in D.W. Blum (ed.) *Russia's Future: Consolidation or Disintegration?*, Boulder, CO: Westview Press.

Spatafora, N. (2001) 'Country study: Russia', *IMF Research Bulletin* 2(3): 8–9.

Standing, G. (1996) *Russian Unemployment and Enterprise Restructuring: Reviving Dead Souls*, Basingstoke: Macmillan.

—— (1999) *Global Labour Flexibility: Seeking Distributive Justice*, New York: St Martin's Press.

—— (2002) *Beyond the New Paternalism: Basic Security as Equality*, New York: Verso.

Stark, D. (1989) 'Bending the bars of the iron cage: bureaucratization and informalization in capitalism and socialism', *Sociological Forum*, December: 637–64.

—— (1995) 'Not by design: the myth of designer capitalism in Eastern Europe', in J. Hausner, B. Jessop and K. Nielsen (eds) *Strategic Choice and Path-dependency in Post-Socialism*, Cheltenham: Edward Elgar.

—— and Bruszt, L. (1998) *Postsocialist Pathways: Transforming Politics and Property in East Central Europe*, Cambridge: Cambridge University Press.

Steel, J. (1996) 'Why Gorbachev failed', *New Left Review* 216, March/April: 141–52.

Stiglitz, J. (2002) *Globalization and Discontents*, London: Allen Lane.

Stone, R.W. (2001) 'Russia: the IMF, private finance, and external constraints on a fragile polity', in L.E. Armijo and T.J. Biersteker (eds) *Financial Globalization and Democracy in Emerging Markets*, London: Palgrave, pp. 177–206.

Stoner-Weiss, K. (1997) *Local Heroes: The Political Economy of Russian Regional Governance*, Princeton, NJ: Princeton University Press.

Sutela, P. (1991) *Economic Thought and Economic Reform in the Soviet Union*, Cambridge: Cambridge University Press.

—— and Mau, V. (1998) 'Economics under socialism', in H.J. Wagener (ed.) *Economic Thought in Communist and Post-Communist Europe*, London: Routledge.

Swedberg, R. (1990) *Economics and Sociology, Redefining Their Boundaries: Conversations with Economists and Sociologists*, Princeton, NJ: Princeton University Press.

Szelényi, I. (ed.) (1998) *Privatizing the Land: Rural Political Economy in Post-Communist Societies*, London and New York: Routledge.

Tabak, F. and Crichlow, M.A. (2000) *Informalization: Process and Structure*, Baltimore, MD: Johns Hopkins University Press.

Tchernina, N. (2000) 'Rising unemployment and coping strategies: the case of the Novosibirsk oblast in Russia', in G.A. Cornia and R. Paniccia (eds) *The Mortality Crisis in Transitional Economies*, Oxford: Oxford University Press.

Tenstr issledovanii rynka truda (2001) *Ekonomika promyshlennykh predpriiatii: Zanyatost', dokhody i l'goty dlya rabotnikov*, Moscow: IE RAN.

Tikhomirov, V. (2001) 'Russian debt problems in the 1990s', *Post-Soviet Affairs* 17(3): 262–84.

—— (ed.) (1999) *Anatomy of the 1998 Russian Crisis*, Melbourne: University of Melbourne, Contemporary Europe Research Centre.

Tikhonov, A. (2002) 'Kriziz kriziza', *Izvestia*, 17 August.

Urry, J. (2000a) *Sociology Beyond Societies*, London: Routledge.

—— (2000b) 'Editor's introduction: sociology facing the millennium', *British Journal of Sociology* 51(1), January/March: 1–3.

—— (2000c) 'Mobile sociology', *British Journal of Sociology* 51(1), January/March: 185–203.

van der Pijl, K. (1993) 'Soviet socialism and passive revolution', in S. Gill (ed.) *Gramsci, Historical Materialism and International Relations*, Cambridge: Cambridge University Press, pp. 237–58.

Vasilchuk, Y. (1996) 'The President is to submit bureaucracy to the interests of the society', *Finansoviye Izvestia* 116.

Veseth, M. (1998) *Selling Globalization: The Myth of the Global Economy*, Boulder, CO: Lynne Rienner.

Vinogradova, E. (1997) 'Sotsial'naya rol' predpriiatii: mneniia rukovoditelei', VTsIOM: *Monitoring obschchesvennogo mneniia: ekonomicheskiie i sotsial'nye problemy* 5.

—— (1998) 'Sotsial'naya rol' predpriiatii: mneniia rukovoditelei', VTsIOM: *Monitoring obschchesvennogo mneniia: ekonomicheskiie i sotsial'nye problemy* 6

—— (1999) 'Problemy sostyal'noi infrastruktury predpriiatii: munitsypalizatsyia sotsyal'nykh obyektov i sotsyal'noe obsluzhivannie rabotnikov', in O. Alle and M. Nikolaiev (eds) *Sotsial'nye posledstviia ekonomicheskikh preobrazovanii i privatizatsiia v Rossisskoi Federatsii: Sotsiologicheskiie issledovaniia*, Moscow: TACIS.

Visaria, P. and Jacob, P. (1996) 'The informal sector in India: estimates of its size, needs and problems of data collection', in H. Bohuslav and W. Stoffers (eds) *Unveiling the Informal Sector: More Than Counting Heads*, Brookfield, VT: Avebury.

Vorobyov, A. and Zhukov, S. (2000) 'Russia: globalization, structural shifts and inequality', Working Paper 19, Center for Economic Policy Analysis, PLACE.

Walder, A. (1986) *Communist Neo-Traditionalism: Work and Authority in Chinese Industry*, Berkeley, CA: University of California Press.

Wallerstein, I. (1979) *The Capitalist World-Economy*, New York: Cambridge University Press.

—— (1991) *Geopolitics and Geoculture: Essays on the Changing World-System*, Cambridge: Cambridge University Press.

Wallich, C. (1996) *Russia and the Challenge of Fiscal Federalism*, Aldershot: Avebury.

Waters, M. (1995) *Globalization*, London: Routledge.

—— (2001) *Globalization*, 2nd edn, London: Routledge.

Weber, M. (1981) *General Economic History*, New Brunswick, NJ: Transaction Press.

Wedel, J.R. (1998) *Collision and Collusion: The Strange Case of Western Aid to Eastern Europe, 1989–1998*, New York: St Martin's Press.

Went, R. (2000) *Globalization: Neoliberal Challenge, Radical Responses*, London: Pluto.

Wertman, P.A. (1996) 'Russian economic reform and the IMF: mission possible?', *Current Politics and Economics of Russia* 7(2/3): 85–94.

White, S. (1994) 'Introduction: from communism to democracy?', in S. White, A. Pravda and Z. Gitelman (eds) *Developments in Russian and Post-Soviet Politics*, London: Macmillan.

—— (2000) *Communism and Its Collapse*, London: Routledge.

Whitley, R. (1999) *Divergent Capitalisms: The Social Structuring and Change of Business Systems*, Oxford: Oxford University Press.

Williams, C. (1996) 'Economic refor m and political change in Russia, 1991–96', in C. Williams, V. Chuprov and V. Staroverov (eds) *Russian Society in Transition*, Aldershot: Dartmouth Publishing Company.

Wilson, W.J. (1987) *The Truly Disadvantaged: The Inner City, The Underclass and Public Policy*, Chicago, IL: University of Chicago Press.

Winkler, R. (1997) 'The size and some effects of the underground economy in Mexico', in O. Lippert and M. Walker (eds) *The Underground Economy: Global Evidence of Its Size and Impact*, Vancouver: The Frasier Institute.

Woodruff, D. (1999) *Money Unmade: Barter and the Fate of Russian Capitalism*, Ithaca, NY: Cornell University Press.

World Bank (2002) *Transition: Ten Years*, Washington, DC: World Bank.

Yavlinsky, G. (1998) 'Russia's phony capitalism', *Foreign Affairs* 77(3): 67–79.

Yorke, A. (2003) 'Business and politics in Krasnoyarsk *Krai*', *Europe-Asia Studies* 55(2): 241–62.

Zaslavsky, V. (1995) 'From redistribution to marketization: social and attitudinal change in post-Soviet Russia', in G.W. Lapidus (ed.) *The New Russia: Troubled Transformation*, Boulder, CO: Westview Press.

Zohoori, N., Mroz, T.A., Popkin, B., Glinskaya, E., Lokshin, M., Mancini, D., Kozyreva, P., Kosolapov, M. and Swafford, M. (1998) 'Monitoring the economic transition in the Russian Federation and its implications for the demographic crisis: the Russian Longitudinal Monitoring Survey', *World Development* 26(11): 1977–93.

Zudin, A. (1999) 'Oligarkhiya kak politicheskaya problema rossiiskogo postkommunizma', *Obshchestvennie nauki i sovremennost* 1: 45–65.

Index

For Product Safety Concerns and Information please contact our EU
representative GPSR@taylorandfrancis.com
Taylor & Francis Verlag GmbH, Kaufingerstraße 24, 80331 München, Germany

www.ingramcontent.com/pod-product-compliance
Lightning Source LLC
LaVergne TN
LVHW011123300926
849160LV00008B/496

* 9 7 8 0 4 1 5 6 5 4 1 4 2 *